"The book is remarkable for many re[...]
understated; the obstacles to accomplishment familiar and yet appallingly new in the retelling; the fortitude and resilience admirable and bold, as children under stress so frequently show us. . . . *Do I Dare Disturb the Universe?* is a success story filled with drama, luck and moxie. . . . Charlise Lyles does not write with sentimentality, but with a cold eye on the reality of what usually happens when people are discarded."
—*Women's Review of Books*

"*Do I Dare Disturb the Universe?* rightfully takes its place among a growing body of memoirs and biographies written by the new generation that is assuming African-American intellectual leadership."
—Benjamin D. Berry Jr., professor of history and American studies, Virginia Wesleyan College

"In a vibrant tale of personal and family triumph, Charlise Lyles reaches back and makes us see how the failure of public housing rains on children's lives. Lyles's rich and powerful memoir of adolescence in Cleveland's King-Kennedy housing project unfolds as a primer on who pays the price for an America hellbent on creating ersatz communities segregated by race and income. Lyles's story of opportunity grasped celebrates a mother's strength, family, and the unsung heroines and heroes who work to pluck black youth from the dual onslaught of racism and urban decay." —Anna Karavangelos

"There is much tenderness and pain in *Do I Dare Disturb the Universe?*. Charlise Lyles writes like a novelist or a poet. Her language is beautiful even though it conveys loss. Here is a story about a daughter's love for her father, who disappears but who leaves her with 'life' lessons. *Do I Dare Disturb the Universe?* is about claiming an education. Lyles also takes us inside the world of public housing and places the city of Cleveland near the center of the universe." —E. Ethelbert Miller

"Lyles evokes the anxieties involved in going from the projects into the world of scholastic upward mobility. But the real subject of her memoir is another kind of education: what she learned as 'a girl growing up Afro and American at the edge of a new era.'" —*Washington Post*

Do I Dare Disturb the Universe?

From the Projects to Prep School

Charlise Lyles

[*Second Edition*]

GRAY & COMPANY, PUBLISHERS
CLEVELAND

This book was originally published in 1994. Part Three was added in 2008, and some of the original text was revised. Some names have been changed. Photographs are from the author's collection except where otherwise credited.

Gray & Company, Publishers
www.grayco.com

Library of Congress Cataloging-in-Publication Data
Lyles, Charlise
Do I dare disturb the universe? : from the projects to prep school /
Charlise Lyles.—2nd ed.
p. cm.
ISBN 978-1-59851-041-6
1. Lyles, Charlise 2. African Americans—Biography. 3. African
American journalists—Biography. 4. African Americans—Ohio—
Cleveland—Biography. 5. Cleveland (Ohio)–Biography. 6. Cleve-
land (Ohio)—Social life and customs—20th century. I. Title.
E185.97.L95A3 2008
305.89607713209'041—dc22
[B]   2008013947

Second Edition
Printed in the United States of America
10 9 8 7 6 5 4 3 2 1

To Ikeda Sensei

Do I Dare Disturb
the Universe?

PART ONE

The Middle

Chapter One

THE NO. 14 BUS runs east on Kinsman Road, straight through the steel heart of Cleveland. I stepped on at East Fifty-fifth Street as the bus headed uptown to Mount Pleasant. That's where the people who worked at the steel mills lived.

They were men forged from cauldrons of molten metal. We lived in Mount Pleasant before we moved to the King-Kennedy Estates public housing project. I used to see them coming home in the evenings, gleaming like tin men, glistening sweat and metal sprinklings. After working all day in dim foundries, they could look up at the grayest sky and feel lifted. Some years, that sky stayed dull as the day after Christmas all year long. Many a soul in this northern city just couldn't take it. But the steel men, they did fine. For they carried home paychecks full of overtime and spent them on long, green Ford Gran Torinoes, Buicks, Chryslers, and sometimes Cadillacs. With the money left over, they bought two-family houses in the nice neighborhood of Mount Pleasant on the East Side, far from the West Side where the white people lived.

And in summer, the black steel men painted the porches of their new homes in shiny coats of red and yellow, blue and green. From my seat in the back of the No. 14, I watched their pretty porches slide by like carnival tents.

"They make that long money working at Bethlehem Steel,"

Momma was always saying. Or, "Republic Steel pays good money, enough to buy a nice house with a porch."

Momma was a hard-working woman, too dignified to pout about her disappointments in life. But some days, disgust got the better of her. And words like lemon and salt squeezed bitter off her tongue, stinging my open adolescent wound—an absent father. "We coulda bought us that house in Mount Pleasant instead of ending up down here in the project if your father coulda got a job in one of the steel mills," she would say, then purse her lips in regret.

But my father, Charles "Skeeter" Lyles, was not a man made of steel. Time after time he had searched, and still no mill would hire him, something about a statement in his Navy discharge papers.

Even when I was in kindergarten, when he still lived with us, he spent his days jobless, out roaming the stratosphere where love and astronomy collide. He looked skyward and swore that the stars were shining in broad daylight. "You just can't see them because the light of the sun is drowning them out," Charles Lyles explained to me. "But they are there. Oh yes, they are."

At night, he gazed on stars and counted. "One, two, three, four, five, six, seven. Those are the Big Dipper, or Ursa Major. See, those seven there are the Little Dipper, or Ursa Minor. They all have names like little girls: there's Maia, Taygete, Electra, Merope, Atlas, Pleione. And see Alcyone, at the bowl and handle there? She is the brightest of them all, just like you. These over here to the east are Cassiopeia. See, they're shaped like a lady in her chair in heaven."

And in winter skies over the shivering lip of Lake Erie was his favorite, the Zeta star. Three times in the course of eight years, Zeta twinkled. It looked like it was winking, just like Marilyn Monroe, the movie star that Charles Lyles liked a lot. The twinkling happened when one star passed in front of another, Charles Lyles said. This was called an eclipse. Zeta could be seen more clearly with something called a telescope—which I imagined was a long pair of glasses. But Charles Lyles could feel enough of Zeta to revel in her light.

"Skeeter, who told you all that stuff about stars?" my five-year-old self demanded to know.

Other times, he pointed to clouds piled up high in the sky like soapsuds mountains and said, "Those are cumulus clouds." Or he would point to a red sky at dawn and announce, confident as a rain dancer, "Gonna be a storm today. Gonna pour down this evening." Or, "Look at those curly ones there, Sugarbabe. Those are cirrus clouds."

"Come on, Skeeter," I begged. "Tell me how you know."

Impressed with his celestial savvy, I reported to my Sunday school class at Mount Olive Baptist Church that Charles Lyles, my father, could find his way around heaven. And that he also knew what kind of clouds God slept on.

That was a lot more than I could say for old bald-head Reverend Berry. For all his preaching, he did not seem to know the real road map that led to the Lord. His face went blank as a turned-off TV set when we Sunday school students gangstered him in the corridor to ask what God's "Great Big Kingdom" looked like. And did God have a living room? And did he have a painted porch to sit on in the evenings and watch the sinners go by on their way to hell?

I was proud that even though Charles Lyles did not make it to church often like some Sunday school students' daddies did, he was obviously privy to special information from heaven.

But it did him no good, his hours idle, his pockets empty. Too often, that sky, gray as a cemetery, descended on his soul, landing him dead drunk off a bottle of Thunderbird wine, hopelessly, painfully earthbound at the Kinsman Bar and Grill.

That is where I hoped to find him as I rode the No. 14 bus up Kinsman Road that summer day in 1974. Nine years had gone by since he had left me, my mother, two sisters and two brothers. Since then, I had seen Charles Lyles only half a dozen times or so—maybe. They are times I could no longer remember. We now lived in the King-Kennedy project, a place of brown brick and cinder block buildings, hallways, steel doors, gritty tiles, concrete and tar-topped playgrounds, ice-cream trucks, rats, murderers, and incinerators. Charles Lyles had never come there to visit us. But at fourteen, I was forgiving.

There was much to tell Charles Lyles. A month before, upon my graduation from ninth grade at Kennard Junior High School, all the English and social studies awards had gone to me. "Outstanding." That's what my teachers at Kennard Junior High School called me. "Miss Lyles is an outstanding young lady."

But most outstanding of all, I had been awarded a $12,000, three-year scholarship to attend the Hawken Upper School in Gates Mills, Ohio, a private school for rich white kids way out in the suburbs. For grades ten through twelve, my books and everything would be paid for.

Hawken, I had been told, was ten times better than East Tech or John Hay, the high schools where most kids from the projects went. Hawken had no more than fifteen students to a class, while East Tech had thirty-five or more. Hawken had a huge library full of books, maps, and magazines. A big red barn stood over cows with moody eyes big as a Kennedy silver dollar. An art studio had a potter's wheel. A theater with dressing rooms was under construction. In the math lab, a computer talked in lighted green letters. Classrooms faced a lush forest that stretched for acres. And the French teacher was really from France. In the spring when I visited Hawken, three teachers, including the French teacher, had told me they wanted me to come to their school.

Plus, I needed to report to Charles Lyles that I would be leaving home to live with a schoolteacher whose house was closer to the Hawken School bus route. Our place in the project was too far away and we had no car, no way for me to get to Hawken. My new bedroom would have flowered wallpaper, a set of books about almost every country in the world, and an electric typewriter.

Plus, Charles Lyles needed to see that I was grown-up now, with real breasts that fit into a regular ladies' size bra, not no training bra. With all my heart, I hoped they would bloom even bigger into beautiful bosoms. My bushy hair now puffed to my shoulders, except on a day like this, when Momma had convinced me to imprison it in a ponytail and braids. (She was worried about boys checking me out.)

So I dropped two quarters in the No. 14 fare box to ride up Kinsman Road. I was going to find Charles Lyles. And I was going to tell him that Charlise—the daughter he had chosen to name after himself—was about to do something brave and remarkable in the world. I thought he ought to know about it.

He would be proud. He would brag about me to his buddies at the bar. They would order another drink to ease their envy. They would scold their own children: "Why can't you win a scholarship to private school like Charles Lyles's daughter did?"

"East 130th," the bus driver called. Too excited to sit any longer, I slid off the vinyl seat, pulled the bell, and bounced down the back steps onto Kinsman, right smack in front of the Shrimp Boat restaurant. The smell of frying fat thickened the air. Sweet ketchup, fries, and footlongs.

The Kinsman Bar and Grill was a few blocks away. The bus pulled away, belching fumes. I headed up the avenue.

My low-top Converse tennis shoes smacked the pavement. Doubt smacked at me. Suppose he wasn't there? Charles Lyles was a traveling man, always moving from one joint to the next. I had heard my Aunt Cora say that. For his whereabouts, my family commonly relied on friends and relatives like Aunt Cora to report infrequent sightings. "Saw Charles the other day on East 130th." Or, "Saw your daddy at the bar up on Kinsman." I relied on this last report.

BEER and wine. Beer and WINE. Pink and green neon beckoned from the window of the Kinsman Bar and Grill.

The wooden screen door slammed behind me, forbidding a fly entry. Inside, it was dark and dank as a basement. A man was parked on a high-standing bar stool.

"Hi. Have you seen Charles 'Skeeter' Lyles?"

He smiled a broad, short-toothed smile. "You Charles's little girl?"

I knew he knew the answer.

"Hey, Pursey," he called to someone on the other side of the bar. "This Charles's little girl."

Pursey appeared around an old Coca-Cola freezer, tickled as could be. "I coulda told you that. She got that Lyles fo'head. Broad and tall, just like Charles's."

"It sho is that Lyles fo'head," the other man mused. "She got them cowlicks too."

"Have you seen Skeeter?" I asked flatly, annoyed, but pleased that the Lyles clan's distinguished features could be so easily identified by total strangers, like royalty or something. "Do you know where he staying at?"

"Ain't he staying up on East 147th Street with Mary?" the nameless man asked Pursey.

"I b'lieve that's where he stayin', lest Mary done kicked his ass out."

"Wait a minute now. Don't be talking like that in front of this young lady."

Yeah. I was an outstanding young lady and hadn't done anything to him. He sounded like he was mad at Charles Lyles and it had nothing to do with me.

"You know what house number on 147th?" I was ready to go.

"I don't know the address," said nameless. "But I know it's the first apartment building, three stories, you come to after you cross Barlett Street. He stay up on the second floor."

"OK. Thank you." On my way out the door, Pursey tried to trip me up.

"You tell your daddy he better come 'round here and pay me what he owe me. Else we goin' have some business to tend to."

"F'get chu, ole pointed head, high-booty thing." I flung the words back, dismissing him with a smart-aleck flick of my wrist, once I was outside and well on my way up Kinsman toward 147th Street.

He had made it sound like Charles Lyles was mean to people on purpose. Maybe he was. Maybe he would tell me to get lost. Or send me back home to my mother.

The strap on my new red vinyl purse dug deep into my skinny shoulder. Packed inside were seven paperback library books that I believed had to be hauled everywhere I went, lest I miss a minute to read.

A No. 14 bus whizzed by, headed back down Kinsman toward King-Kennedy, toward home. Maybe I should turn back. There was lots to do. The summer reading contest at the library had to be won. The first team to read and report on fifteen books would win two tickets to see Al Green at Blossom Music Center. Those books had to be read. I could visit Charles Lyles some other day—after me and Desiree Kincaid, my reading partner and best friend, won the contest. There was really no time for this unpredictable man who was supposed to be my father.

And who was this Mary woman? What if she was a mean old bitch who answered the door, just outright lied and said Skeeter wasn't home?

Even my big sister Linda had said it wasn't worth trying to go visit Charles Lyles. "He was no 'count," she said. "Never sent us no money." It was true. He did not take care of us the way Fred Mac-Murray on the TV show *My Three Sons* took care of his kids.

After four blocks of frenzied indecision, I looked up. East 146th Street. Too late to turn back now. Some force mightier than my better judgment pulled me up the avenue.

My black tennis shoes, accented by two-toned socks (red and blue) bounced me down East 147th Street. Hugging my narrow hips were red low-rise, elephant-legged jeans, flapping like propellers as I stepped. Outlining my bosom's progress toward womanhood was a knitted tank top from Petries Apparel, downtown. Pulling at my shoulder was the shiny red vinyl b.k.a. "wet leather" purse from S. S. Kresge, also downtown. My hair was cornrowed tight as crochet stitches. Though new wire-framed, stop sign-shaped glasses, just like Don Cornelius wore on *Soul Train*, I looked straight ahead. Past porches. Past geraniums. Past aluminum-framed lawn swings rocking in the stale breeze. I was going to find Charles Lyles. I had something important to tell him.

The purse of paperbacks pressed my arm numb. Finally, after crossing Barlett Street, I approached the three-story apartment building, cautiously. Inside the glass door were six narrow metal mailboxes. Number 4 said "Mary Robinson, Theodore Taylor." Penciled in over Mr. Taylor was Charles Lyles's name. I touched the button. It spit a buzz.

At the top of the dimly lit stairs, a door creaked open. What if he peeped out, saw it was me and went back inside? What if he didn't recognize me? What if he mistook me for one of those Girl Scout cookie peddlers or some square selling candy to pay for a class trip to Washington, D.C.?

This was stupid. I should just go on home. Linda had told me not to take my butt up on Kinsman anyway.

"Who knock?"

"It's me, Sugarbabe."

A pair of dusty, square-toed loafers stepped onto the landing. "Who is it?" It was a man's voice, deep, demanding, and annoyed.

He leaned over the railing and studied hard. The dim hall hid his face, but I felt my presence in his and knew he was my father. He did not know me.

"It's me. Sugarbabe. Lillian's daughter. Charlise Lillianne."

"Well, ain't this something. Sugarbabe come to see old no good Skeeter—talkin' 'bout you Lillian's daughter," he faked it. "Like I don't know who you are."

Not a bad comeback, I thought. He seemed real happy to see me, excited even. I wished he wouldn't say that "old no good Skeeter" stuff.

Standing akimbo at the top of the steps, he towered like a man with untold powers, whole planets at his command.

"Come on, Sugarbabe. Come on up."

The book-load on my shoulder fell away to feathers. I had come all this way.

As I climbed up, there he was, radiating at the top of the stairs, his smile beaming light out of darkness deep in his life. Gapped but otherwise perfectly straight teeth grinned that irrepressible grin that Charles Lyles had bestowed like a crown on all his children. And a beacon shone from the sheen on his brown, broad forehead—that Lyles fo'head.

Beyond the glow, my father's face was a funny cross between Al Green and Ray Charles, with just as much rhythm and just as much blues. Old-timey sunglasses shielded his eyes. Surely, at any minute he would break out singing and stepping a Temptations tune.

He led me into a dingy room where a black and white television blinked a bad picture, then pointed me to a sagging, soiled sofa. I sunk into its worn embrace.

"You sure have grown up since the last time I saw you. How old are you now, Sugarbabe?"

"Fourteen. My birthday was June first." Stupid, I scolded myself silently. He probably knows when your birthday is. He was there the day you were born, the day the flash floods put all Cleveland under water.

"I know when your birthday is." He turned toward the television. "Hey, I'm getting ready to watch the Indians beat the hell out of Minnesota." Silence. "So how you been doin', Sugarbabe?"

"Fine. How you been doin'?"

"Just fine. How's your mama?"

"Fine."

"How your brothers and sisters doin'?"

"Fine."

I sat. He smoked Lucky Strikes, unfiltered. I stared at his yellowed fingertips and the cigarette between them like a piece of chalk. He sipped something from a dull green, plastic tumbler. He looked bored and kind of sad, his eyes vacant.

I decided to tell him the good news right away. That would cheer him up.

"Hey Skeeter, guess what?"

"What, Sugarbabe? What you got ta tell?"

It all gushed out on a geyser of excitement.

"I won me a $12,000 scholarship to Hawken School way out in the suburbs and if I get good grades, I might be able to get me a scholarship to go to a good college, any one that I want to, even out of state, like New York or Massachusetts or Washington, D.C., or someplace famous like that, if I can be admitted."

"Well that sho is something, Sugarbabe." He beamed that smile. "I always knew you were the smart one. The way you useta ask me questions all the time. Hawken? That's that school where them rich Jewish kids go, ain't it? That sho is somethin.'" His delighted laughter echoed off the empty walls.

I was still unclear about Jews. Though I had read the diary of Anne Frank, I still wasn't sure about why the people in Germany wanted to kill them so bad. But I nodded my head. Yes. Hawken was where the rich Jewish kids went to school.

There was more to tell.

"Plus, since the Hawken School is so far from where we live, I'm gonna be living with my biology teacher, Mrs. Moore, from Kennard, my old junior high school. She offered to let me stay with her because otherwise I wouldn't have no way to get to school."

"And where do she live?" Charles Lyles was curious about my life.

"Out off Lee Road in the Lee-Harvard/Seville area." That's where all the black people who were schoolteachers or social workers lived in nice little houses with trim.

"Well, ain't you somethin', Miss Sugarbabe."

I sure was. And I wanted Charles Lyles to know it. And now he did.

He smoked some more, blew rings toward the ceiling, then glanced over at me, looking kind of puzzled.

Maybe he thought I was going to ask him for some money or something. Momma said he ought to help me out a little bit. But I wasn't worried about it. My summer job with the City of Cleveland cleaning up playgrounds would help pay for school clothes and whatever else I needed. That's how I paid for my new stop-sign glasses from Dr. Frederick's Optical, downtown. I would put his mind at ease.

"The scholarship is going to pay for my books and everything, and for me to ride the school bus near Mrs. Moore's house. And I been working over at Aunt Cora's house all summer cleaning. Plus, I'm in the summer jobs program—we clean up playgrounds all over the city—so I'll have money to buy my own school clothes."

There. That ought to stop him from worrying. Though Momma had said he ought to help, she had also taught me, "Don't go around beggin' people to do things for you. You'll make folks hate you." I was loyal to that lesson.

Everything was quiet again. And that bored, distant look seeped over Charles Lyles's face again. Maybe he didn't like my hair in these stupid cornrow braids.

"What's that you got all lumpy in that purse, Miss Sugarbabe?" he asked. "Look like you carrying 'round a load of bricks."

"Those are my books I'm reading for the contest."

"What contest?" he asked. He really was kind of interested in me.

"Me and my friend Desiree Kincaid, we entered a contest at the Woodland Branch Public Library. Whichever team reads the most books in six weeks and writes the best reports on them will win two tickets to see Al Green in concert at Blossom Music Center."

I was in love with Al Green. I started to add that Al Green was sexy and his songs made me tingle in the hip area. But I discerned that this would not be an appropriate thing for an outstanding young lady to say on her first visit with her father. It might be too sophisticated for him.

"What books you reading, Sugarbabe?"

"You wanta see 'em?" I unzipped, unsnapped, and unbuckled my vinyl purse. *Rich Man, Poor Man, A Connecticut Yankee in King Arthur's Court, One Flew Over the Cuckoo's Nest, A Hero Ain't Nothing But a Sandwich, The Autobiography of Miss Jane Pittman, Go Ask Alice,* and *The Learning Tree* poured out, all in paperback. Title by title, I laid each out for display on the dirty sofa. Then I babbled on about how *Go Ask Alice* was about a girl who ran away from home. "I think she takes dope," I explained of the heroine. And on about how *Cuckoo's Nest* was about a man who got put in the crazy house by accident.

"Is that right?" Charles Lyles took in my report. Then he was quiet for a moment. "You like to read, huh?"

"Yeah, me and Desiree both. But she like to read them old-timey books like *Wuthering Heights* about this man and this lady that fall real deep in love and then they go stand on the hillside in the wind."

"Follow me," Charles Lyles said, rising and walking across the linoleum floor that creaked like a midget's box spring under a giant. To the rear of the apartment and his bedroom we went.

The stale, suffocating funk of my father's inertia clung to the walls of his room—wine, sweat, and some lust that had not been for my mother smothered the air. It was a funk that Charles Lyles could not camouflage with Irish Spring soap and aftershave.

But on the floor beneath the cracked, water-stained walls was a treasure trove: books and books and books lined up along the baseboard. They traveled the length of the wall, turned the corner, and continued on down the adjacent wall. On they went: tall books, short books, paperbacks, hardbacks, thin books, fat books, novels, textbooks, Reader's Digest Condensed, Time/Life Mexico, A, B, F, S, and T-U-V World Book encyclopedias, history books, a book about airplanes, a book about stars, books.

I sucked in the intoxicating breath of discovery. Then rejoiced silently: My father could read books. Charles Lyles read books!

Even though Momma said he dropped out of school in tenth grade, Charles Lyles read books!

But everyone said he was such a good-for-nothing. Momma didn't mean to say it, but it slipped out. My sister Linda had said it too. Even that man at the bar had badmouthed him. But Charles Lyles read books. How could someone who read so many books be bad?

All the money never sent home to take care of us kids—here it was, spent on books, precious books that Charles Lyles had saved for this moment when he would share them with me, not my sisters, not my brothers. But me alone, his Sugarbabeeeeeeee!

It was I who had stumbled upon the true Charles Lyles, a man who read books, hundreds of them. A man with a library of his own like a president or a millionaire in a murder mystery. "Go on. Take any one you like," he urged.

I wasn't no sucker. "Which ones are best?" I asked cautiously, testing to make sure he had actually read them.

He pointed to a hardback with a picture of a mean-looking bulldog of a man leaning on a cane. "This one is about Winston Spencer Churchill, the prime minister of England during World War II." It was a tome, fatter than anything I had read so far, even *Rich Man, Poor Man.*

"You read that whole book, Skeeter? No you didn't."

"I sho did, four or five years ago," he said too proudly to be telling a lie.

He picked up another, thick as the Bible, with a white paper jacket yellowed at the edges. *Hirohito, Emperor of Japan.*

"This man is still living," my father said of Hirohito. "Read this one. It's good. Tells you all about World War II."

All I knew about Japanese people was that there had been a war and they had been bombed real bad with a new type of bomb. Winston Churchill seemed closer to home. His mean muzzle growled at me. "Can I take this one?"

"Go on. You can take it home with you if you promise to bring it back."

"OK. I promise. Hey, Skeeter? Where you get all these books?"

"Saved 'em. Bought them at the Goodwill store up on Kinsman and down on Buckeye Road. Or people give 'em to me 'cause they know I like to read. Go 'head. Take another."

I was a disciplined reader. "Nope. Not till I finish this one, then I'll come back for King Hirohito."

"Emperor Hirohito," Charles Lyles corrected.

We parted with my promise to read Winston Churchill in a week or two and return it.

I was hardly out the creaky door and down the dim stairs when my celebration began. Just wait. Oh, praise be to me and my serendipity. Charles Lyles was a great man of knowledge, practically a man of letters, a man of the world who knew of powerful men in faraway lands. The bus ride home was a movable jubilee. I snapped my fingers to the music of my discovery, music only I could hear. To the beat, I bobbed my head and twisted my butt, strutting my stuff in my seat—not caring if others saw me, in the back of the bus, by myself, acting a fool in public just like Momma told me not to do.

That night, I couldn't wait to tell my big sister Linda with her signifying self. She was going to Case Western Reserve University way across town on scholarship, but stopped in as usual to "borrow" some soap powder. Momma wasn't anywhere around. I turned Bob Barker on the TV up louder just in case, and took an icy sip from my cup of Kool-Aid.

"I went and saw Skeeter today up on Kinsman. He got a whole lot of books and stuff and he let me take some of them with me."

Linda's jaw dropped just for a moment: Yes, her little sister had the audacity to hunt down Charles Lyles. Then she cut to the point. "Did he give you any money?"

"Nope. But look." I propped the Churchill book up on my lap for display. "See? He let me borrow this book."

Linda snatched it from me, ran her forefinger along the binding, breathed in the aroma of the old book, studied its cover front and back, then promptly returned it to my lap. "Who wants to read about an old bald-head white man smoking a cigar?"

"Skeeter said he was the president of England during World—"

"I don't care what Skeeter said. He shoulda gave you some money if he wanted to give you something so bad, instead of some useless book."

I was ashamed to admit that I had decided not to ask about money.

"Where is he staying at, anyway?" She sat down at the kitchen table, which was not in the kitchen because the kitchen was too small.

"Somewhere up on Kinsman." I deliberately withheld all details. What if Linda showed up demanding compensation for a lifetime of unpaid child support? She might scare Charles Lyles away from me. He would never trust me again.

"Where up on Kinsman?"

"I forget exactly where. You know I don't know my way around up there too good and stuff."

"What was it near?" She poured Kool-Aid and sipped. I could see plots racing in her almond eyes.

"The Two Cousins beauty products store," I lied.

"Oh." By now, Linda was highly annoyed with me. She busied herself opening and slamming cabinet doors in search of soap powder. "Well, I just as soon not know where Charles Lyles lives anyway. Ain't going to do me any good anyhow." Slam. It wasn't in there. "Why couldn't you just leave him alone? You see that he doesn't want to have nothing to do with us so why don't you just leave him alone?" Slam. Not there either. "Why do you always have to go disturbing things?"

"There it is." I spotted the detergent just as she was about to slam another cabinet. She grabbed the box, poured three cups into a plastic bag, slammed the door to Number 129, and was gone. The soap dust made me sneeze.

Linda was right, I thought, staring into the tall dark cup full of Kool-Aid. I was always disturbing things, as she put it. And I felt bad about that, for a little while. Just a little while.

Chapter Two

PRESSURE PICKED UP IN the library reading contest. Rumors circulated that Gwen Johnson and William Jackson had taken the lead after finishing *Jubilee*. Plus, I had heard that the librarian, Miss Smith, had marked their reports "Excellent." Desiree and I would have to do some hard reading to move back into first place. But I wasn't worried. We were only six books away from winning from seeing Al "Let's Stay Together" Green live in concert. The mere thought made my earlobes warm in July.

I read quickly through Churchill's life, alternating with *Rich Man, Poor Man*. The saga of Rudy and "rich man's weather" answered my curiosities about love and luck. Churchill was a different story. It kind of bothered me that he did not seem to care much for black people. But old Churchill did have something in common with me. He had been a chubby, redheaded, stuttering schoolboy who ended up running the whole country. And I had managed to climb out of the slow class, a dungeon for academic rejects, to become a big-time scholarship winner.

I pressed on to finish Churchill in two weeks as I had promised. At the ready was a dictionary to decipher big, unusual words like *hegemony*. By eight A.M. each morning, I was up and out the door to work for the Cleveland summer jobs program. A brigade of teenagers with brooms and rakes, we were dispatched in busloads to clean and groom the grounds of public playgrounds. As the bus bounced through the city, my head bobbed over the books.

Two weeks went by. The No. 14 bus deposited me again at the corner of East 147th Street and Kinsman. A fast walk, a quick buzz, a creaky door, and once again I was in Charles Lyles's light. "Hey Sugarbabe, what chu doin' up this way again?" He looked blank, surprised to see me, red "wet leather" purse and all, as if I had had no intention of keeping my promise.

"I finished it."

"What, Sugarbabe?"

"Winston Churchill. In two weeks. Just like I said I would. Plus, I finished *Rich Man, Poor Man* at the same time. Here, I brought it back so I could take another one. You said I could, remember? I know all about Churchill now."

"Alright, Miss Sugarbabe. You done proved yourself a woman of your word."

My lesson began. Was Churchill an imperialist, Charles Lyles wanted to know. And why did he believe the British should hold on to India as its colony, even though the Indians wanted them out? Was Churchill a warmonger or peace lover? And why was Churchill determined not to surrender in the face of imminent German invasion?

Most of my teachers at Kennard Junior High School had never asked these kinds of questions. They had wanted names, dates, or places.

Charles Lyles's questions were my chance to show him how smart I was. To make him proud of me. Correct answers were crucial, else my confidence to compete at that private school way out in the suburbs would be crushed. But instead of waving her hand wildly to be called on by the teacher, the outstanding young lady squirmed, frustrated, without answers.

"I don't know, Skeeter. Why don't you ask me about the important dates and stuff like that?"

But Instructor Lyles refused to alter his lesson plan. My intellect was dull and brittle from too much junior high school memorization and regurgitation. Charles Lyles detected this and challenged me with his flexible mind, which whirled way out there in space where intellect and soul merge.

He was trying to teach me how to think. Not about dates, places, and other rote matters. They were secondary in Charles Lyles's lesson plan. Rather, he was concerned that I learn about souls, conscience, character, dilemmas, decisions, how men dealt with destiny and dying.

These exercises seemed prepared especially for me, like the banana pudding with vanilla wafers and whipped cream that Momma made. At the same time, Charles Lyles fork-fed me knowledge, the facts, pure and fortifying as rice. I ate greedily, famished for fatherly affection. Plus, it was fun.

Down East 147th Street I walked, worrying about Charles Lyles's mind, a mind that could streak quick as a comet and then be gone; a mind left lightheaded, dizzy from the glow of a nebula on a page in a Time/Life book; a mind that puzzled over the complex beauty of a poem; a mind that could be irritatingly attentive to detail and weird equations that had nothing to do with my existence—or so I thought.

He scratched "$E=MC^2$" on a piece of paper. "What does that mean, Sugarbabe?"

"Algebra," I guessed.

"That's what they call the Theory of Relativity."

I shrugged my shoulders and wondered where Charles Lyles had gone wrong in the world.

At night I slept, dreaming jobs for my father. Not pressing metal or stirring molten steel, but jobs that would keep his restless mind happy and use all of his books; jobs that would make him lose the constant urge to sip from the green plastic tumbler in the middle of the day when most men were at work; jobs that might make him want to come home and be with us forever. History teacher, scientist, librarian, lawyer.

Sunday, while Momma was making apple-cookie pie, string beans, and potatoes, and the aroma of goodness rose in the kitchen like a warm prayer, the questions took possession of me.

"Momma, how come Skeeter couldn't find no job? I went over to where he stay last week and he seems real smart to me." I had decided against mentioning the library. It might make Momma upset, since Charles Lyles never sent us any money.

"What were you doin' up on Kinsman by yourself?"

"Momma, I'm fourteen years old. I know how to cross the street."

"And who told you how to find Skeeter?"

"Nobody, I just found him myself." Telling Momma about my visit to the Kinsman Bar and Grill could have been the end of me.

"And why did you do that? So he could tell you he ain't got no money and try to borrow what little bit you got?" Momma shook her head, amused at me and sorry for me at the same time.

"Momma just answer the question. How come he can't find no job?" Plain as cauliflower or sweet as Alaga brand syrup, there was no in between with Lillian Wardean Lyles: She would speak the truth. Strained seconds ticked by while she locked into place her will not to speak ill of my father.

"You know Skeeter taught me how to cook," she said finally. "He taught me how to make turkey dressing, and macaroni 'n' cheese, and barbecue, and how to make bread dough with yeast. Aw yeah, your father could really cook, you hear me? He knew how to use those spices. He put just the right amount of sage in the dressing.

"He was smart too. Always had his head in one book or another, reading about this or that." She was speaking in the past tense. Was Charles Lyles dead in her heart?

She went on. "In a lot of ways, Skeeter was a perfectionist. He straightened up the house just as good as I did sometimes. He organized everything perfectly, just like he was getting ready for a Navy inspection or something professional. Not a speck of dust could you find. All the dishes stacked in the cabinet. Everything in order. He was a better housekeeper than I am."

That really wasn't saying much, I thought, leaning against the wall, shifting on my toes from one Converse to the other. Where had Charles Lyles gone wrong? This was the question. But it was unwise to interrupt Momma. She would take her time, answering her way.

"Yep, your daddy was a perfectionist," she continued, talking to herself more than me. "Whenever he got a job painting houses, everybody would talk about how straight he could paint those lines. He could paint the windowpane trim without tape, and do that two-toned painting.

"But it was that Mattie Lyles that messed Skeeter up. I b'lieve he would have been something today, if it hadn't been for Back."

"Back" was Momma's crude but accurate nickname for my estranged Grandmother Lyles. Her spine was rounded as Lil Bo Peep's staff. It kept her shoulders stooped and her head bowed to the ground as if she was in perpetual prayer. According to Momma, Back's god was gambling in bars, drinking, and living the high life. (I had heard portions of this sermon before when Momma warned us of the evils of card playing.) With a deck of cards, Back was deadly dexterous. And she drank gin in houses where good women didn't go—or good men, either.

My daddy, Momma explained, had made the mistake of choosing his mother to admire, rather than his father, hard-working Wallace Lyles who labored at Republic Steel all night long and brought home the money to his card shuffling, gin-swilling wife.

"Skeeter started hanging out in those bars with Back when we were still going to John Adams High School over on East 116th Street," Momma went on. "He dropped out. Started drinking beer. But I didn't see that as anything that could mess up a marriage. I loved my skating. But I wasn't quite sure how to go about making steady work out of that anyhow. So we went on ahead and got married. Right after your big brother was born, Skeeter started drinking that Thunderbird wine. Next thing I knew it was whiskey. Not too long after you were born, I started finding those Old Crow bottles behind that gray davenport we used to have when we lived on East 123rd Street in Mount Pleasant."

Momma's words roused memories in me that wished not to wake: The attic apartment in the house on East 123rd Street; the Old Crow bottle with the black bird perched on the label, a devil indifferent to the damage he did, and the whiskey, clear and pure-looking.

Every afternoon seemed sunny back then, and Momma disappeared for hours every day to a place called "work," leaving me in Charles Lyles's care.

While my big brother and sister dug and threw dirt on the weedy lawn, I sat upon a special throne. On the downstairs porch, painted red, my father cuddled me in his lap, rearing back on the hind legs of a lawn chair. We went rocking away. He was goofy drunk and gentle, teasing me like Donald Duck with big buck teeth and wide eyeballs. I laughed wildly, like a seagull flapping my wings on a beach.

"Daddy, do that again. Daddy, make me laugh. Daddy, do Crazy Guggenheim from *The Jackie Gleason Show*. Daddy, do like the clown on *The Red Skelton Show*."

His eyes rolled with silly sadness. He stretched his mouth wide, ear to ear, like a rubber band, and stuck his chin out like a goon. "Good night and may God bless." Then his fingertips waved good-bye.

"Huc, huc, huc, huc," I hiccupped with delight. "Daddy, do Moms Mabley."

Out of nowhere, an old paint-spattered work hat frumped on his head. This time, those eyes bulged wide out of orbit, marbles gone berserk. Lips tucked over teeth made him toothless.

"All you chil'ren know Moms. An' you know a ol' man cain't do noooooothin' fo' me." Pause. Charles Lyles had perfect timing. "But bring me a message from a young man." He growled laughter like an old granny with time and phlegm caught in her throat.

No matter that the joke was too grown for me to get, I giggled wildly, ridiculously.

By bedtime, Momma was home. And with hardly a good-bye, Charles Lyles was out the door on his way up Kinsman Road to a bar and grill where pretty colored circles blinked in the window, soap bubbles bursting. His evening departures left Momma calm in the kitchen, frying hamburgers over a hot stove and humming way off-key: "Stag-o-Lee shot Billy through the head / Shot that poor boy bad."

This is when Momma loosened the white cotton bra straps that had pinched her shoulders all day long as she worked. Those straps slipping to the soft flesh of her forearms meant that her work was done for the day. Whether scrubbing houses in the suburbs or running elevators at Sterling-Lindner-Davis, a big downtown department store, her day was done. And it was her time now, not mine or my siblings'. They played quietly on the living room floor. And I would not whine to be held or demand attention with a self-provoked tantrum. It was Momma's time and she took it, dozing into evening to the lullaby of Walter Cronkite and the *CBS Evening News*.

In the night, only Charles Lyles's voice returned, deep in the craw of Old Crow. From my bed, I heard it rage up the stairs to our attic apartment, cursing, sputtering, slobbering like some awful creature angry because it had not been born a human being. The voice pounded down the wooden door, then unleashed fury, hurling and smashing things about in the kitchen, some precious, some replaceable.

Above my blanket in the other room, the air cracked and split.

I moved my lips to repeat the words Momma said: "Skeeter, stop. Stop it."

The jar of grape jelly, my favorite in the whole cupboard, was smashed into sugared shards of glass, splintering our chances for sweet toast and harmony at breakfast.

The hot breath from the voice heaved through the living room, hovering closer to my bed, tucked in a tiny makeshift bedroom at the roof's lowest point. The breath was grapey and sour, like a vine rotting in late summer, its grapes never picked. The sounds persisted. Then there was whimpering like a wounded sparrow trapped in a tree.

Morning brought colorless quiet, soft moans, and the swish of restless sheets. After his drunken slaps burned Momma's face, Charles Lyles's touch could still be tender to her. With no other man in my universe to love, I too forgave him much too easily.

Two more babies got born after me, one year apart. They made five. A sister, Beverly Caroline (named after President John F. Kennedy's daughter). She quickly became known as Tinky (though nobody quite knows why; it may have been one of Charles Lyles's drunken utterances that stuck). And a brother was born. He arrived in November 1964 and was named John after the assassinated president. Charles Lyles's search for a job in the steel mill still hadn't panned out. He peered longingly, painfully into the white braided bassinet at his sleeping son and was gone for good.

The kitchen grew warmer as Momma turned up the oven to bake her crust. She rolled the apple-cookie pie dough on the table and nodded, her forehead sprinkled with perspiration. Telling how Charles Lyles had gone wrong had drained her.

"Yep. Skeeter probably could have been something brilliant if it hadna been for Back. I b'lieve that to this day. But Skeeter could sure cook. He sure could cook," Momma affirmed one more time, as if cooking was the skill of Charles Lyles's redemption.

Chapter Three

MY NEXT LESSON: SHAKESPEARE.

"Uuhmmmmm, I didn't do too well with this one," I 'fessed up as soon as the creaky door cried open.

"C'mere, Sugarbabe," Charles Lyles thumbed through the tome. "This one here is *The Merchant of Venice*. Listen. This is Antonio talking."

The odor of wine in his room seemed to give way to the fresh, resplendent air of a star being born. The water stained walls darkened to deep maroon curtains. And when the velvet fluting parted, there stood Charles Lyles, Shakespearean actor, upon a stage that rose from the scaly linoleum floor. The performance began.

> In sooth, I know not why I am so sad.
> It wearies me, you say it wearies you.
> But how I caught it, found it, or came by it,
> What stuff 'tis made of, whereof it is born,
> I am to learn.

Charles Lyles had barely glanced at the page for that smooth delivery. He flipped a page, took two steps back, and whispered an aside.

"Now this is Bassanio. He blew all his dough on stuff he didn't need. So he's broke and owes everybody money. Understand?"

"Uh-huh."

Charles Lyles the supporting actor took over:

> . . . But my chief care
> Is to come fairly off from the great debts
> Wherein my time, something too prodigal,

(Another aside: "That's when you waste all your money.")

> Hath me gaged. To you, Antonio,
> I owe the most in money and in love,
> And from your love I have a warranty
> To unburden all my plots and purposes
> How to get clear of all the debts I owe.

Charles Lyles took a deep bow. "Ain't that something, Sugarbabe—'to unburden all my plots and purposes'? Shakespeare knew how to say somethin', now didn't he?"

The poetry left him near tipsy, a glass of wine ten times finer than a bottle of T-bird.

"I just thought you might like old Shakespeare's poems, Sugarbabe. That's all."

That uncomfortable quiet slipped over us. I filled it with the notion that my non-aptitude for Shakespeare had disappointed Charles Lyles and that I should take my leave soon for the No. 14 bus. "Hey, Skeeter? I know a poem by heart just like you know Shakespeare."

"What poem is that, Sugarbabe?"

"It's by Langston Hughes. You heard of him?" He didn't seem to ever mention any black writers like the ones I knew about.

"'Course I know Langston Hughes. Which poem you know?"

"'Ballad of the Landlord.'" If he asked me to recite it, I could show off my dramatic talents, for which I had been highly praised at Kennard Junior High School.

"Well, go on. Let me hear you say it."

I stood. The velvet stage curtains parted once again. House lights down. Stage lights up on the set: a sagging staircase of a sorry tenement. My costume: curlers and bathrobe. The actress inside me stepped out. I huffed and puffed, manufacturing anger for a fiery, irreverent delivery:

"'Ballad of the Landlord,' by Langston Hughes. 'Landlord, landlord . . . '" I smacked a hand on my hip and railed about the leaky roof, the broken down stairs, and the no-good, low-down landlord who eventually sends his tenant to jail.

On and on I rampaged in rhyme till the poem was through. When my head bobbed up from a deep, gracious curtsy, I saw Charles Lyles grinning like grinning was going out of style. The thespian in him lived on in me. But there was no applause.

"That was good, Sugarbabe. You pretty good at that." But there was no hug. No kiss on the cheek like on *The Brady Bunch*. Just another dry "Sugarbabe."

Well, I wasn't going to feel bad about it. I let Langston Hughes carry me down a different track.

"Hey, Skeeter? You got any books that black people wrote?"

"I got a few, Sugarbabe. They're in there with all the rest of 'em. Lemme see, I got *Mr. Black Labor: The Story of A. Phillip Randolph, Father of the Civil Rights Movement*, *Yes I Can* by Sammy Davis Jr., *Why We Can't Wait* by Martin Luther King Jr. This one here is a good one," he said, showing me *Stride Toward Freedom* with King stepping and smiling on the cover as if facing high-pressured fire hoses and rock-pelting racists was a pleasure.

I knelt on the floor by the books, sifting through titles and pages. No, these were not the kind of black books I was talking about. I meant real black books, like the ones the Afro Sets in the project used to read, like H. Rap Brown's *Burn, Baby Burn* and Eldridge Cleaver's *Soul on Ice*—those books that made you get really mad at white people.

Maybe that wine had warped Charles Lyles's mind so bad that

he had forgotten the white man's dirty deeds. Forgot that he was on an eternal path to destroy the black man. Maybe my own father was a traitor, an Uncle Tom. That T-bird and Boone's Farm had done it. Never, ever would I touch it if that's what it was going to do to me.

"Skeeter? Do you have any *real* black books?"

The afternoon was ticking away to five o'clock. Birds in an elm tree outside slowed down their song, ready to slip into darkness. Charles Lyles was quiet and still, staring at the water-stained wall.

I walked toward the bus stop on Kinsman Road. I had hoped Charles Lyles could help me figure out how I was supposed to feel about the white people at my new school. Should I roll my eyes and be mad at them for all the dirty stuff white people had done: slavery (I still hadn't gotten over it since learning about it in Mr. Salo's social studies class), Jim Crow, causing riots that nearly burned down the whole city and upsetting our black mayor, Carl B. Stokes, so bad that he didn't want to be mayor anymore, plus upsetting the Afro Sets? Their silly prejudice just made me sick. Or should I let them slide and try to be nice to them?

But there were no angry black books on my father's makeshift shelf, though racism had whipped hard at him. Maybe Charles Lyles saw life through a different lens, one that refused to focus on "the white man" as misery maker.

The library reading contest hit the home stretch. Desiree and I read until our eyes ached and turned bloodshot as winos'. Finishing *Cotton Comes to Harlem*, we pulled firmly into the lead. Finally, we went to see Al Green, leaving Gwen Johnson and William Jackson coughing on the fine dust of our hard-driven victory.

In a see-through rose lamé jumpsuit, Al Green gyrated across the stage, tossing armloads of roses till scarlet petals rained down on his wailing, love-afflicted following. Only a few floated to our sandaled feet. Convulsing with desire, one woman almost jiggled free of her halter top. Al Green kept right on strutting, hopping on one foot and singing close to the microphone as if kissing a lover. "Here I am baby, wontcha come and take me?"

I don't know about Desiree, but I tingled shamelessly. In a moment of frenzied abandon, another fan tossed her drawers to the stage. We L-O-V-E *loved* Al Green, alright. Yes, we did. But not enough to publicly relinquish our pastel panties, purchased in three-packs with $2.99 of our hard-earned summer job money at Woolworth's, downtown.

Miss Smith, the librarian—also a closet Al Green fan—dropped us off home at one A.M., the latest we had ever stayed out. Girlish dreams of love and happiness guided us to sleep, wilted rose petals pressed in our palms.

The contest won, I was now ready to take Hirohito home. This would please Charles Lyles.

Japan was a strange world of shrines and people bowing in deep deference. I was consumed by it until a neatly folded note written on dime-store tablet slipped from between pages 294 and 295. It was yellowed as cake batter. Blue ink in what had to be my father's hand read:

Nov. 4, 1961

Dear Charles S. Thomas
Secretary of the Navy
I served in the Navy from 1954 to 1958. I received an honorable discharge. But because of something in my discharge papers, I have not been able to find a job. I need work to support my wife and family. Is there anything you can do to help me

The letter stopped right there, as if he had given up in midstroke. Why hadn't he finished it? Why hadn't he mailed it? What did his navy discharge papers say? Would he tell me? Or should I return the book and pretend I had never come across the letter? Maybe Charles Lyles planted it there for me to see. Sneaky. Trying to make me feel sorry for him.

Once I arrived at the rooming house, we got right down to the business of Hirohito.

"How old was Hirohito when he became emperor of Japan? Why do the people believe he is superior?" Charles Lyles quizzed.

I fired back answers to the first two questions. Then I asked one of my own. "This book says the people is—are—Buddhists. What does that mean, Skeeter?"

"Well, Sugarbabe, some people believe God is outside you and some people believe He's inside you. Now, what do you think about that?" He laughed way down in his gut.

I didn't have too much to say.

The quiz continued: What was the Manchurian Incident? If Hirohito was a peace-loving man like he said he was, why did he sign the papers to bomb Pearl Harbor and start World War II?

These questions left me squirmy and confused. "I don't know, Skeeter," I owned up.

Though I didn't know the correct answers, I wanted Charles Lyles to know that I was grateful to him for introducing me to the majestic Orient, a land of silk robes, cherry blossoms, shogun dynasties, ideas of utter darkness that could make a short man on a white horse a divine king, and philosophies of supreme enlightenment, different from Reverend Berry's God. As if this might be my last chance, a sudden rush to please this man who was my father pushed me to redeem myself.

"Skeeter, I remember the poem—I mean, the haiku poem that Hirohito recited before the war started.

Throughout the world
Everywhere we are all brothers.
Why then do the winds and waves
Rage so turbulently?"

"Hey, Miss Sugarbabe, you pretty good at that poetry, now," he exclaimed. And Charles Lyles hugged me close to him, close enough to hear laughter welling up from that darkness deep inside, resonating from his rattly lungs and choking in his cigarette-smokey throat. A happy ghost, it leaped out of him and inside of me, taking possession. I laughed. He laughed. We laughed the laughter of communion, a coming together of father and daughter.

The poem, gentle and spontaneous off my lips, was a kiss, a surprise topped with a shiny red bow, the only gift I ever gave my father.

In the excitement, I abandoned my plan to ask about the unfinished letter that I had found inside the book. Instead of my questions, it was my admiration and affection that Charles Lyles deserved. For, all summer long he had been the man of my dreams, my Sidney Poitier in *A Patch of Blue*, and I, Laura, the blind girl in the park, waiting for him to bring his light.

Such was the hyperbole in a silly schoolgirl's heart yearning for a father's love to affirm her, to assure her that she did indeed merit a special place in his universe.

School would start in two weeks. I was busily packing, getting ready to move to my new home near the suburbs. President Nixon had resigned. Momma insisted, despite my busy protests, that I sit and watch on TV with undivided attention as a hunchbacked Nixon waved a wounded victory sign, and boarded a helicopter on the White House lawn with his family for the last time.

"The president of the United States of America is resigning," Momma announced through the living room in her dramatic, high-strung style. "Sugarbabe, you better come watch this right now. This is history. Those white kids're probably going to be talking about it out at that school you're going to."

One of my last chores was to return a book borrowed from my father's library: *Introducing the Constellations*. I had tried to match the star patterns in the night sky to the book's illustrations, but without much luck. Instead I ended up gazing on fireflies that sparkled like dust from a fairy's wings.

When no one answered the buzzer, I took the stairs, two at a time (easy this time, since I was free of my big bag of books). I knocked on the door. It cracked open, and a jet-black wig poked out. Underneath was a woman with an upper lip hairy as a Musketeer's. She had not been around during my previous visits. What could my father possibly want with this furry-faced woman? My mother was ten times more beautiful. "Skeeter here?"

"You Charles's little girl, ain't you?"

It was August. I was irritable. I wasn't no damned little girl. Need I let her know that I had breasts that would fit into a grown woman's bra, including hers? Thank you. Plus, I had hips and had gotten my ears pieced at the May Company Department Store, downtown.

But I wasn't going to get into all that. "Miss, is Skeeter here?"

She leaned against the slight opening, blocking the sagging sofa from my view.

"Naw. I haven't seen Charles in 'bout two or three weeks. She shook her black head fast, a peruked woodpecker in reverse.

I didn't believe her. "Well, do you know where he staying at now?"

"No, I sho don't," she said, a smooth finality to her tone. "Charles don't never leave no address when he go. He just go."

Maybe he was in there sick, sick from the sweet T-bird, doubled over and unable to rise up from his bed to greet me. And this kind lady did not have the heart to tell me that my father was ill, perhaps even dying. Surely that must be it.

"Is his—*are* his—books still here? I have to return one. I told him I would bring it back."

"If you want, I'll take it. Maybe I'll see him around somewhere."

She took the book, confirming my worst suspicions. Charles Lyles was there, but had finally tired of me and did not wish to see me. I was boring and he didn't like me with my silly poems. He had only been faking when he laughed so hard and hugged me. He was done with me now. Maybe he was just on the other side of the door sniggering, the way I had hidden as a child from undesirable playmates. And he had instructed this strange, fuzzy-faced woman to send me away, to get rid of me. Plus, she was clearly jealous of me. The whites of her eyes burned pink with envy. Her breath stank of it.

"You don't have no address for him?"

"Uh-uh, honey. No. I sho don't."

Don't play that "honey" stuff with me, I started to say. "Do you think they might know up at the Kinsman Bar and Grill?"

"I don't know, baby. You can sho ask 'em."

I pounded down the stairs, my Converses stomping each step. Where had he gone? Why had Charles Lyles left without telling me? How would I explain to my siblings that Skeeter had "skyed up" on me? Surely Linda would have the last laugh at me for building Charles Lyles up to be so much. A tantrum gathered momentum in my chest then swirled to my head, heating it hot enough to burst.

Where had Charles Lyles gone? Didn't he like me anymore? Didn't he want to follow my progress in prep school? Know what my grades would be? And what a decent hockey player I might become? Didn't he want to show me off to his buddies at the Kinsman Bar and Grill and tell them that I was going to that white school way out in the suburbs? And that I might even win a big scholarship to go to college? Most importantly, wasn't he proud that I had grown up to be an outstanding young lady?

I rampaged down East 147th Street. Checking the bar would do no good. Those men would just be there, waiting to tell me how Charles Lyles was no good and now he had proved it, skying up on his own daughter. Tears blurred the green and red painted porches to flames as I took off running toward the bus stop. By the time I reached the corner, there was only the thin blue smoke from a Lucky Strike cigarette into which Charles Lyles had vanished.

"F'get you then, Charles Lyles," I told the smoke and defied his disappearing act with a fast flick of my smart-aleck wrist. "Old wino. Old punk drunk who beat up on my mother. Shoulda kicked your butt back then. F'get chu. Even if you do have books. Even if you are smart. F'get chu."

Why had I wasted my time fooling around with Charles good-for-nothin' Lyles? I tried real hard to hate him.

In the summer of 1974, programs and promises born of the civil rights and Great Society eras beckoned to "bright" black kids like me. For some reason unknown to me, I had hoped that my father possessed wisdom that would help me negotiate the unknown path ahead. I did not understand then that Charles Lyles had no references for the opportunity that had come my way.

But the lessons from Charles Lyles's library lifted me, pointing out questions that had to be asked, teaching me how to think, daring me to gaze up and wonder, telling me to seek out my own path. Those lessons became my reference point for confidence in life.

That summer years ago, I wanted a father's hand to guide me through the new world into which I had somehow managed to gain entry, determined to prove myself a very outstanding young lady. But as the No. 14 bus bounced down Kinsman Road, past the bar and grill, past the Shrimp Boat, past Palmer's Record Mart, I swallowed hard on the ache in my throat and accepted that there would be no such hand. The voices inside Charles Lyles's life, Churchill, Shylock, or others more insidious, had called him away and he had gone, forgetting that Charlise, the daughter whom he had named after himself, was about to undertake the biggest challenge of her life.

So I held my own hand, one folded in the other propping my head against the window. The colorful porches of Mount Pleasant slipped by. And I remembered the past that had brought me to this fifty-cent bus ride, straight through the steel heart of Cleveland.

PART TWO

The Beginning

Chapter Four

EVERYTHING CHANGED AFTER THE summer that the river caught fire. I turned ten on June I, 1969. Twenty-one days later, the Cuyahoga burned on a gray, moody Sunday that promised rain but never delivered. A cool breeze blew the sheer curtains. Curled up on the couch, Momma dreamt of gardenias and dancing, bubbles from yesterday's *Lawrence Welk Show* still floating like shining, transparent pearls in her head.

Then a TV bulletin flashed the news. Momma sat upright. Her thick, wavy black hair fell from a French roll.

"Shorty. Come here. Quick." She yelled to me washing dishes in the kitchen. "The news just said that the Cuyahoga River caught fire today. I just can't believe that—a river catching fire. Lord, what's going to happen to Cleveland next?"

"Momma, can I go? Can I go see that river burn?"

No. I could not go with Edward Mims, Ruthie Clark, and a bunch of other, older kids to actually see the flaming, burning waves, the black smoke. The gang would report back to the whole neighborhood on East 123rd Street in Mount Pleasant. Momma's decree came as a relief. Standing on the shore of a burning river might be bad for me. Surely a veil of stinging smoke and ash would blind all who dared come near enough to witness the wonder.

The Cuyahoga was an oily eel of a river that slithered through the Flats, the city's industrial alleyway, and then on into Lake Erie.

It separated the East Side, where we lived, from the West Side, home to poor white people who, according to Momma, came from Russia and Eastern Europe and liked to bake and sell sweet, sticky pastries.

Sitting on the porch steps, I shut my eyes tight and conjured images of a fiery wedge dividing the city in two like something from one of Reverend Berry's Sunday sermons at Mount Olive Baptist Church. How deep could the waters of a burning river run? Would the river evaporate into a rainbow? I squeezed my eyes tighter to find the colors of the firmament over a burning river.

Of course, TV supplied logical, adult explanations, something about government regulations or violations and dumping by irreverent industrial tenants. But Momma and other neighbors seemed to blame themselves. I went right along with them. Heaven had perpetrated an unnatural act upon our city, and therefore upon us. Bewildered, we puzzled over what sin had brought this bizarre punishment down on our house and whether it should be perceived as prophecy.

Everybody on East 123rd Street searched for an answer. Next door, old Mr. Fletcher, who labored at a steel mill by day, drove a pale yellow 1960 Cadillac home from work in the evenings, and tinkered in his basement "laboratory" by night, believed the burning river was part of a conspiracy. "You know, Miss Lillian, Cleveland done become the dumping ground for de whole worl'," he said over the fence to my mother as she hung sheets and drawers on the backyard clothesline. "And the more colored people you get in here, the more they going to try and dump these poisons on us, till you won't be able to drink no water 'r breathe no air. The birds won't be able to fly. I b'lieve that. Yes, I do. Pretty soon, we won't even be able to take a decent bath. A river catchin' fi'. Now, who ever heard of such unusualness?"

Some awaited the next Sunday, when Reverend Berry would preach a sonorous sermon from the humble pulpit of Mount Olive Baptist that would surely explain everything.

Momma was not one for showing up at church every Sunday, though she was faithful at sending me and my older sister and brother. After Sunday school, they fled. I stayed. It wasn't so much fear of Reverend Berry's God that made me stay, though it seemed he wanted everyone to be afraid of the Lord. Instead, it was my own spirit trying to find a force, somewhere, maybe even inside, that would help me be smarter in school and never flunk a grade again like I had done in third.

"It was ek-tra-or-dinary sinning that caused this ek-traor-dinary fire—a con-fla-gray-shun—burning upon the very waters that Jesus hisself once walked upon," Reverend Berry declared. He wiped slight perspiration from his bony forehead and kept right on preaching. "And the only way to cease these ek-tra-or-dinary fires is to cease our ek-tra-or-dinary sinning. You may not b'lieve it. But it ain't no less the truth."

I did not believe for one minute that Jesus Christ himself had ever walked on the Cuyahoga River. His white robes would get filthy dirty walking out there on water that wasn't even fit for fish to swim in. Plus, if Jesus was out there, why didn't he stop that fire? There was no one to consult on these matters.

I sat in the pews, scrunched between two broad-bosomed and well-powdered ladies with dead-headed foxes slinked over their shoulders. The ladies sort of hummed softly to themselves, hmmm-mmmm. As Reverend Berry preached, I imagined myths that could have set the river afire. A mischievous sun had sneaked beneath the horizon just long enough to strike fire to the river. Or a falling star had sparked the flames while the moon over Cleveland looked on coolly. Or perhaps an expelled angel was to blame. Hurled out of heaven with such force that her wings must have ignited, setting fire to the river as she plunged toward hell. Or a demon had managed to climb up 500,000 leagues from the depths of the lowest hell to reach the river's surface and flee, leaving an unidentified soul smoldering on the waters.

In July, Momma and all of us gathered around the TV and

watched a man walk on the moon like he was floating in his own dream. Wherever he was, I knew Charles Lyles was watching too, wondering what it would be like to step out into the stars. But the man on the moon was no wonder compared to the burning river. It was closer to home and therefore more worthy of my pondering.

I could hardly make sense of the mystery at hand. All I knew was that this wasn't the first time Cleveland had burned.

The first match had been struck to Cleveland in the summer of 1966. I was seven then. Smoke and ash eclipsed the noonday sun. Across town in a place called Hough, "Negroes were riotin', fightin', and carryin' on," Momma said.

For three days straight, Momma watched the riot reports on our secondhand TV. She left only to report to her job as an elevator attendant at Sterling-Lindner-Davis department store, downtown. All evening, she smiled at well-to-do shoppers and in a pleasant voice asked, "What floor please?" (She had practiced at home in front of the mirror.) At closing, she rushed to catch the No. 14 home to watch the riot. She settled in front of the TV, spread a blanket at her feet for my toddler siblings to play on, then turned on the dull gray screen.

Grainy as ghosts, men and women ran down streets, hurling rocks and sticks and yelling. One man looked right into the TV camera. His eyes bulged big and ugly as the bogeyman's. One boy pulled his striped shirt over his head, struck a match to it, and threw it in a storefront. A white fireman held up a hose that had been slashed in two.

Momma was a practical woman. Having been married to Charles Lyles, a man who spent his days out roaming the cosmos, Lillian Lyles couldn't help but have her feet planted firmly on the planet. She had five children to raise by herself: John, three; and Tinky, four; me; Linda, thirteen; and Scharlton (who was known as Dynamite because of his bad temper), fourteen. She had to pay the rent, heat, and electricity for the first floor of a drafty three-story house. And she had to do it with a welfare check and any menial job—

cleaning for $10 or $20 every other Saturday or running elevators a few nights a week. An just in case Tinky began convulsing in an asthma attack, $5 or $10 had to be set aside for a cab or a jitney to speed the whole family to the St. Luke's Hospital emergency room. For some reason, Momma did not feel she could count on the city ambulance.

Occasionally, Momma swooned when she heard Gladys Knight sing about love. And sometimes, she ducked out to a Heaven and Hell Party: hot foods and fast music ("Devil with the Blue Dress On") downstairs; sweets, love songs, and slow dancing upstairs. But when it came to matters of money, Lillian Lyles shook herself and her children back to reality with her special brand of practical poetry.

When we forgot to switch lights off in a room, she'd say "Wasting electricity. That's like throwing money up a wild hog's ass."

"Momma, do you have ten cents so I can buy a candy necklace from Mr. Bets's store?"

"Child, I'm broker than the Ten Commandments."

"Momma, do you have some money for me to get me some soap bubbles?

"Girl, my money is low as hens' teeth."

"Momma, I need new shoes."

"I'll get them just as soon as I can spell *a-b-l-e*."

Being such a practical woman, Lillian Lyles couldn't help but be political. From watching the Dorothy Fuldheim show, she had learned to be hard on politicians and call them liars right to their faces on the TV screen. Dorothy Fuldheim was a hard-bitten and feisty local news commentator who made her reputation trying to wring the truth from Cleveland politicians. We kids cried to see cartoons when old Dorothy Fuldheim's wrinkled horse face appeared on the TV screen. But Momma shushed us up. "Dorothy Fuldheim may be not so good looking, but she knows something about this world and she doesn't let these lying-assed politicians tell her just anything."

When Momma talked about the politics of the riot her voice was dry with disgust, like she was looking at stale cigarette butts in an ashtray.

"None of this would have happened if they had gotten rid of that damn Mayor Ralph Locher and let Carl B. Stokes be the mayor," Momma said to the TV screen as she tied John's shoe and wiped his spitty chin. That boy was always slobbering.

"Negroes are mad enough to fight and burn down their own neighborhoods and that Mayor Locher is trying to pretend not a thing is wrong. He's hurtin' the whole city. And he still gets to hold on to a good job."

From the intense look in her eyes and the way she pursed her mouth, I believed that my Momma could have run the whole city from her rented living room while watching her babies and snapping green beans into a bowl. Momma's practical soul and solid will could have righted all Cleveland's wrongs, mended all its incorrigible divisions.

On the third day of watching the riots, I reasoned that Momma might want to talk to me instead of the TV.

"Momma, why do the Negroes want to fight?"

"Why do *we* want to fight," Momma corrected, keeping her eyes on the blurry, blinking picture on the screen while she dusted an old secondhand table scarred with cigarette burns.

"Why do we want to fight?" I repeated, not quite catching on that Momma had included me in with the Negroes.

Momma was quiet for a minute like she was when her children asked about things that only adults needed to know about. "None of your business/Cut your chitterlins/Hadda been a white girl you would mine your own business," was the answer I expected. But Lillian Lyles was just taking a minute to mourn the way a mother must when she can no longer keep from her children the secret of skin.

"Because the white man don't want to treat Negroes right no matter what we do," she said quickly, moving to a shelf to dust plastic flowers. The edge in her voice cut my curiosity. I did not wish to know more.

Unless they were on television shows like Lawrence Welk or Ed Sullivan, "the white man" seemed to make Momma and everybody else angry. And my big sister Linda had said that once you grow up, that's when they really start treating you mean. Other than Mrs. Bryant, my kindergarten teacher, I hadn't had much to do with the whites. And I planned on keeping it that way since nobody liked them.

Down the street in front of Mr. Bets's corner candy store, men long retired from the steel mills sat in cheap aluminum lawn chairs on the sidewalk, arguing about the riot all day. When I popped in to purchase a nickel's worth of penny candy for me and my doll baby, named after Tabitha on *Bewitched*, my favorite television show, I heard them.

"You know what got the whole thing started, don't chu?" Mr. Willie Joe loved to "talk controversial." He was itching to get the "'cussion" going.

"Oh, yeah. I know what got it started, alright," said Mr. Paul, nodding his head and spitting into a Red Man snuff can. He was not quite as smart as Mr. Willie Joe and knew it. "It was when that niggah, drunk off of red wine, went into that bar and asked fo' a glass a water. Man that own the place told him, 'No water for the colored.' Then he put a sign on the do' that said, 'No Water for Niggers.' That there is when the trouble broke out."

Leaning against Mr. Bets's big storefront window, I listened. "A niggah drunk off of red wine." Could it have been Charles Lyles? Momma had said that he liked to drink wine too much. That is why the year before she had gone downtown to a stone building, big like a palace. Inside was a judge. According to Momma, the judge said that Charles Lyles could not come back home anymore and teach me about stars and planets in the backyard late at night because now he was divorced from Lillian Lyles. Even if he did cause arguments, I had liked having Charles Lyles around and I missed his sour grape-smelling whiskers and wide, gap-toothed smile. I wondered if he still liked me a lot. The judge had ruled that Charles Lyles could visit only once a week—if he wanted to, Momma said. But he never did. Now maybe Charles Lyles was way across town, setting the city afire. I listened for more telltale signs of my father. There were none.

"Now, see, I b'lieve you wrong there. That niggah, drunk off red wine, was just the tip of the iceberg," piped up Mr. Soodie MacIntyre. He was retired from Republic Steel mill but still wore his blue uniform every day.

"I b'lieve the whole thing was brewin' for a long time. Remember way back in January when the whites and the Negroes was fighting over there in Sowinski Park?"

"You right. You right," Mr. Jeffries said finally, as if he had weighed all the evidence.

"Well, I b'lieve you wrong," said Mr. Willie Joe. "The whole thing started 'cause the police didn't want them colored children meetin' over at that there John F. Kennedy House, learnin' about Negro history, Africa, and what's his name? Jomo Kenyatta. People at city hall don't want them kids congregatin' and talkin' 'bout Africa. They tried to bring the psychologists and the psychiatrists in on them. Say they need to be studied."

"I don't b'lieve none of it would've happened if they had gone on and elected that boy Carl B. Stokes for the mayor," said Mr. Soodie MacIntyre.

"You right. 'Cause this fella we got in here now, Locher, he act like a ostrick with his head in the rocks." Mr. Jeffries slapped his skinny thigh and rested his forearms loosely at his crotch the way I had seen old men do.

"And you know that boy Carl B. Stokes is qualified. The boy's a lawyer," said Mr. Paul. "But naw, they can't stand the thought of a colored man sittin' down there at city hall, runnin' the show. But I sho b'lieve you right. Stokes could've kept the peace."

After the smoke cleared, the riot had merely singed the surface. Deep down, Momma said, nothing had changed in Cleveland. It was like meat that burns to a crisp on the outside but inside remains bloody raw.

The fires came again when Martin Luther King was killed.

The night it happened, I was watching *Bewitched* on television. Eudora had cast a spell on Darren that made his ears grow every time he told a lie. And he was telling plenty to cover up a surprise present for Samantha. His ears were as large as two of Momma's skillet-wide flapjacks when a man in a suit blinked on the screen and said that a "Reverend Dr. Martin Luther King Jr." had been shot right in the neck and was dead.

Momma came home from her elevator-operator job smiling. Thursday, April 4, 1968, was payday, and Momma had brought us a treat, a white and blue Hough Bakeries box of coffee-glazed doughnuts.

I promptly reported the most recent trauma in my life: "Momma, they cut the *Bewitched* show off right in the middle because Mr. Reverend Dr. Martha Lutha King got shot in the neck and he is dead."

Momma was a pretty lady with her pink shift dress on, fair skin and long dark hair and glittery dime-store earrings and bracelet. I felt bad for telling her something that made her cry.

At Lafayette Elementary School, teachers wept too. Even cheerful Miss Ruth Collins, with her rouged cheeks and large, happy, bobbing bosom that boys poked fun at, broke down and cried. A special assembly was called. A boy named Augustus Peeples sang a gospel song with no music. A girl in a plaid skirt and ruffled white blouse played a sad song on her violin. The whole student assembly stood to sing "We Shall Overcome," our hands held over our hearts, our faces shining with tears and the sheen of Vaseline.

The men at Mr. Bets's corner store were mad about the killing for days that turned into years. As they spoke, I nodded my head and bit down hard into peanut butter Mary Janes and green-apple rock candy, three for a nickel.

"The Negro ain't never gonna get his freedom now," Mr. Jeffries said.

"All America's gonna burn now," Mr. Willie Joe prophesied. "Yes it is. I b'lieve it is. I can see the flames coming."

"Naw. Naw," Mr. Jeffries insisted. "I b'lieve now that our boy Carl B. Stokes is the mayor he'll to be able to keep these Negroes under control. Them niggahs may burn up Detroit and Chicago, but in Cleveland ain't gon' be no fire this time."

Momma believed in Carl B. Stokes too. After one failed campaign, he had finally been elected "the city's first Negro mayor," she explained as we ate dinner and watched television—just in case some riots came on. In fact, Momma said, passing the cast-iron skillet of hamburgers soaked in onion gravy and pouring icy orange Kool-Aid, Carl B. Stokes would keep Negroes in Cleveland from rioting. "Here, you all take some of these potato sticks." She dumped them straight from the can onto my plate. "See that right there," she pointed when smoke and ashes and people running popped on the screen from other cities. "It won't happen in Cleveland." Momma shook her head, certain and proud. "Because the Negroes in Cleveland have got Carl B. Stokes. Yes, we do." She settled down and sipped her Kool-Aid.

Punching the air over his plate, my brother Dynamite pretended to be Cassius Clay, the boxer. Linda stroked freshly pressed bangs hanging unevenly over her big furrowed forehead. John and Tinky played with their food. I had heard the word before, but for the first time, I felt it was important to know how to spell it. With a potato stick as my pencil, I spelled it out in the air. K-n-e-e g-r-o w.

"No, siree." Momma was overjoyed enough to repeat herself. "We've got Carl B. Stokes in Cleveland."

Three months later, blue smoky clouds rose over Glenville on the northeast side. Momma's usually darting, laughing eyes darkened.

Dynamite was nowhere to be found. Through the evening, Momma asked, "Lord, where is my son? Where is my boy?" Around midnight, Dynamite came home, his clothes sooty and sweaty, his face blank and strangely calm. He never told. We never asked.

"You would think them niggahs wouldn't've gone crazy like that, knowing we got a black mayor downtown at the city hall trying to help the colored peoples," said Mr. Jeffries. He sat on his lawn chair outside Mr. Bets's store, chomping on fresh gray peels of Juicy Fruit chewing gum.

"That's why whitey let him get in there in the first place, thinking he could keep these niggahs under control 'fo they burn down the whole damn city." Mr. Soodie MacIntyre spoke his mind between nibbles of pungent, reddish sauce meat and crackers.

"Sho did. That's the only reason they voted for him in the first place," agreed Mr. Paul.

"But you know what? Niggahs is crazy," Mr. Jeffries said. "And that—what's his name? the one who started the whole thing?—Fred 'Ahmed' Evans. He crazy as a chinch. So is the rest of them militant niggahs."

"Now don't put your mouth on them boys," said Mr. Willie Joe. "They just fed up with this stuff. They ain't like we was. They shooting back now."

"Yeah, TV called 'em 'snipers.' Say they had carbines like the cavalry. Lord have mercy! Shootin' dead at the police. Can you b'lieve it?" Mr. Paul was getting all excited, like he was watching the Indians win a baseball game.

"I sho can't blame them. I'd join the damn black nationalists myself if I wasn't so old and good for nothin' but to set up in this here store every day," said Mr. Willie Joe.

"The steel mill messed me up, you know," said Mr. Paul. "But if I could join 'em, I sho would, 'cause we need a revolution in this country."

Mr. Soodie MacIntyre unfolded his analysis of the situation. "Police coulda started the whole thing. Mayor Carl B. Stokes is colored. But the policemens is still all white. 'N you know they'll knock a niggah upside the head in a minute. 'N even if they did start the whole thing, I bet ain't no investigation in the world going to ever tell the truth about that."

"You know what I b'lieve?" Mr. Soodie MacIntyre always talked like he was in on a big secret. "I b'lieve Carl B. Stokes hisself is a militant. And at the right moment, he going to seize the power. 'Cause he went right out there and marched with them black nationalists when they had that big parade on the anniversary of the Hough riot. Remember? He was right there in the newspaper, smiling next to one of them militants who was carrying a rifle. I'll never fo'get it long as I live."

"I tell you one thing though," said Mr. Willie Joe. "You can bet Carl B. Stokes won't be mayor for too much more longer. Whitey ain't going to let him get back in there again if he can't keep these niggahs from shootin' and burnin' up the damn city."

Just outside the swinging screen door, I listened and sucked hard on a SweeTart till the top of my mouth went raw. The riots, the way the flames darkened the sky like dust, were all like a bogeyman to me. They made me so upset that I wanted to leap into Mr. Soodie MacIntyre's lap and hide my face in the jacket of his steel mill uniform.

Before the death of Martin Luther King and the riots, neighboring women hardly ever spoke to Momma. They had hard-working husbands who earned good money in the steel mills. That woman who rented the first floor of 3220 East 123rd Street was on welfare and divorced from a "no-good man who never could get or keep a job," so the talk went. Her brood of five children was practically fatherless. We were regarded with turn-your-head pity, as if born with whole arms and legs missing.

But the killing of King and the riots left everyone on East 123rd Street talking to each other—in the line at Lawson's store, where Momma stopped to buy baloney, white bread, and orange juice, or over the backyard fence with Mr. Fletcher.

"The whole thing is just a damn conspiracy. Makes me so disgusted that I don't even want to put my teeth in." Old Mr. Fletcher pouted and kicked gravel in his driveway. "Just like when they killed my boy John F. Kennedy."

Lillian Lyles had no time to talk. She was rushing off to run elevators at Sterling-Lindner-Davis or to clean houses in the suburbs for fifteen dollars a day and bus fare home.

Still, enough for five children was hard to come by, and plenty was an impossibility. Toward the end of each month, our cupboards were bare. While Momma worked, we fed ourselves fried potatoes, grits, white bread, and slippery sardines. Some days, Dynamite bagged groceries at the Pic-n-Pay on Buckeye Road and returned home with potted meat, crackers, Kool-Aid, and a five-pound box of Domino sugar.

When the steel mills paid, we watched through the windows as neighbors unloaded big grocery bags full of bananas, Sugar Crisp cereal, hamburgers, buns, and pies. We didn't actually see pies, but imagined they were there, full of syrupy blueberries. On Saturdays, Momma brought home a paper bag of kosher wieners, a gift from the Jewish lady in the suburbs whose house she cleaned.

More and more often, Aunt May Jane, from Momma's side of the family, came to our doorstep, bearing pots of nourishment. Aunt May Jane was born with six fingers on each hand, as if Reverend Berry's God had crafted them to give more than other people's hands. Her favorite offering was an iron pot of nasty, sweet-tasting spaghetti. We sucked down every red noodle.

The summer of the burning river, I heeded lessons from Deacon Roach, my big biscuit-eating Sunday school teacher. He convinced me that baptism might save me and my family from the hell of hunger and poverty, and even stop the city from catching on fire.

On the third Sunday in August 1969, Momma graced the pews of Mount Olive Baptist Church with her rare presence. She wore a simple blue shift and no hat on her head. She had come strictly to witness her child's acceptance of the Savior.

"Take me to the waaaaaaters," the choir commenced. "Take me to the waaaaaaters to . . . beee . . . baptiiiiiized."

Behind the pulpit, the baptismal "candidates," in white gowns sewn from bed sheets, lined up like wingless angels. A hefty woman stood in front of me, her gown seams stretching over flabby sides. As we marched toward the tub, she sang out: "Oh, Lord. Oh, my Savior. At last, I come to thee."

"Take me to the waaaaaatahs. Take me to the waaaaaaatahs to . . . be . . . baptiiiiiized." Mrs. Circee's deep-fried Southern soprano flew high above the chorus into the rafters. "Take me to the waaatahs. Take me to the waaatahs . . ."

As the choir sang, I recounted the deal to myself. In exchange for my soul and "excellent" behavior in word, thought, and deed, my family would receive food all the time: bananas, Sugar Crisp cereal, hamburgers; buns, and pies, all kinds. Charles Lyles would return home—steel mill job or no steel mill job. The Negroes and whiteys would be happy together, no matter what. And the city would cease to burn.

But nothing changed after Reverend Berry's holy hands dipped my swim-capped head into his lukewarm redemption pool. So I remained prone to mischief. I swore that old Mr. Fletcher, next door, peed in the vanilla ice-cream cups that he offered us kids, though I had no proof. I slandered and secretly hated my best friend, Carmen, because she was simply too much prettier than I. Remorselessly, I ate the candy that Dynamite was supposed to sell to raise Boy Scout money.

"That baptizing didn't change you one bit," Momma scolded one afternoon as I scraped the grape jelly jar, leaving none for my siblings. "You're still as contrary and selfish as ever."

I intended to remain contrary until all terms of the baptismal deal had been met. So far, Charles Lyles had yet to return home. Plus, we were still poor and getting poorer. And Aunt May Jane didn't smile so sweetly anymore when she dropped off her vat of spaghetti. Instead, she wrung her six-fingered hands and shook her head.

Momma looked to her own savior. Mayor Carl B. Stokes was a more practical god, a gleaming god come to save the city. She was enamored of his charm. He sparkled when he walked; moved masses—Negroes and whiteys, East Side and West—when he spoke perfect sentences through perfectly straight teeth. Wherever he appeared, citizens worshipped at his feet, intoxicated by political promises. Momma was a believer. She made up songs about how Mayor Carl B. Stokes was going to make a miracle in Cleveland. "Gonna be a change in this old town," she warbled off-key as she dusted artificial flowers or the chrome television stand. "And I know the man who's gonna make it so."

Momma was always talking about how much had changed "in this factory town" since Lillian Wardean Sullivan arrived in 1946 from Aberdeen, Mississippi, a tiny city of antebellum mansions on the Tombigbee River where cotton floated on its way to Mobile, Alabama. "We exchanged white folks' hatefulness for that icy wind off Lake Erie. Either one could slice right through you like a razor." Back then, according to Momma, the whole town was banging and clanging, alive with industry and opportunity. Down the Cuyahoga River came coal and iron. Men on barges worked into the night to widen, deepen, and straighten the crooked Cuyahoga. In winter, a season new to Momma, people pulled wool collars to their throats and walked swiftly down streets that seemed to gleam as if paved with steel. I could just see my mother, a girl again, "Little Lil'yan," pulling at her wavy plaits, bedazzled by electric street lanterns that could make a city shimmer like a crown.

But nowadays when Lillian Lyles took her daughters downtown on the No. 14/Kinsman Road bus, silent factories and smokestacks without smoke slid by. "I remember when Cleveland used to be something," she said to herself.

It still was something to me. "What is that tall building, Momma?"

"That's the Terminal Tower. It's the tallest building in Cleveland. Fifty-two floors."

"Why do they call it the Terminal Tower? What do that mean?"

"That's where all the trains used to pass through." There was also mystery on the rooftops of Cleveland's tall buildings. "What are those giant pots, Momma?"

"Water tanks."

Bridges carried us over what looked like giant silver sliding boards. "A chute for coal to come through," Momma explained.

At night, a few smokestacks still puffed out thick white clouds like pillows for every soul in the city to sleep on. And the May Company department store, downtown, would sell you anything you wanted if you saved up enough green Eagle Stamps, including a chocolate malt and hamburger with mustard and dill pickle. Cleveland was just fine with me.

The No. 14 huffed and puffed uptown past abandoned storefronts. "My man Carl B. Stokes is gonna change all this. Yes he is," Momma said, promising herself. "Cleveland is going to be something again."

Momma put her faith in "Cleveland: Now!," the mayor's multimillion-dollar urban renewal campaign. And she bragged about more and more Negroes being appointed at city hall. That last riot in Glenville had made the mayor look bad, but he vowed to resurrect Cleveland from the ashes, Momma said. He swore to unite the city, the blacks and the whites. Everyone would have their fair share. He promised summer jobs for "underprivileged" teenagers, like Lillian Lyles's children. He promised decent, low-cost public housing projects on the white West Side and on the East Side where the black social workers and teachers lived.

Both our saviors kept one promise. Once the flames died out in Glenville and the fiery river was quelled, the city ceased to bum.

That was when Momma announced that we were moving to the King-Kennedy Estates public housing project. It was named after her favorites, President John F. Kennedy and Martin Luther King. (I had seen both their big funerals on TV. Beautiful white horses had pulled Mr. Kennedy's coffin through the streets; a mule pulled Mr. King's.)

"We made it. We made it," Momma practically sang one night in September at the beginning of the school year. Our name, Lyles, had risen to the top of a year-long waiting list for an apartment in the new King-Kennedy, built by the Cleveland Metropolitan Housing Authority. It was public housing. Lillian Lyles's eyes were shining and flashing. She had done something remarkable for her family.

King-Kennedy was our chance to get ahead. Momma chattered on and on about it. What an opportunity it would be. At 3220 East 123rd Street, all six of us were crammed into two bedrooms, one of them makeshift. In the project, we would have three "nice" bedrooms and pay a lot less rent. The heat bill would be paid automatically by CMHA. Momma planned to save up money, find a better job, maybe even enroll in community college and develop a career. King-Kennedy was a chance she dared not miss. In the project, there would be "programs" designed to help people like us, if we worked hard. Maybe some day we would move back to East 123rd Street in Mount Pleasant, where the steel mill people lived. We would buy our own two-story, two-toned house with a bright painted porch and, in the evenings, sit right out on it. Strangers would pass by and envy us.

Chapter Five

MOVING MEANT LEAVING LAFAYETTE Elementary School. Conveniently located right across the street from 3220 East 123rd Street, Lafayette was the only school I had ever known—and loved, from the first day in wacky Mrs. Bryant's kindergarten to the day that I flunked third grade.

My father's comings and final going had distracted me from the serious third-grade tasks of reading and arithmetic. No equation would add up with yelling, screaming, and jars crashing to the floor at night when Charles Lyles returned home from the Kinsman Bar and Grill. In the morning, I reported to class, my arithmetic homework paper blank but for blue lines and my uncoordinated signature. My teacher, Mrs. Hexter, shook her head, sad but fairly certain that giving up on me was the best she could do.

I was held back for one year, during which I grew taller than every third grader at Lafayette Elementary School. I looked down at my elfish classmates as they compared my giant, size five loafers to their sizes three and four. This did not assist my efforts to disappear. Too humiliated to answer questions, I studied my knees when the teacher called on me.

Somehow I managed to make it to fourth grade. There I was rescued by the magic inside Miss Collins's bosom. She was perfumed, rouged, tall, and very slender, with breasts that bounced jauntily down the hall, a full ruler length ahead of her. They had a life all their own. You could almost hear fun Disney tunes playing in the background as Miss Collins bobbed along like Baloo the bear.

The teacher who had flunked me had been flat-chested and factual. But Miss Collins's merry bosom was full of imagination. Old, scoldy women used their broad bosoms to tuck away coins tied in white lace handkerchiefs. But Miss Collins's bosom harbored song and surprise.

"Good morning, children. I feel good today. Don't you?" Miss Collins was always ever so fresh, as if she had awakened in a bed of daisies, breakfasted on honeydew, and ridden a sunbeam to work and parked it right in front of the school. "To start the day, we're going to do the Navajo Indian rain dance. It will fill our minds with colorful, magical thoughts. Up, up, everyone on your feet."

"Miss Collins she so pretty/She got meatballs for her titties," came taunts from nasty, unruly boys who sat in the back of the classroom. "She got bacon and eggs between her legs/And that's why she so pretty."

"Now, you young men in the back, I'll bet you know a nicer song than that to sing," was her gracious reply. Disappointed that their disrespect had hardly ruffled the indomitable Miss Collins, the boys in the back fell silent.

Taken with my dramatic talents and poetry reading skill, Miss Collins selected me to lead the chorus line in her original Mother's Day production, *Give My Regards to Mother*. But even before that, my grades had begun to improve. There were no signs of brilliance, but I was alert and attentive, adding and subtracting, reading and writing, showing and telling, even though my feet were still the longest under all the desks.

Some day, I would grow up and sprout a bosom just as joyful as Miss Collins's, bringing merriment to all fourth grade girls and boys. Parting from Miss Collins would be hard. She had rescued me from my first failure in life. For that, I owed her and Lafayette School my eternal presence. How could I simply pack up and move to another school?

And what about my big brother Dynamite? How would he know where we had gone? Not long after the last riot, he had been sent away to a place called a "detention home." That summer, he had seemed restless, confused, and ripe for trouble. One warm night in September, a policeman had knocked at the door. When Momma opened it, red siren lights streaked across the living room, the TV screen, and her frightened face.

"Is Mr. Charles Lyles in this evening?" asked a deep voice that came from a skinny boy in a blue uniform. I pressed my face to the living room window to see his face. It was long, narrow, and speckled with pink bumps like chinch bug bites. He was a white. Some whites had called on the telephone before to ask Momma about bills—I could tell they were the whites by their voices. But this was the first white to ever come right up to our door, except for Momma's insurance man.

"No, Mr. Lyles is not home." Momma never volunteered the information that this was no longer Mr. Charles Lyles's residence.

"Well, are you the mother of Scharlton Lyles, alias 'Dynamite'?" asked chinch-bug face.

"Yes. He's my son," Momma said.

"Your son is being held in juvenile custody in connection with a burglary tonight, Mrs. Lyles. That's correct? You are Mrs. Lyles?"

"Yes. I am."

"We'll need you to come downtown to the juvenile court building tomorrow morning, first thing, for arraignment on these charges."

Momma huffed as she closed the door quietly and leaned against it. It was after nine o'clock at night, no time to be crying and carrying on. Quickly, Momma formulated a plan and threw it into action. "Linda, I need you to stay home from school tomorrow to take care of Tinky and John. Sugarbabe, I want you to go on to school, but help your sister out when you get home. Hear me?"

After many trips downtown, Momma sadly reported that a judge had found Dynamite guilty of breaking into a store and stealing cigarettes and a jar of pigs' feet. He would be sent to Hudson Farms, a detention home for boys. If he was good, he could come home in two years.

"Hanging around with the wrong crowd got him in trouble," Momma said. "Watch who your friends are."

"Momma, what is the detention home?" To me, it sounded like a mean place, like something in an old army movie.

"The detention home is where they send you when you won't do right to try 'n straighten you out."

"Can you have pets at the detention home?" Without pets, lots of them—dogs, fishes, turtles, rabbits, hamsters, white mice, snails, birds (everything except cats)—my brother Dynamite would not be happy, even if the detention home was a friendly place with nice people.

For he was rescuer, caregiver, and lover to every stray animal to be found on East 123rd Street, in garages, backyards, sheds, and gardens. Ever since he was old enough to dig in dirt, Dynamite had bestowed upon me worms, snails, wood lice, big black ants that had wandered from the colony. He advanced from invertebrates to reptiles. Striped garter snakes slithered along my hopscotch game. From one of his first trips to Woolworth's five-and-dime store, Dynamite returned toting a clear plastic bag full of water and three fishes that shimmered golden orange, like little living sunsets. He nursed, cleaned, and cared for each, all the while reminding me that every creature truly belonged to me, a big brother's gift menagerie.

Homer, a shaggy black and white stray cocker spaniel, was the last gift from my brother before his banishment to the detention home. Homer had made his share of bad causes in life: eating Hoover, a stray, red-eyed white bunny rabbit, and leaving her remains on the back steps to horrify Miss Annie Lynn, the cranky woman who lived upstairs; dismembering a nameless, disoriented turtle who had escaped his bowl, never to return; plus, snapping at the goldfish in Dynamite's aquarium.

For each act of brutality, I beat Homer bad with a plastic hair brush. After the flogging, new affection for him flooded my heart. Despite his growling threats, my arms ringed his neck and we were friends again.

Then Momma announced: No pets would be allowed in the project. The Cleveland Metropolitan Housing Authority had said so. We would be as miserable as Dynamite without pets. From listening to Momma as moving day drew near, it became clear that CMHA ruled the projects like a king. The kingdom now included our lives. CMHA would tell us what we could keep to love and what we must discard.

A few days before the scheduled move, my fifth grade class went to Severance Hall to hear the Cleveland Orchestra play music that only fairies in crinoline could dance to. When I got home, Homer was gone. His old mangy tail wagging up, down, counterclockwise was nowhere to be found. My throat tightened. Tears were a waste of time. Instead, I wondered just what kind of place were we going to that wouldn't allow a girl to have her a dog?

Plus, how would I remain friends with my best friend, Carmen, if we moved to the project? She was pretty with a pointy nose. Mine was flat and lumpy. But her free-hearted hands were always sticky with a blue-green Freeze Pop or a sugary candy necklace just for me.

One night in late October, while trying to doze off in my dismantled bunk bed, it came to me. Moving to the project was not such a good idea after all. I tippy-toed across the icy linoleum floor to tell Momma. She slept in a room that had been built to be a dining room.

"Momma." I put my face right up to her pillow. "Momma."

She stirred and sniffed. "Did you brush your teeth before you went to bed?" Nothing roused Momma's wrath more than a child delinquent on tooth brushing. "Go in there right now 'n' get the baking soda and brush your damn teeth before they fall out of your

Do I Dare Disturb the Universe? / 61

head. You hear me? The Lord has blessed you with nice teeth. But if you keep treatin' 'em the way you do, you won't have any."

"But Momma—"

"I don't want to hear your excuses. Just go in there and brush your teeth. All kinds of germs are growing and crawling all over your teeth right now."

Goodbye to the backyard of 3220 East 123rd Street. To the big dark garage where Mr. Fletcher tried to show little girls like me his "experiments" until his wife found out about it and in the quiet of their living room one evening poured a bucket of lye over his head that shriveled his left eye like a turkey butt.

Good-bye to the wise men at Mr. Bets's store.

Good-bye to the droopy clothesline that cranky Miss Annie Lynn loaded down with her large-sized panties, girdles with silver hooks, brassieres, and occasionally a red hot-water bottle.

And good-bye to the backyard's sweet-smelling grapevine, the intoxicating plum tree, wild peppermint weeds, and morning glories so lazy they opened at noon.

Good-bye to Reverend Berry, who taught me that God was the father of a blue Jesus who sat in a stained glass window in the rear of the church, the sun shining brightly through his robes.

Good-bye to big, biscuit-eating Deacon Roach, whose Sunday school class taught me how to sing, how to hope, and how to pray.

But Momma had made it clear: The move to the project did not mean good-bye to our blue-collar aspirations.

She scheduled a moving date and issued instructions. From Mr. Bets's store, we were to fetch cardboard boxes, the biggest we could find, then pack up the secondhand dishes, cast-iron skillets, assorted cracked bric-a-brac, dusty bouquets of aging artificial flowers, worn blankets, the straightening comb, the almost-paid-for set of encyclopedias, the pair of run-over, paint-spattered house shoes that Charles Lyles had left behind, every piece of our lives.

When the King-Kennedy Estates public housing project officially opened in November 1969, Lillian Lyles and her children were one of the first three families to move in.

Project. I did not like the name. It sounded like an experiment for science class: You proved your premise, dissected the insects or frogs, disposed of them, and then the whole thing was done with.

King-Kennedy stretched from East Fifty-ninth Street to East Sixty-sixth between Scovill and Woodland avenues. It lay just a few blocks east of some of Cleveland's oldest and largest public housing projects, the Carver and the Portland-Outhwaite homes. The House of Wills, a funeral parlor painted pale pink, stood right between the new project and the old.

All along, I had known that no real trees were going to grow in a place called a project. Instead, thirty-two three-story brown and yellow brick buildings sprung up over acres of frozen, cracked earth, tough flowers on a desert in winter. The buildings' concrete edges cut sharp into a white sky. I squinted my eyes at the starkness. Roofless and windowless, more than a dozen buildings were still under construction.

I grieved the loss of the trees on East 123rd Street just as lilies mourn the end of spring. There would be no shade of poplar in summer. No spooky shadows of elm in autumn or crispy leaves to crackle underfoot. No oak branches to drape colored lights on at Christmas. Where was I supposed to climb? Pick plums? Hunt acorns? And stock up on sour stink bombs to hurl at newfound enemies?

There were only frail, crippled, never-grow-into-nothing-looking saplings, hooked up to braces to keep from blowing away in a mild winter wind.

Momma saw hope in the project landscape. King-Kennedy was "urban renewal at its best," she said. It was a vision fulfilled, as promised and fought for by her favorites, John F. Kennedy, Martin Luther

King, and of course, Carl B. Stokes, even though she admitted that he didn't have much to do with the building. "You know it's good if the federal government built it." Momma bragged as if she were advertising the projects in a commercial.

Each building in King-Kennedy had been assigned a number and letter, B-10, A-18, C-6, as if the people inside were units of warehouse inventory. There seemed to be no rhyme or reason to the numbering, just some senseless code that the all-seeing CMHA used to keep up with everybody.

The Lyleses were assigned to 2530 Bundy Drive, Building A-11, Number 129. One of twelve units, four to a floor, Number 129 was our brand-new, never-lived-in-before, three-bedroom apartment.

Living in A-11 was like living inside a vault. The place seemed specially designed for me to play secret agent woman or "The Girl from U.N.C.L.E." To enter Number 129, I had to go through three heavy metal doors. Each led deeper into the stark cinder-block sanctum of the building. Slamming and echoing behind me, each locked out some dreadful counteragent who sought to eliminate me and steal my files. The first door opened to a long hallway of cinder block and steel stairs. Overhead was a high plaster ceiling with naked white light bulbs. Underfoot was an antiseptic tile floor. Next, a steel door with a small window (like on *Get Smart*) led to an inner chamber and finally the door to Number 129.

In the hallway, I met my new friends. Dee-Dee Saunders was gap-toothed, tall, wiry, and agile, with a short shock of black hair like a cantankerous cockatoo. She could swing from the second floor stair landing then let go, leaping at least nine feet to the first floor. She dared the rest of us to do likewise. Her physical prowess shamed us, even the boys. Her malicious mischief scared us. She was a girl operating without a god, a bully from birth.

Dee-Dee's family (eight sisters, one mother, and a short man with crooked teeth, bright pink gums, and reddish eyes), had packed up their lives out of the ashes of the Glenville riots to move to the project. Other families had come from the old Hough neighborhoods, where the first riots had struck. Others, like us, had come from uptown neighborhoods where the steel men lived.

The Williams brothers, Antoine, twelve, Darryl, thirteen, and Keith, nine, had come from just down the way, off Woodland Avenue and Sixtieth Street. On bus rides downtown with Momma, I had seen their old neighborhood. There were rows and rows of houses so old they seemed to slant in the wind, and so weather-beaten that they faded right into gray skies in late autumn. According to Antoine, moving to the project had made the Williamses the envy of all their friends. "Them niggers think they something 'cause they moved to the project." Others marveled: "'Oooooooh. The projects are real nice. I heard some of them apartments got two bathrooms. One day, we going to move in there too.'"

But the names of those left out of King-Kennedy had been too far down on "the list," Momma had explained. (I imagined a single sheet of paper as long as a roll of toilet tissue.) My mother, queen of efficiency, had signed us up long ago, when she was certain that she would not allow Charles Lyles to come back and when heating bills were way too high for her to pay enough to keep my sickly, asthmatic baby sister Tinky warm in the dead of an Ohio winter in our drafty flat. Surely life in a warmer apartment where wind didn't blow right through raggedy window seals would help Tinky sleep through the night without waking up wheezing for air. And Linda and I wouldn't have to worry anymore about Momma coming home and finding Tinky gasping for breath, her lungs collapsed, her dark eyes frightened of death. Now Dee-Dee, the Williams brothers, and I were the chosen, lucky enough to live in a brand-new project. We thought we were something.

The Williams brothers were long and skinny, like black licorice string. They were cool. Plus cute. They made me feel like I wanted to be somebody's girlfriend. All the time, they bragged about what a good job their mother had working at a restaurant across town. Real early every day, she left for work in a starched white uniform just like a nurse or a barber. In evening, the Williams brothers waited in the hallway to greet her as she walked vigorously up Bundy Drive in her white stockings and polished white shoes, lightly spattered with sauce after a hard day's work. In her hand, she carried a white grease-stained box of barbecued ribs.

And there were the Pierces: five teenage girls and L'il Joe-Joe. First came his squeaking, like a tin man badly in need of oil. Presently, seven-year-old Joe-Joe would come creaking around the comer, his twisted legs buckled into malfunctioning braces bought secondhand. Dee-Dee and the Williams brothers, athletic and sturdy, crowed cruelly at L'il Joe-Joe. Trying to get in good with my newfound playmates, I teased and mocked him too. "Hey, crip cool." It felt good. But the part of me that listened when Reverend Berry preached knew that I was just being a punk.

As we taunted him, L'il Joe-Joe lowered his metal-bracketed limbs on to the hallway's steel steps, clutched his set of secondhand bongos, and sobbed.

L'il Joe-Joe, Dee-Dee, Antoine, Darryl, Keith, and I became playmates by default; ours were the first families to move into Building A-11. Except for a few schoolmates, my circle of friends never grew much beyond them even as the projects filled up.

Winter days grew shorter. Mothers called children in earlier and earlier. One night in early December, just as our hallway playground was about to close down for the night, L'il Joe-Joe gripped his bongos between his knees and got up enough courage to play. His misshapen hands beat out a rhythm like blood pulsing syncopated through the four chambers of the heart. And songs we had never heard before—not on the radio, not by the Temptations or the Supremes—songs that seemed old, ancient, and full of vibrato rose from within L'il Joe-Joe.

Dee-Dee, the Williams brothers, and I stood. We were suddenly remorseful for our abuse and silenced into shame by L'il Joe-Joe's cinder block rhapsody.

The teachers at my new school, Dike Elementary, did not have bosoms full of joy, fun, and fantasy like Miss Collins at my old school. Gray-haired Mrs. Smith spat when she spoke, spraying me with a dose of harsh reality. She assured me that I would go nowhere—not even to sixth grade—until I understood that "organization is the key to success." I would also have to overcome a tendency to fantasize answers to serious questions with a perfectly straight face. "What did the Pilgrims do to make sure their crops grew?" asked Mrs. Smith. My hand shot up in the air before anybody else's. "They used special magic juice that came from their spit," I answered confidently. Saliva had become my latest fascination, so I thought it would provide an interesting answer, since most people had to spit sometime and they usually did it on the ground or in dirt. At the same time, I knew it was a risky answer because I was not quite sure whether the Pilgrims were able to get enough water to make good spit.

Chester Davis, a nappy-headed boy who always had flaky white stuff around his mouth, burst out laughing. My other classmates giggled, apparently pleased with my answer. Andrew Jefferson chewed on his fingernail and squinted his eyes, waiting to see if my answer was correct.

"Miss Charlise, that is a ridiculous answer," Miss Smith said. "I have told you time and again you're not allowed to make up answers to history questions or any other questions. Young lady, do you understand the difference between fact and fantasy?"

"Yes, Mrs. Smith. Facts are what really happened and fantasy is when you make it up. Right? And when you read a book it could be either one. Right?"

Mrs. Smith could not be made to understand this. She was frightfully serious and insistent that my classmates and I grow up to be responsible adults before passing to sixth grade. As she saw it, we were a generation about to encounter the greatest opportunities yet available to our race. There were to be new scholarship and aid programs designed especially for bright Negro students. So she had no tolerance for our silliness and fidgeting.

And of course, my schoolmates and I did not understand Mrs.

Smith's sternness. We believed pure evil drove her to be the meanest, oldest, moliest woman on earth, black or white, as she forced us to forget our fantasies and face a not-so-friendly world with hope, courage, and confidence.

The school principal, tall, wavy-haired, kind-faced Mr. Taylor, was just like Mrs. Smith. Even with all the aid and programs that were to come our way, he seemed forever sad-eyed, as if he knew something about some of our destinies that we didn't know and that made him want to weep.

In Mrs. Smith's class, Sheryl Turner sat right next to me. Her desk was full of dreams. Once during geography lesson, she lifted the smooth, shiny desktop. Inside were Crayolas, pencils, spiral notebooks, grape Now and Laters, gum erasers, Elmer's glue for making fake fingernails, and a worn record album cover. On it were four grinning brown men wearing matching vests and balloon-sleeved shirts.

"Sheryl? Why do you keep that record in your desk?" I whispered as Mrs. Smith pointed to Massachusetts and explained, "Now this is where the Pilgrims lived, boys and girls."

"That one is my daddy," Sheryl whispered, pointing to the smiling brown man in the middle. He was dressed differently from the rest in a Nehru-style jacket and turtleneck, like Sammy Davis Jr. wore. "He is in a singing group," she explained. "They made this album in New York City. My daddy can sing real good. And he is going to make a whole lots of money and send a lots of it to me and my mother. I'm getting a Christie Doll for Christmas."

Three rows behind me sat Wendell Wilson. He always acted like a brainiac know-it-all whenever Mrs. Smith asked questions. During recesses, he blabbed about his big brother being able to sing real good. "His name is Edwin Starr and he's going to sing for Motown records and stuff," Wendell stated, as if he was giving a book report.

"If he's your brother how come his last name is Starr and yours is Wilson?" I challenged, trying to catch old Wendell in what was dearly a lie. Plus, I was jealous. None of the Lyleses were making records or anything.

"Because he wanted a name that would make him famous, a name like nobody else's. That's why," Wendell Wilson snapped back. I could believe that, since Wilson sure wasn't the kind of name that could make anybody famous.

Regina Dots was the baddest girl in the class. She was pretty with a dimpled chin and moody, dark eyes. She acted up all the time. One day in the lavatory, I found Regina tossing sopping-wet paper towels to the ceiling where they stuck and dried. I washed my hands and gave Regina an I'm-gonna-tell-on-you look.

"I don't care if you tell on me." Regina confronted my reflection in the long mirror over the sinks.

"Your Mama's probably going to end up having to come down and talk to the principal." I tried to scare her into doing right.

"My mother can't come down to school to talk to no principal," Regina stated boldly. "My mother can't go nowhere 'cause she died last summer from the Hong Kong flu." With that, Regina ripped another paper towel from the dispenser, drenched it with water, and sent it sopping wet to the ceiling. It wrinkled and stuck like a wrecked angel wing.

I felt like a fool, and a cruel one at that.

All in all, school was good, especially because we now received free food every day. For breakfast, orange juice, cereal, and milk. At recess, we got graham crackers and milk. This was because Dike School was something my Momma and the teachers called a "Title One" school. More and more, teachers and others in charge whispered about us. We were "low-income," I heard them say. We were "underprivileged." We would need "government aid."

After-school chores were more exciting in the project than on East 123rd Street. There, dumping the trash had meant a boring trip to the backyard and a large, smelly, banged-up aluminum can—and a possible encounter with old Mr. Fletcher and his pissy vanilla ice-cream cups. If you were lucky, for your amusement there might be curly white maggots like little pieces of moving rice. But in King-Kennedy, dumping the garbage was an exciting trek to the eternal flame.

Every full garbage can was my chance to get closer to the incinerator. "Momma, can I take out the garbage?" I volunteered on boring winter nights, even when I could see that the plastic bag was only half-full of potted meat and pork and bean cans, empty Kool-Aid packs, white bread wrappers, and greasy meat drippings. "No. Wait until it's full or you'll use up all the plastic bags." But as soon as Momma was out of sight, I zipped up my hooded red fake-fur jacket, grabbed the garbage, and slipped out the door.

With my bundle slung on my back, I hurried past Building B-10 toward the incinerator. January cold bit at my bare fingertips. From her second-floor window, Dee-Dee laughed at me having to take out the garbage. I swear, that girl's imagination was in a coma. She couldn't see what I saw in the incinerator.

A small brick room full of flame, it burned hotter than all the riots put together, hotter than all of Reverend Berry's sermons on the depths of hell. The iron door was the size of our kitchen oven, the handle hot and heavy as a skillet. For a moment, the heat held me, blasting orange and blue. The flame moved like a woman dancing wildly, privately. She was sultry, liquid, licking off the sooty walls and gently murmuring some incantation. I let go of the garbage bag and stood back. The green plastic melted to a bright green flowy syrup. Our lives' debris disintegrated before my eyes. Flecks of black ash fell on my face and I was exalted.

At night, in Number 129, a metal contraption along the floorboards banged and clanged, exhaling heat. Undisturbed, we slept a warm, deep sleep that we had never known in the drafty flat on East 123rd Street. In the project there was no high gas bill to pay. With more money for groceries, our bellies were full. Momma had kept her promises. Still, I was not sure that every little thing would be all right.

Before lying down to sleep in the heat, I prayed to Reverend Berry's God. We had moved so far away that going to Mount Olive Baptist Church was no longer possible, but I still believed in Reverend Berry's God, even though he was not very likable. He seemed to always be in a bad mood and spent his time thinking up mean punishments and insisting that we really bad people slide. Plus, there was reason to suspect that he was white because the picture of Jesus hanging in Mount Olive Baptist was white. This meant he could not be trusted, if everything Momma and the old men at Mr. Bets's store had said was true. Secretly, I hoped to find out about another, nicer God, who was black like me, and switch my prayers to him. But so far, Reverend Berry's was the only one known to me. So I stuck with him since he had answered at least some of my prayers.

Did he know that we had moved? I could not risk having my prayers going unanswered due to us being unlocatable. "Dear God, we have moved to the King-Kennedy Estates project," I reported at the end of each evening prayer. "We live at 2530 Bundy Drive off Woodland Avenue. It's near East 55th Street—in Building A-11 in Number 129 on the first floor. You have to go through the hallway to get here. In Jesus' name. Amen."

Spring came. The moon eclipsed the sun and there was darkness in the day. This strange occurrence in the heavens in March 1970 sent some people hiding in their apartments. They peered out of windows in awe of a moon that dared to cross the sun. Dee-Dee, L'il Joe-Joe, the Williams brothers, and I stood hushed in the hallway, amazed at our absent shadows.

"You scared?" Dee-Dee, by now an aspiring career bully, always wanted to know who was scared.

"Naw. I ain't scared," I said, cocky. "My father, Charles Lyles, taught me a long time ago what a eclipse is. It happens all the time to the stars. It's when one star passes right over in front of another. That's what makes 'em twinkle."

"The sun ain't no star," Dee-Dee snapped back. "It's too big to be a star."

In five months of playing in the hallway with Dee-Dee, I had learned not to challenge her authority for fear of a butt kicking. But on the subject of astronomy, in which Charles Lyles had schooled me, Dee-Dee would have to reckon with me. "Yes, it is a star."

I had dared to defy Dee-Dee. Surprised, the Williams brothers and L'il Joe-Joe waited tensely to see who would win.

"The sun is just a big ball of burning gases. That's what every star is." I wasn't backing down.

"Sun ain't no gases," Dee-Dee spat back. "The sun is the sun. Period." To prove her point and stave off public embarrassment at her own ignorance, Dee-Dee laughed and let go a loud fart, wrapping me in a warm draft of odorous humiliation.

"*Is too* gases that burn in giant spheres," I insisted through the lump in my throat and the burn in my nostrils. "Think you know everything, but you don't know about the stars. *I* know about the stars. I know that every one of them has a name. That's what my daddy, Charles Lyles, said and he knows what he's talking about."

"If your daddy knows so much, why come he ain't here right now to 'splain it?" Dee-Dee was digging deep, trying to get me mad.

Because Charles Lyles is an astronaut and he has a lot of important things to do. That's the lie I started to tell. Instead, I shut my mouth and stood quiet in the darkness at noon.

Chapter Six

"YOUR LEFT. YOUR LEFT. Your left. Right. Left." From my perch on the hallway stairs, I heard the steps, stomping up the avenue. But I did not know yet the rhythm of "The Revolution" when I heard it. "Your left. Your left. Your left. Right. Left."

Surely, a parade was dancing down Bundy Drive. Or maybe, just maybe, the flamboyant, the fabulous East Technical High School Marching Band was high-stepping in their bad brown and gold uniforms, strutting and twisting golden tubas from side to side. Remaining at my post on the stairs became an impossibility.

Taken by twos, threes, and a flying leap over the last four, the stairs still wouldn't move out of my way fast enough. I flung open the red steel-plated door. There they were: millions and millions of black men in black clothing marching up the avenue. Row after row after row, they came like blackbirds ascending an autumn sky.

Your left. Your left. Your left. Right. Left.

From Woodland Avenue they advanced in a diagonal wedge formation, cutting a swath of Bundy Drive in black. *Your left. Your left. Your left. Right. Left.* From the sidewalk, a man called cadence. He wore dark glasses. A tam tilted atop his head at a gravity-defying angle. He never missed a step.

In black-jacketed solidarity, shoulders swayed in sync, flowing into one graceful wave, like the wings of birds sailing south. *Your left.*

Your left. Your left. Right. Left. Shades shielding their eyes from the midmorning sun, the men looked mean, mysterious as thunder.

Closer. I wanted to be closer to them, and took off running down the street.

Dee-Dee whirled and twirled toward the strange pageant, laughing and spitting between the gap in her front teeth the way she always did when excitement took hold of her.

L'il Joe-Joe took off behind us, trying to run in those creaky braces. Slightly off balance, backward and forward he went like a porch rocking chair in a windstorm. "Who is it?" L'il Joe-Joe demanded to know.

What did they stand for? Would they take me by the hand and lead me to the magnificent place for which they were surely bound? I wanted to be with them.

We reached the curb. I was near enough now to reach out and touch the moving black men, their stoic cheekbones outlined like onyx against the azure sky, their rebellious goatees and righteous fists clenched at their sides.

People spilled out of apartments, hallways, parking lots, trailing the marchers. Little girls skipped alongside them, swiveling Hula Hoops on narrow hips. Big boys toting transistor radios trotted to keep up. Women hauled babies on sturdy hips. Two old, tired, mangy strays yapped back to life.

"Black Power," someone in the crowd cried out with urgency. Suddenly every black fist rose in the blue sky, a million medallions swinging toward the sun.

"Revolution now," came another voice.

"Liberation," came another. "Freedom. Liberation. Now." If these men were bound for "Liberation," I wanted to go. It sounded like an excellent place to share with these men of power and grace.

A tall, thin boy, barely whiskered, brushed right by me. Not all the marchers were grown men. But there was manliness in the way they held their shoulders and locked their jaws so still and determined.

Your left. Your left. Your left. Right. Left. Highly polished brogans slapped the asphalt with insistence. *Your left. Your left. Your left.* Hands, big and small, clapped out the cadence. Like something being born, my heart pounded to the drumbeat of "The Revolution."

On the sidewalk, a man stood transfixed, his fist still raised to the sky. "Black Power," he intoned, bowing his head as if in prayer. "Black Power. Now!"

Bringing up the rear, a row of men held aloft a red, green, and black striped flag. It was the banner of our new-found freedom, flapping transparent and ephemeral in a sooty breeze. "Your left. Right. Halt," came the command. The marchers snapped still to attention, waited a beat, and recited in unison:

> Black is your color.
> Red is your blood.
> Green is the ground you walk upon.

A moment of stillness. In the silence, I saw slavery for the first time: a million muscled, gleaming men moving off ships, nigger-eyed and enraged.

"Hey bro," Keith whispered, trying to stir the attention of one marcher. But the man stood immovable, looking straight ahead through dark glasses as if Keith did not exist. This man's mission was too great. He could not be distracted by a chump kid like Keith. Fool. Couldn't Keith see that these men were not about playing in hallways and other jive? They were bound for liberation! Glorious liberation! Whatever that meant.

On cue from the cadence caller, the stepping started again, up-tempo, double-time: "Your left. Your left. Your left. Right. Left." Row by row, the marching men were leaving me now. I watched their shoulders and backs shifting gently left, right, left. Should I follow? Momma's "and-I-mean-business" warning replayed in my head: "Don't go anywhere past Building A-11."

The marchers rounded the comer at Scovill Avenue, disappearing into the dull spring day. *Your left. Your left. Your left. Right. Left.*

Dee-Dee, Keith, and I rushed back to A-11, erupting into a celebration of newfound black pride. Rapt by the rhythm of "The Revolution," we stepped, imitating the militants. "Your left. Your left." My baby brother John joined in. "Left. Right. Left."

We tried out our new oath:

> Black is your color.
> Red is your blood.
> Green is the ground you walk upon.

That verse pumped us with pride in a way that the Pledge of Allegiance never had.

"Unh ooom gawah, Black Powah," Dee-Dee chanted, gyrating her hips in a victory swivel.

I skipped about, snapping my fingers. The marching black men and their defiant presence had left me feeling what old ladies seemed to feel after Reverend Berry preached his best Sunday sermons. I had found a new faith—in what, I wasn't exactly sure.

"Them was the Black Panthers," Dee-Dee announced.

"No they ain't. Them was the Afro Set," Keith declared without pause from his marching spasm. "And they are black nationalists and they got guns."

"You don't know what you're talkin' 'bout, boy. They're the Black Panthers. Don't tell me. I saw it on TV. And they said they ain't got no guns." Dee-Dee thought she had set the record straight.

"Yes they do got guns," Keith persisted. "I heard it on the TV too. They said they got caches of guns."

"Aw, shut up, boy, before I kick your butt. They just marchin'. You don't know what chu talkin' about." Dee-Dee insisted that she knew what she was talking about.

"When did you see it on TV?" I asked Keith at the risk of being shot down and humiliated by Queen Dee-Dee.

The marching party quieted. Dee-Dee stopped leaping from the first step to the third and back. I settled on the steps. Keith leaned against the cinder block.

"My mother is the one that saw it." Keith started getting closer to the truth when it looked like we were going to be asking him some real serious questions.

He swallowed hard. Then Antoine, his older brother, jumped in to save him. "I saw it on TV too," Antoine stated boldly.

I suspected he was lying. But I listened. Maybe he could clear up some of the confusion.

L'il Joe-Joe creaked up to A-11, out of breath from following the marching militants. He leaned against a fire hydrant, those ever-present bongos tucked under one arm and his deformed hand held close to his chest. He had admired the marching men, moving left, right, left, moving in a way that he could not, moving like music. He stared through thick black-framed glasses, wanting to understand more about the men.

"Yeah," said Antoine. "We saw it on TV the other night. They got guns out in California, machine guns and rifles. A whole lots of 'em in a warehouse."

"See there, I told you." Keith couldn't pass up a chance to show up Dee-Dee.

"What they going to do with all them guns?" asked L'il Joe-Joe.

"They going to shoot wit 'em," answered big know-it-all Antoine.

L'il Joe-Joe pressed. "Who they going to shoot?"

"White people, stupid. They going to get them back for slavery, Martin Luther King, and everything," explained Antoine.

"They still got slaves?" L'il Joe-Joe was a little unclear on that one.

"Naw, you fool," Antoine and Dee-Dee chorused in mutual disbelief at L'il Joe-Joe's ignorance. "Don't you know nothin'?"

"Gheeyawd," Dee-Dee exclaimed in disgust.

"There ain't no slaves anymore but people are still upset about it," Antoine went on, taking pride in his superior grasp of history.

"Why come?" L'il Joe-Joe still needed more.

His ignorance was too much for Antoine. "Because, fool. The nationalists said that white people are still trying to treat us like slaves, still trying to oppress us."

"Right," chimed in Dee-Dee like she had seen the full picture all along.

"Oppressed? What do that mean?" L'il Joe-Joe was only seven going on eight. He remained confused.

"It means they got control of everything and only way we going to get it is to do some shootin'. That's why when I turn sixteen, I'm joining up with the black nationalists," declared Antoine. "Yep, going to haveta get me a tam," he added, sounding for a moment like an old man who had made up his mind about something. "Yep. I'm gonna join the Afro Set."

"OK then," L'il Joe-Joe agreed, nodding his head. He had grasped the basics. Now he needed time to process it all. So did I.

We never figured out just what group the marching militants represented: The Black Panthers? The Afro Set? Or some other nationalists? And we hadn't a clue on the political differences that divided them.

I decided that the militants were the Black Panthers. I liked the name. Panthers. It conjured images of fierce, sleek creatures moving from a center, full of energy yet in control. When I grew up, I planned to marry a Black Panther.

The marching militants were the harbingers of my black consciousness. Along with everyone in the crowd that day, I had felt the mystique of black American masculinity, the pain, passion, and power born of their oppression. Revolution, liberation—their vocabulary was beyond me. But in my heart I knew and now accepted that there was an enemy.

Neither my mother's tears over the death of Martin Luther King nor smoke rising in the sky over riots had made me understand truly. All I felt was sad and fearful. But the rhythm of those brogans stepping down Bundy Drive made me bold and strong against a clear enemy. *Your left. Your left. Your left. Right. Left.*

I traded in the bliss of childhood for the serious business of blackness and was better for it. Never again could I play innocently with blue-eyed, blonde, ruddy-cheeked baby dolls, though some looked like my mother. Never again would I pretend to be Bridget, Jeremy's wife on *Here Come the Brides*, my favorite Friday night TV show. Bridget was white. And therefore against me. Tabitha, Darren, Endora, and Mrs. Kravitz on *Bewitched* were against me too. *The Partridge Family. The Brady Bunch.* All my friends on TV who lived in nice houses were against me now. And I had to be against them. Captain Kangaroo, Dancing Bear, and Mr. Green Jeans. My younger siblings, John and Tinky, loved them. But I would have to break the news that they were white and against us. And Miss Louise on *Romper Room*, she was against us too. At the end of the show, when she looked out through her unstrung tennis racket at all the children of the world, Miss Louise had probably overlooked our names on purpose all those times just because we were black. Walt Disney, Tinkerbell, Mary Poppins, Dr. Doolittle, Chitty Chitty Bang Bang the car, all of them, against us.

Chapter Seven

THAT FIRST SUMMER IN the project, life was bright. The Black Pride movement empowered us and the goodness of federally sponsored programs lifted our lives.

For two years, Momma had listened closely for whispers, rumors, promises of opportunity that old men like Mr. Fletcher said would come flowing from the blood of Martin Luther King Jr. and others felled on the civil rights road. Church sermons prophesied it. Newspapers reported new "programs" and acts of Congress. Once Lillian Lyles got word of "funding" or "grants" or "initiatives"—or other words that I did not understand—she investigated immediately. Would it, could it benefit any of her five bright-eyed children?

Articulate, nitty-gritty, charming yet cautious, Momma deftly maneuvered her way through the public housing, social services, and educational bureaucracies to get at opportunity. She scoured community and recreation centers, the principal's office, and, on occasion, a church bulletin board. Once she uncovered opportunity, Lillian Lyles called on her every resource and skill to see that we took advantage.

For my big sister Linda, there was the Upward Bound program.

As soon as school was out in June, Linda, now "fifteen going on sixteen," stripped the Jackson Five, Stevie Wonder, Sly and the

Family Stone, Jimi Hendrix, and Chicago from the walls of the bedroom we shared. She and her posters were Upward Bound. The program offered two summer months of college education and living at Case Western Reserve University, way across town. Sponsored by the federal government, Upward Bound aimed to prepare "underprivileged" minority teenagers for college. If Linda worked hard, Momma explained, she might win a scholarship to a good college, and someday become a social worker.

"Linda is going to college." Momma practically made up a song about it.

I couldn't imagine Linda a social worker, whatever that was. Her outlook on life seemed limited to the day when the East Technical High School Scarabs basketball team would win the state championship and she would lead the majorettes down East Fifty-fifth Street, twirling and tossing her baton.

Twirling won Linda dubious respect from leather coat-wearing basketball players, band members, and a panoply of characters who dressed exclusively in Army-Navy store clothing and recited humorous ditties about the war in Vietnam: "Gotta doodoo/Gotta doodoo/If you're stuck in Vietnam/Use your finger to avoid a jam." In our small living room, Linda tossed and twirled that baton, just missing Momma's red and gold matador lamp. In front of the TV, she struck acrobatic poses, imitating skinny white girls in leotards on *The Gene Carroll Show*, the local Sunday afternoon TV talent search.

When Momma worked on Saturdays cleaning in the suburbs, Linda baby-sat John, Tinky, and me. She enthroned herself upon a high-backed floral chair, part of our new living room set from Kurtz's furniture store, downtown. The baton gleamed silver across her lap, a scepter. Transfixed by Angelique on *Dark Shadows* or one of half a dozen television shows that she called "my soap operas," the queen was not to be disturbed. One rattle, squeal, or other disturbance out of us and the scepter became a staff. Between her graceful fingertips, it whelped through the air, landing on our legs, booties, or the palms of our hands. Our revenge: the covert removal of the rubbery white baton ends that she scrubbed and polished to keep white.

Linda had nicknamed herself "Buster," which I assumed was a reference to her burgeoning breasts. She was thick-limbed, light as the flesh of a walnut, and freckly. Her breasts had definitely come in good (boys who hung out in the hallway had said so). I was determined that my own would grow in even better.

Linda was a good big sister. But I suspected that she had "done it." There was just something about her, a knowing. And each month when Momma did her "big grocery shopping" there was a lavender box, like a gift for Linda. On it, a suspiciously serene-looking woman smiled from a soft powdery-purple heaven. (Maybe she had just "done it" too.) The box was shrouded in silence. Linda simply accepted it from Momma or found it tucked under her pillow. I wasn't stupid; I knew that box had something to do with "doing it."

A young woman of enterprise, Linda always found work, including a summer job for underprivileged youth that spun off Mayor Carl B. Stokes's "Cleveland: Now!" campaign. Or she created work, like her home-based business crocheting red, green, and black tams for the Revolution. At least once a day, some fashion-conscious militant knocked on the door of Number 129. "Hey, is Buster there?" a male voice asked. "I want to order me a black, red, and green tam for four dollars." (The Revolution was not cheap.) In one night's sitting before the television, Linda could crochet up a tam. She assigned Tinky and me to place the finished product in a clear plastic bag for complete customer satisfaction.

For Linda, Black Power was mostly a fashion statement. The hippie and black militant movements met at her end of the closet we shared. She had sewn black, red, and green scarves into dashikis and knitted her own black, red, and green tams. Black-fisted medallions hung from hangers. She ripped up pants legs and T-shirts and called them fringed. She bought some clothes already torn up, like a suede vest and fringed moccasins. Other T-shirts displayed the cryptic proverbs of her post-hippie era adolescence. "Turn On, Tune In, Freak Out." The butts of her britches relayed other messages. "Yield." "Stop." "Go."

Linda and I lived in different worlds. She didn't invite me into hers and I wasn't curious enough to force entry. When she happily packed her posters and bizarre wardrobe that summer, I hoped only to follow in her fringed footsteps someday, upward bound, even though I knew that I wasn't nearly as smart as she was. For my big brother Dynamite, there was the summer Job Corps program, a dubious reprieve after two years in the detention home.

Dynamite had been my favorite sibling, bestowing upon me every manner of stray pet. But his crime of breaking into a store to steal pig's feet and cigarettes had left me upset with him. When he ended up in the detention home, as far as I was concerned, he was bad, doomed to hell, no longer worthy of being my brother.

But Momma had insisted that we visit him there. Once every three months, Momma, Linda, Tinky, John, and I had risen early on a Sunday morning. Momma wrapped fresh fried chicken in wax paper and carefully placed it in a shoe box. Like a Christmas gift, she wrapped three packs of Fruit of the Loom men's underwear. And we were off to Hudson Farms School for Boys. We met the Red Cross bus on East Fifty-fifth Street. "Lyles," a nun called off our name along with the names of four other families. We boarded the bus. She was the driver, charged with hauling us two hours or so east to Hudson, Ohio, and back.

What was this nice nun doing driving people to a detention home for boys who did bad things like my brother had done? Nuns were supposed to pray and care for innocent, pure children. Plus, she was white. With all five families on board, the petite nun slid into the driver's seat. Her back rounded slightly, she gripped the wide black steering wheel, mashed her black oxford down on the gas pedal, and sped east toward the interstate. Pale cheeks and lips without makeup, her face was stark, her eyes steady. Wind through a window filled her habit like a sheer curtain on a breezy spring day. It did not tickle her attention from the road. Across the aisle, scrunched between Momma and Tinky, I stared all the way to Hudson at the tough young angel, finally and reluctantly concluding that there must be some nice white people. I could tell that the nun was a woman who could fall humbly to her knees and compose prayers for the souls of the most damned, a woman who could pray away doom, even from my big brother Dynamite.

At Hudson Farms, buildings were numbered, just like in King-Kennedy. On one spring day outside Building 3, scores of boys, shaven-headed and bony, gathered behind a fence greeting visitors. Above them, concertina wire coiled like strange steel blossoms. "Ma." "Mamma." All the shaven heads, black and white, but mostly black, called out. At the far end of the fence, squinty-eyed, pointy-eared, and thick, stood Dynamite, an overgrown imp in state-issued dungarees.

Dynamite hugged Momma, took the shoe box of fried chicken, and led us into Building 3. It was a long, low cinder block structure that looked like a never-ending corridor. A huge blue-green circular sink stood at the center of the lobby. "I sure am glad y'all came all the way out here to see me," Dynamite said. We settled in blue plastic and chrome visitors' chairs. I looked around for tables with colorful magazines. There were none.

"Hey, Sugarbabe, girl. How you doing?" he said to me. "Are you taking good care of that dog I gave you? Yeah, old Homer. He's a good dog, you know."

I opened my mouth to tell him Homer's fate all because we moved to the project, but Momma shot me one of her "Don't-be-dirty-and-break-his-heart" looks. "Yep. Homer is fine," I lied and felt bad about it. Up close, I could see that my brother's nose had been badly bashed.

"What happen to your nose, Dynamite?" Momma asked, alarmed. "It looks like your nose has been broken."

"Naw, I'm all right," Dynamite said. "Got into a fight—an altercation—that's what they call it out here. I got into an altercation with one of them little punk white boys. That's all it was."

"They got a doctor out here, don't they?" Momma pursued it.

"Yeah. I went to the doctor after it happened. He said everything is fine. My nose just needs to heal. That's all."

My brother's nose never healed correctly. Nor did his spirit. He was no longer the slightly twitchy boy who bestowed every living stray creature upon me. He picked and gnawed at bloody nails bitten white way below the quick. His eyes, beady and deep-set, darted about the room. He leaned forward and pulled a pack of Kools and matches from his pocket.

"Dynamite? You done started smoking?" Momma asked, worried.

"Yeah. It ain't much else out here to do. They ain't tryin' to teach us nothin'. I'm supposed to be gettin' out of here by late summer if I keep up my good conduct record. Yeah. I should be home by August or September. That's what my counselor was telling me the other day."

John, Tinky, and I surveyed all the fuzzy-headed brothers in the big room.

"Ma, do you think I'll be able to get me a job so I can get me some nice clothes 'n' things when I get out?" Dynamite puffed nervously on his cigarette, squinting his eye from the smoke.

In July, Dynamite came home to Building A-11 for the first time. To his name, he had the white shirt and khaki slacks that Momma had bought from Sears and sent to Hudson. Since news of his return, Momma had been on the prowl for job programs for him. She found the summer Job Corps.

At first, Momma worried that the militants might lure Dynamite away to some revolutionary mischief. (I still wasn't sure what they did all day, and I had heard that some of them really did have guns.) But when they marched down Bundy Drive, my pointy-eared brother stood at the curb with us kids, in awe and angry at himself. He had neither the courage nor the will for the Revolution.

Picking up trash in parks and other public places with the Job Corps, Dynamite earned his first paycheck. Long before it was issued, he had composed a wish list: a Delfonics album, an aquarium and five tropical fish, a bright balloon-sleeved shirt, and a pair of black leather knee-length boots like the ones the Temptations wore. In the living room, Dynamite modeled his new outfit in front of the whole family while singing his falsetto impersonation of the Delfonics, "Didn't I blow your mind this time?"

Momma doted on her boy, "workin' a real job like a grown man now and wearing nice clothes." Dynamite was happy. I was happy.

We filled up the aquarium and named the fish. Blue, orange, and yellow, they were nothing more than streaks of fire as they swam back and forth. "That one there is named Sugarbabe," Dynamite said, pointing to the fish that kept bumping into the glass. I forgave my brother all his crimes.

Two weeks later, he came home early, his bashed-in face long and dejected. He waited two days before telling Momma: The supervisor had dismissed him. The reasons were unclear. He hung his balloon-sleeved shirt in his empty closet. All the tropical fish died. Dynamite couldn't bear to flush them down the toilet so I did it for him. We never talked much after that. Alone in the bedroom he shared with my baby brother, Dynamite passed the summer of 1970 smoking Kools, playing Delfonics albums on a cheap component set, and singing falsetto, "Didn't I blow your mind this time? Didn't I?"

For Tinky and John, there was Head Start. Momma promptly enrolled them in the preschool program for "underprivileged children," a new word in Momma's program vocabulary.

Head Start promised to prepare Tinky and John to excel in real school. Early each morning, a beige, nondescript van, marked HEAD START in huge letters, pulled up and they skipped on board to the center of the laughing load of snotty-nosed preschoolers. Each afternoon, the van deposited them at the curb, more pre-cocious than the day before.

Tinky was a clever-witted darling with three bushy pigtails orbit-ing her head. She was ticklish and gregarious. Full of the alphabet and an advanced preschool vocabulary, she spared no one her adult insights. She was also peculiarly punctual for a kid who had not yet learned to tell time. Up to fifteen minutes before *Truth or Conse-quences*, her favorite game show, was due on, she parked in front of the TV. "I'm getting ready to watch my show," Tinky would say.

Momma credited Head Start: "That program is teaching these kids to be on time," she said. "You sure can't get anywhere being late. My babies are going to be on time in life."

Tinky learned to read well before age six. Scanning beauty maga-zines was her pastime. Evening entertainment often included her recitations of the bogus ads. "'In ten weeks with the Mark Eden breast developer, I went from a size 26A to size 36DDD. And you can too!'"

John was a quiet and curious boy. His oval-shaped head, shaved closely under Momma's orders, looked like a fuzzy kiwi fruit. Head Start taught John colors, sizes, and most of all, shapes.

At first, no one could figure it out. Just a few months after John began attending Head Start, oddball household objects began to disappear. Tablespoons, jar tops, cookie cutters, pin boxes, coins, spools of thread. Gone. Under the dinette set, the couch, the record-player stand—they were nowhere to be found. Household chores led to eruptions: "Where is my damn spool of thread?"

John was the culprit.

Late one night, he lay curled on his side in a baby bed long out-grown, but all Momma could afford. Clasped in his hand was a crumpled brown paper bag like a sack of Halloween candy. Momma and I followed a hunch. Without stirring our shaven-headed cherub, one by one, we peeled his small fingers from the bag. Inside clinked and clanged the cache of John's collected household items: pepper box, measuring cup, a soy sauce top. Head Start had taught John to identify shapes. Upon recognizing each one as he went about the house, he carefully deposited it into the crumpled paper bag collection: circles, squares, rectangles, triangles.

Within a week of our discovery, caps to aerosol deodorant cans, spools of thread, forks, a can opener, my brown oval-shaped barrette, and Linda's curlers were lost again and found inside John's special brown bag. Again as he slept, we confiscated his assorted paraphernalia. He never questioned its whereabouts. Instead, he waited patiently for Momma, me, or someone to take a trip to the store. Upon our return, John retrieved a fresh paper bag from the garbage can and began his collection anew.

Our ordinary objects were my brother's extraordinary treasures. A triangle cookie cutter was a silver pyramid, piercing the clouds. A jar top was a giant windmill spinning tornado gales. Head Start taught him the shapes of the world, real and imagined.

Whenever she had occasion to mention her precious children's smarts, Momma marveled and blushed like a maraschino cherry. "Oh, yeah. My Tinky was in that Head Start program and she could practically read before she got to kindergarten. And John, he knew all his shapes and colors and animals. Ain't—isn't that something? What a difference one little program can make?"

Of course, I took this boasting about Tinky and John to mean that I was not so bright. There had been no Head Start for me. I had flunked third grade, bringing disgrace on the family and my permanent record. And now, I wasn't doing so hot at my new school, Dike Elementary. Maybe I was destined to flunk again. John and Tinky wouldn't flunk third grade or any grade. Groomed for grade school by Head Start, they were bound to glide through with straight A's on their permanent records. Momma's unabashed bragging about them left me jealous and dejected.

But one afternoon, as I sulked on the hallway steps of Building A-11, it came back to me. The rocking and singing, goofy laughter, and astronomy lessons learned in Charles Lyles's lap—lessons Tinky and John would never know because Charles Lyles was gone now.

And I felt sorry for them. They could have their Head Start van rides, field trips, shapes, colors, and alphabet. Those Head Start teachers didn't know a thing about moons, stars, planets, and eclipses—not the way Charles Lyles did. I bore my sister and brother no envy. Head Start had nothing on Charles Lyles.

Momma also scouted opportunities for herself. Head Start workers singled her out as an attentive, "on-the-ball" parent. By virtue of her children's participation and her close attention to their well-being, she had become an expert on Head Start procedures. Would she like to interview for a parent-counselor position at the Community Services Center?

Even Momma's walk was more prideful after she took her new position, at a $2,000-a-year salary. (With adjustments for our new income, we continued to receive welfare. It was not something Momma was proud of, but Tinky's almost weekly spasms of asthma made it impossible for us to go without the Medicaid insurance benefit the monthly stipend provided.) She kept her "day work" cleaning at the home of a Jewish family in the suburbs every other Saturday. In her new role as a parent counselor, Momma was challenged to go beyond the mere mechanics of interacting in the elevator or cleaning. This job required insight, creativity. It was Lillian Lyles's chance to shine, to be somebody.

It was also the first time she had ever worked around "college-educated black folks," as she called them. They impressed her up and down, from their stylish clothing to their subtle perfumes. She marveled at their polished vocabularies and eloquent mastery of social service bureaucratese.

The people who worked at the center were called social workers, Momma explained to us over a dinner of pork and beans and wieners. That meant that when people had problems, like we had problems, social workers were supposed to help. But you could not get help if you had too much money, real nice clothes like a leather coat, or your boyfriend had a nice big car like a Brougham. At least, that's how I thought Momma explained it. Those people would just have to figure out their problems by themselves, because social workers were forbidden to help them. If they sold or gave away all their nice things, then maybe they could be helped, but not before.

The parent-counselor position was the beginning of Momma's career in social work. She joined many working poor who became part of the social services network that administered an assortment of poverty programs to other needy people in the 1970s. Experts in eligibility forms, "in-take," and welfare protocol, they processed the needy in and out.

The new job took Momma to big meetings in hotels. She called them conferences. Scores and scores of social workers stood up on stages to talk about poor people and how to help them. Momma met police officers, schoolteachers, and others who were part of the social service network.

After bearing five children, Lillian Lyles was still a fox, tall and fair-skinned with a neat French roll of wavy black tresses coiled to the nape of her neck. I feared she might meet a nice schoolteacher or other and marry. Then Charles Lyles would have no chance whatsoever of coming back to live with us. Nearly six years had gone by since he had gone for good—or so Momma said. Besides an occasional phone call, which I usually missed while outside playing, we had not heard much from him. Still, I believed that a good job in a steel mill might make Lillian Lyles think twice about him, regardless of what that judge downtown had said.

With daily access to the Community Services Center, Momma became a living index to programs. She knew about this one and she knew about that one. One for old folks and one for young. Programs for little girls and programs for little boys. Programs for smart kids and not-so-smart kids. Which were free. Which required sliding-scale fees. How much the federal government had "appropriated"—another of her new words. How much the state of Ohio would receive. How much would come to little children on the East Side of Cleveland. Lillian Lyles could tell you. And her children would be among the first, if not the first, in line.

Parent-counselors also received special perks. In fall, there were free tickets and a bus ride to the Apple Butter Festival in Burton, Ohio. We rode far from gray city streets to Amish country, a green place of rolling hills where all the men looked like Abraham Lincoln. They had pale skin, square beards, dark loose suits, and high-standing hats. A lady in a long dress and bonnet said that the Amish made their own soap out of grease (yuck) and would rather ride in a horse-drawn buggy than a car. John took it upon himself to remind her that cars go faster. With sticks as long as paddles, the women in bonnets stirred huge brimming cauldrons. Cinnamon-scented steam wafted into the chilly air. "Come here, young lady," one of the Abraham Lincolns beckoned. "Taste this," he said, holding out a crudely carved wooden spoon. On it was something gooey and brown as you-know-what. But Momma nodded "OK." The tip of my tongue tasted apple butter for the first time, smooth and sweet.

Before Christmas, Momma flashed four tickets to the Ice Capades. There in the bleachers, Momma left us. The sharp-eyed budgeter who could feed five children on a government check, a $2,000-a-year job, and weekend cleaning gig disappeared. In her place was the girl who wrote in the 1953 John Adams High School yearbook that she would some day be a professional skater. Her body lithe and swift, the girl whirled out on white ice that sparkled like diamonds frozen together. With silver-bladed feet she kicked up a dazzling frost, amazing in her grace. Then, before thousands, she turned faster, faster, and faster, spinning into speed, energy, light.

In the dead of winter, Momma flashed tickets to see Disney on Parade. Even in fifteen-degree weather, she insisted that we be "exposed" to the Disney panoply at the Cleveland Arena downtown. John and I bought a hotdog to share and sneaked up close to the railing around the stage area. Scores of kiddies beckoned to Goofy.

"Please, Mr. Goofy, come over here." He poked and danced about in that floaty, slow-motion way that giant puppets move. I could feel Goofy staring at me, like he was looking right through me. I was eleven going on twelve, older than the others, old enough to know that Goofy was just a grown man in a ridiculous suit and hat. I stared right back just as hard, looking through the gaps in Goofy's big buck teeth, till I could see two holes in the mask and a pair of eyes. They were blue.

In the grand finale, Snow White, Mickey Mouse, all of Disneydom sang "It's a Small World." We filed out of the arena, past rows and rows of white people from the West Side and suburbs, the ones the Panthers didn't like. Momma's smile was simple and satisfied. She had provided an extravagant treat for her children. Any minute, she would swell up with pride and float away like a balloon big enough to ride five people. Then I broke the news. "Momma." I tugged at her nice dark green coat worn only on special occasions. "There's a mean white man inside of Goofy."

"SURPRISE!" In spring, like a magic trick, Momma pulled from her blue vinyl purse four tickets to the Karamu House Theater. It was a special place, Momma explained, "Because when blacks couldn't do plays nowhere else they could do them at the Karamu House. That's where Ruby Dee got her start. You know she was in *Raisin in the Sun*." (The long movie about a black family squabbling over moving to a white neighborhood had put me to sleep on more than one occasion.) "And Brock Peters—he's a good-looking man now—started out right here in Cleveland at the Karamu House on East Eighty-ninth and Quincy Avenue."

Thus, on our first trip to the Karamu House Theater, Momma thought it appropriate that we wear our Easter clothes.

In our suits from Sears, we sat waiting at the bus stop. Mine was a yellow mohair coat and knit skirt with spongy lining. Metal heel taps weighed down my black patent leathers like paperweights, tugging lacy socks to my ankles. Our faces shone with drug store-brand petroleum jelly. John's luminous skin beamed atop his tan coat and red tie. The day was sunny, the avenue dingy with litter and bus soot. We waited half an hour. Still no bus. John played happily with a toy truck, oblivious to our tardiness.

"Momma, are we going to miss the play?" the ever-punctual Tinky asked, sucking on two fingers.

Momma peered down the avenue empty of traffic. "I don't see anything coming. These are the slowest buses." She swung John up on her hip. "Come on. We're walking."

We didn't know, but Momma knew that the Karamu was twenty-four blocks away. Lillian Lyles wanted her babies to see theater, to see culture, and no late city bus or hauling a forty-pound boy on her hip was going to stop her. Momma walking with the weight of my brother worried me. The varicose veins that ached inside her legs every day and required thick opaque stockings stoked my imagination. What if her legs split open like cheap wieners over-boiled?

"Momma, I don't want us to go—your legs might start hurting." I whined my best. "Let's go home. We can watch Ed Sullivan tonight. The Supremes are going to be on."

A "damn-Diana-Ross" look blipped across Momma's face. She started up Quincy Avenue. Stepping down the concrete, her feet swelled slowly, puffing out of cheap patent leather pumps like loaves of bread rising in a pan. Momma's grace was amazing. Six blocks later, the bus caught up to us.

Hidden in a neighborhood of three-story houses, some painted brightly, others weather-beaten and battered, the Karamu was a secret palace. There famous people had donned makeup and costumes, rehearsed, acted, sung, danced, and dreamed. The play was *The Sandalwood Box*, an oriental fable that was cast in brown. Gently fragrant sandalwood perfumed the theater. Actors in costumes adorned the stage. I wanted to be like them, golden and glittering, more beautiful than myself. They spoke in voices full of virtue and power, trained to the purity of song. In the Karamu's curtains, we saw a majestic imitation of our lives, all splendor and spirit.

When the curtains closed, with us in tow, Momma made her way to the lobby bulletin board. Signs there said the Karamu had programs for boys and girls who wanted to become dancers, singers, actors, costume designers.

"Sugarbabe," Momma called me. "How would you like to take acting lessons? Remember how good you were in Miss Collins's play, *Give My Regards to Mother*?"

I nodded. It didn't take long to figure out that Momma was looking for a way to bring her daughter back to academic life. Playacting had worked before when I flunked third grade. Now at my new school, Dike Elementary, I was progressing slowly. Momma figured awakening my imagination would work again.

Bluish white and wrinkly, Ted and Helen Hedwick arrived grinning from Lyndhurst, a suburb northeast of Cleveland. Mr. Hedwick jumped out of his funny, square car. He wore kiwi-green slacks and white patent leather shoes. He smiled a stiff all-tooth smile like he was getting ready to brush his teeth, shook Momma's hand, and introduced himself. "We're the Hedwicks. And this young lady's going to have a great time with us." I didn't like him. He talked funny, like he had a mouth full of something. Before I could speak up, Mr. Hedwick had locked my brand new flowered suitcase from Kresge's in the trunk of his shiny, square car and was urging me to the backseat. The Hedwicks were taking me to Friendly Town.

Bent on broadening our horizons still further, Momma had signed me and Tinky up for Friendly Town as soon as she found out about it from one of the local community centers. A one-sided socio-exchange program, Friendly Town exported inner-city kids to white suburban households for one week. It was a benevolent-spirited effort put together by integration-minded blacks and whites. To Momma, Friendly Town was our chance to learn young the mechanics of dealing with white people, lessons she had learned late in life. Plus, we would get to see how nice they lived way out in the suburbs. Maybe we would hope to live that way too someday. And even though she was still mad at the whites for the riots and a whole lot of things, Momma believed in Friendly Town as yet another opportunity that her babies just couldn't pass up.

The idea appealed to me too. My bossy hallway playmates, Dee-Dee in particular, had grown boring. A week away from the project would do me good. Plus, Momma said that the Hedwicks would teach me how to swim and play new games. Still, there was nervousness. The Hedwicks were definitely white, and besides Mrs. Bryant, my kindergarten teacher, I hadn't really gotten to know too many white people. The Panthers who marched through the project each Saturday had said it was better not to get to know them. But Momma said the Hedwicks were the nice kind of white people who were sorry for all the lowdown, dirty things their ancestors had done and were trying to make up for it by being in the Friendly Town program.

First, Mr. Hedwick drove to the Carver Homes, another project not far from King-Kennedy. There we picked up Denise, nicknamed Neecee. She was to be my Friendly Town sister. She was cuter than I, with thick, wavy hair and big, round brown eyes. I didn't like her.

After a half-hour highway ride, Mr. Hedwick's big, square car rolled into a quaint green town with a gazebo like someplace on TV, which was my only real reference for the world of white people. We stopped at a drugstore for ice cream cones. The pinkish man at the counter smiled. I didn't like him. (By now, I could see that white people looked better on television than in person.) "So, Mr. Hedwick," the counter man said. "Are these the new young ladies you have for Friendly Town this year?"

"Yes, they sure are. This is Miss Charlise and this is Miss Neecee," said Mr. Hedwick. "They are very nice young ladies from the King-Kennedy and Carver homes in Cleveland."

"And they are very intelligent young ladies," chimed in Mrs. Hedwick, nodding her head. She was a nice lady in a checkered, seersucker dress with a bow. Bright pink lipstick lacquered her sweet smile. Her eyes were as blue as those of the white man inside Goofy.

How did they know whether we were intelligent or not? I had yet to tell them that I had flunked third grade and passed sixth only by the skin of my teeth. And Miss Neecee didn't look all that sharp either. Otherwise, I liked the introduction.

Back in the car, I inquired: "Mrs. Hedwick, do you have any white children for us to play with?" Momma had said the Hedwicks were nice white people, but had not mentioned any children. I wanted to know because in the Saturday speeches, the militants had warned us to beware of little white boys and girls who might be "junior oppressors."

"No, Miss Charlise, I don't have any children," said Mrs. Hedwick, smoothing her hand over the white patent leather purse on her lap. "But for this week, you and Miss Neecee will be my children."

"Are your children all grown up now, Mrs. Hedwick?"

"No. I've never had any children, except you and my other Friendly Town children."

"Oh." I felt sorry for Mrs. Hedwick. Even if she was white, she deserved to have children, even if they did grow up to be junior oppressors.

"And we're going to have lots of fun this week, just like I've had with my other Friendly Town children, so you'll have lots of memories," said Mrs. Hedwick. "We're going to go to the zoo and the aquarium."

"My brother used to have an aquarium," I blurted out.

"Oh really," said Mrs. Hedwick.

"And we're going to play putt-putt golf. And we're going to go shopping and to the movies and lots, lots more."

The Hedwicks kept every promise. By day three, Miss Neecee and I were exhausted and grateful to spend one evening at home in the Hedwick's long, rambling brick house, which they called "the rancher." It was four times bigger than Number 129 and it stretched the whole length of Building A-11. We barbecued hamburgers on a grill in the lush, deep backyard. Just beyond the patio in a forest of tall trees, courting fireflies flickered like stars fallen from heaven. In the twilight, Mr. Hedwick spoke to us of dreams.

"What will you young ladies become when you grow up?" he asked.

Trick question. I knew it. Back home, Dee-Dee had said that all white people expect us to be pimps or hoes who let men feel on us for money.

Dumbfounded, Miss Neecee eyed me. She was cute, but so quiet that I seemed outspoken by comparison, a bold presence, curious, and way too talkative. Quickly, I could answer white people's questions with exciting remarks that made their blue eyes sparkle. Naturally, I answered first.

"I plan to be an actress and I would like to marry a Black Panther for my husband," I resolved. Surely such lofty goals would impress. But Mr. Hedwick's pale face blanched.

Immediately, I wanted to take back my marital aspiration. Momma had told me not to go saying anything about the black militants while at Friendly Town. Mention of the militants might scare the Hedwicks or hurt their feelings, she said. But my true heart's desire had just slipped out. Momma's oft-repeated warning replayed in my head: "Your mouth is going to be your ruin. Your mouth is going to be your ruin . . ."

Mr. Hedwick must have thought better of messing with that aspiration. "Well," he said with uncertainty, "those sure are big goals you have, Miss Charlise." Unable to chew another morsel, I slumped back in the lawn chair, disgusted with myself but trying not to show it. The Hedwicks probably hated me now.

That night in my nice bed with flowered sheets—at home we had only white sheets—I was angry with myself and sorry for the Hedwicks. To me, their white lives seemed dull and joyless, bland as boiled potatoes without a speck of salt. And there was nothing they could do about it. Even when we went swimming and they lay out in the sun, instead of getting darker, they turned a scary, pinkish shade of red, like raw meat. When Friendly Town was over and Miss Neecee and I went back to the projects, the Hedwicks would sit each night over their dull dinner—no Vienna sausage, potted meat and crackers, or pork and beans and wieners, greens or apple-cookie pie. "Jesus wept," Mr. Hedwick would say in that marshmallow-mouth voice. And they would discuss "securities,"the only thing that seemed to excite them.

Poor Mr. and Mrs. Hedwick. They had no color in their lives. No women who danced with sultry shoulders and swaying hips. No children who jumped about and whistled James Brown through thick lips and jumped double-dutch. No Jackson Five. And no Afro Set full of power and passion to march through their lives.

What would the militants think of the Hedwicks and me?

Despite Momma's trust in Friendly Town, I believed what the militants taught: The whites were against the blacks. The Hedwicks were white and therefore against me. But being mad at them was hard with Mrs. Hedwick up early in the morning baking oatmeal raisin cookies for "her Friendly-Town daughters," substituting us for the children she never had; plus Mr. Hedwick coaxing us into the community pool to splash and play even as his neighbors stared as if we were extraterrestrials.

Maybe the militants would change their minds if they could go to Friendly Town and meet nice white people like Ted and Helen Hedwick and play croquet in their big backyard. Or maybe we could have Friendly Town in Building A-11. The Hedwicks could come and stay for a week, talk to the Panthers themselves and see if they could work things out.

Sunday was the last day of Friendly Town. We went to a towering, silent church where Jesus sat in a golden and scarlet stained glass window. A few members of the congregation smiled tolerant but not-so-Friendly-Town smiles at Miss Neecee and me. We were dressed in our Easter clothes in July. The pale, spooky looking gray-eyed minister intoned, "Let us pray." I bowed my head to try and understand the Hedwicks' true hearts and why I should hate them. By and by, I came to understand that the Hedwicks were good white people trying to overcome the best way they knew how.

That winter, weeks before Christmas, the postman left a yellow slip. There was a package at the post office for Miss Charlise Lyles, my first parcel. The next day, Momma escorted me to the post office on East Fifty-fifth Street, next door to the House of Wills funeral home. Through the snow all the way home, I held tightly to the oblong box.

When I could wait no longer, Christmas Day arrived. I tore away the shiny blue wrapping. Inside was a pair of dark blue corduroy jeans, a striped shirt like all the girls were wearing at school, and a tiny white card: "Merry Christmas. From Helen and Ted Hedwick, your Friendly Town Mom and Dad."

Chapter Eight

DEE-DEE, L'IL JOE-JOE, KEITH, Antoine—none of the others in Building A-11 had gone to Friendly Town. And they did not go on trips to the Ice Capades or to the Karamu. Their mothers were waitresses or maids, not parent counselors like Lillian Lyles. Mercilessly, I chattered about the Hedwicks, my rendezvous with the Amish Abraham Lincolns, and even my peculiar up-close encounter with Goofy.

My playmates were silent. They had no references for my adventures. Then Dee-Dee piped up. "Did you see the black nationalists marching last week? They was baaaad."

"They sho was," said Keith. "I'm going to get me a tam and some brogans and join up."

"Did you see Stokely Carmichael on *The Dick Cavett Show*?" asked Antoine. "He's a famous black nationalist and he was baaaad. He told that white man off. I was laughing."

The Panthers' pride had taken hold of the King-Kennedy Estates. Saturdays were their day. Fearlessly they marched down Bundy Drive, facing the oppressive but unseen white man. *Your left. Your left. Your left. Right. Left.* Sometimes I mistook their unity for perfection.

One Saturday in July, on cue from the cadence caller, the men halted at the playground. Then a tall, slender figure cut from the ranks. As he moved before the gathering crowd, I could see his face, smooth as chocolate. He was just a boy. With the energy and grace of a trained soldier, he hopped on a playground bench and stood lean and towering. From somewhere in the crowd, a rigid arm propped a megaphone to his mouth, and he spoke with a power that put Reverend Berry to shame. Surely this boy, a project playground his pulpit, was closer to whatever god there was in the world.

"Black People," the militant man-child summoned us. "I said Black People!" He paused strategically. "Afro-American People!"

"Yes," we called out as if recognizing the sound of our own names for the very first time. "Yes. Yes."

His was a presence that stood us still. From apartment windows, women stuck inside with babies looked down on the playground. Swings stopped swinging. Basketballs ceased bouncing. The see-saw sat balanced. For blocks, people stopped in their steps. Suddenly, the clarion had sounded on this most mundane day. By now, nearly everyone in King-Kennedy had seen or heard about the militant marchers. But on this day, their message seemed more urgent than ever.

"Black People! Beautiful People," the militant called out. This was our revolution, *the* Revolution, and he was here to lead us through it.

We answered, "Yes. Yes." We were Beautiful Black People. We were brothers and sisters. Oppression was our mother, struggle our father.

"I want you to repeat after me, my Beautiful Brothers and Sisters!"

"Yes." We were now under his spell, for he had bestowed beauty upon us all, from nappy-headed FeeFee, a wild-acting girl who lived in Building B-9, to L'il Joe-Joe with his twisted limbs. We were all beautiful. Even me. Up till this moment, my flat nose, squinty eyes, and broad forehead had been ugly. Everyone agreed. "Don't smile so widely or your nose will look flat and homely," Momma always cautioned before school portraits were taken. On occasion, she reminded: "Your face is nothing special, just a piece of dough with some eyes thrown in."

The man-child asked again: "Please, my People, will you repeat after me?"

"Yes. Yes, we will."

"We are Beautiful Afro-American People!"

"We are Beautiful Afro-American People," came the echo from the basketball court, from the hallways, from the curbs.

"We are out of Africa."

"We are out of Africa."

"*Wa tu wa zuri* means Beautiful People."

"*Wa tu wa zuri* means Beautiful People."

Our chorus was a collective affirmation, a libation pouring blessedly down upon our heads. From our own hands, the nectar flowed like honey in the sun. We were a blue-black, nappy people, bubble-lipped, with broad bosoms and big asses. We deserved to love our black selves. And the militant man-child dared to give us permission to do so.

According to him, there was a "Black Power agenda": Swahili would be taught in the schools. "Our children must speak the language of their heritage." More preschool and lunch programs. "Nutrition and education for our people: Strong body, strong mind." And economic prosperity to the people. "A new day has come," he proclaimed. "But to advance, we must be of one mind. We must be united in solidarity. United in the struggle. Black Power!" He declared.

"Black Power." We confirmed.

"Black Power."

"Black Power."

Standing by the monkey bars and tire swing, I was close enough to reach out and touch the black militant's tam as he spoke. At last, I understood. "Black Power." It wasn't so much that we were against the whites as we were for our black selves: The way we dressed so foolishly bright, danced and sang so passionately, spoke so soulfully, prayed so feverishly, and felt life so deeply.

This was not about black rage or anarchy at all. The militants had delivered us culture and most of all pride in our authentic American selves. They were our liberators, freeing our psyches from the spell of racial self-hatred.

Flyers, newspapers, leaflets flapped through palms in the crowd like hand-held funeral home fans in church on humid Sunday mornings. "Subscribe to *The Liberator* now," called a man in dark shades. "Order a hand-carved mahogany Black Power symbol," said a leaflet that landed in my hand, "Powerful! Black! Beautiful!" the ad promised. Medallions were $3.95 and a Tiki, whatever that was, cost $2.95.

I bathed in the Panthers' pride. I daydreamed of marrying a black nationalist, just as I had told the Hedwicks at Friendly Town. My militant husband would dress in a beret worn sloped to the side atop his Afro, black leather jacket, olive drab fatigues, and brogans bought from the Army-Navy store downtown. And maybe, just to keep the white man in line, he would tote a machine gun and bullets like some other militants I had seen on TV. But he would never use it or bring it in the house because deep inside he would never want to shoot anyone. At night, my black militant husband would lay down beside me, place his beret on my pillow, and kiss me goodnight.

BRING THE WHOLE FAMILY. ALL DAY AT GEAUGA LAKE. The flyers were posted in the hallway of Building A-11. The black militants and some other community group were sponsoring a trip to the amusement park just outside of Cleveland. The Revolution could and would be fun.

"I'm going to Geauga Lake and I'm gonna wear all black," said DoeDoe, an older girl who lived up on the second floor. "Black jeans. Black tank top. Black belt. Black tam. My black earrings shaped like Afro picks. And I'm going downtown tomorrow to get me some black patent leather brogans from Coles. Do you want to come with me?"

From somewhere deep inside, DoeDoe replied to the call for Black Power. She was a plain girl with sallow, acne-pocked skin and a chipped front tooth. In Building A-11, DoeDoe had been the first to free her hair from the weekly hell of the straightening comb. One humid gray day, DoeDoe had gotten caught in the rain. Her hair, once straightened to greasy stringiness and heat-curled, contracted to her scalp like a bush of bean sprouts.

"I'm gettin' me a 'Fro," DoeDoe had announced, an edge of defiance in her voice. "Come on," she had commanded me.

An Afro had to be groomed with specially purchased supplies. Without an umbrella, DoeDoe marched three blocks through the pelting rain to Marshall's drugstore on East Fifty-fifth Street. I trailed behind. A fifteen-cent plastic rain scarf bubbled over my greasy, straightened bangs and pigtails, the bow tugged at my chin. And I watched the rain, magic silver droplets falling upon Doe-Doe's hair.

She was fifteen years old—old enough to establish dominion over her own hair. Having just turned twelve, I was fully aware that Momma still maintained hegemony over my scalp, pores, and hair follicles. For now, my hot-pressed tresses would remain enslaved to the white man. (That's what the Panthers had to say about straightened hair.) Besides, I liked the rubber bands and ridiculously colored barrettes. I hoped the Revolution would not pass me by, and that the Panthers would not be mad at me for it.

On the eve of the Geauga Lake trip, DoeDoe and I went shopping for black brogans, hoping to buy our Black Power.

Downtown, every five-and-dime store was selling accessories to the Revolution. Black wool berets were on display in the dead heat of summer. Black, red, and green scarves, Afro picks, and "Black Power" pins lined racks and tables. In the windows were posters of unnamed men who sat regal with big, wide Afros radiating Black

Power. And in the "Beauty Aids" section, the Revolution had its own shelf: Afro Sheen spray, shampoo, and conditioner, plus "Blow Out" kits for super-duper Afros.

At Coles Shoe Store, the nice white salesman showed us several styles of brogans, designed with young black revolutionary women like us in mind. The soles were manmade, the uppers patent leather. DoeDoe picked a pair that laced to mid-calf and struck a pose in front of the mirror, her fist in the air.

"They look good, don't they?" DoeDoe displayed her chipped front tooth in a flash of conceit.

I nodded. "Those are baaad, girl. Now see if you can march in them," I advised. Softly, for I had never done so in the presence of white people, I sang the cadence: "Your left. Your left. Your left. Right. Left." On the gray shoe store carpet, DoeDoe stepped in place, all the while watching her feet moving in the mirror, ready now for revolution.

"Miss, would you like that pair?" The salesman reappeared.

"Yes, please. And I want a set of those red, black, and green shoestrings too, please," DoeDoe said. "When are you going to get you some brogans?" she asked me.

"I don't know if my mother will let me," I hedged. The bubble-toed boots looked just fine on the militant men marching through King-Kennedy, uniformed and ready to war against racism. But I wasn't so sure brogans belonged on my narrow feet. I didn't want to get DoeDoe mad so I didn't say it, but I liked my summer sandals.

To earn the ten dollars to go on the militant trip to Geauga Lake, I sold "freeze cups." A product of project ingenuity, enterprise, Dixie Cups, and Kool-Aid, freeze cups brought in fairly big bucks on hot summer days.

A small paper cup of frozen Kool-Aid went for five cents, large, a dime. We set up stands in front of buildings, on basketball courts, and playgrounds. Competition grew stiff. Invention cut costs: "Freeze cubes" without cups were sold. Grape-orange, cherry-lemon-lime, we dreamed up rainbows of exotic flavors. Mothers returned from grocery stores with ten, eleven, twelve packs of Kool-Aid. Kitchen floors shone with sticky red and purple puddles.

The freeze cup business brought out the ambitious entrepreneur in Hattie, a jobless young woman who lived next door to us with her four children. After a month of successful freeze cup sales, Hattie bought thirty ice trays and announced that she was saving to buy a big meat freezer in which she would mass-produce freeze cups.

All day on the burning playground blacktop, Hattie happily sold freeze cups, cubes, and cookie cutter shapes. Drinking and angry men had taken Hattie's teeth early in life. But that didn't stop her from smiling, flashing her brown gums each time she made a sale. By early afternoon, Hattie's big apron pocket jangled with coins. By dinner time, it hung low like an udder. At dusk, she folded up her card table and chair and disappeared into apartment Number 131, Building A-11.

Soon afterward, inside Number 129, we would hear a sad Gladys Knight tune turning on Hattie's cheap record player. "Promises at night are so easily made." Over and over it played, staticky and slightly warped. I lay in my bed, wide awake, listening.

"Hattie, turn that damn record player off," Momma would shout at the thin wall that divided her bedroom from Hattie's. But Gladys's song didn't quiet till the first opalescent strokes of dawn. Hattie's heart was still broken over some long-ago affair. Before noon, she was back on the basketball court calling: "Freeze cups, everybody. Freeze cups for a nickel. It's hot out here today and Hattie's got your cool freeze cup for a nickel."

The night before the militant outing to Geauga Lake, Momma suddenly had second thoughts about letting me go. She definitely preferred the black nationalist vocabulary. She had traded in "Negro" for "black." But "some of that black nationalist talk" rubbed Lillian Lyles the wrong way. Just what did they mean by "the Revolution"? And did they have to call the police "pigs"? "It's only going to make them madder at black people," she reasoned.

"What if they go out to Geauga Lake and start some trouble with that marchin' and carryin' on?"

"But Ma, they ain't going to start no trouble. They're just going to have fun. Just because they're black militants doesn't mean they don't like to have fun." I pleaded my case. "Plus, I'm going to be with DoeDoe the whole time." DoeDoe had a respectable reputation as a good student and a junior high school track star. "I can stay with DoeDoe. Ain't nothing going to happen to me. Please, Momma. I promise."

The next morning, I met DoeDoe in the parking lot across from Building A-18. As promised, she was decked out in black from beret to brogans. After the militant lieutenant called the roll, we filled up two charter buses and were off.

I was thrilled to be on board with Ronnie, the militant minister-in-charge who had delivered the rousing Saturday sermons of self-celebration from the playground bench. The bus huffed and puffed up Woodland Avenue. Everyone talked excitedly. Through the tinted bus windows, we saw the unfortunates staring in envy as we embarked on our excursion.

In the back of the bus, I recognized some of the militants as older brothers of my schoolmates at Dike Elementary. Andrew Jefferson's big brother TeeCee was there, and so was Chester Davis's brother. He had changed his name to Amalwand, an African name, and wore a dashiki all the time. DoeDoe crossed her brand-new, highly polished girl brogans in the aisle so everyone could see them. Radios blared: "Smiling faces, smiling faces," and "Ooo ooo child (things are going to get easier)."

Then Ronnie rose, walked to the front of the bus, and stood akimbo. All fell silent.

"We are Black People," Ronnie declared as if we had yet to really realize it.

"We are Black People." Like a great Greek chorus, the whole bus sang back. "We are Black People."

"We are Beautiful Black People," Ronnie replied.

"We are Beautiful Black People." In harmony, we all agreed.

"We are Beautiful, Beautiful Black People," Ronnie insisted.

"We are Beautiful, Beautiful Black People."

It was the truth. And we knew it.

"Now listen up, my people." Ronnie was about to give critical instructions on the public conduct of Beautiful Black People. "As you know, today we will be amongst those who oppress us. Many of them may appear to be nice to us. But many will be pigs who could and would harm us. Is this not true, my brothers?"

"That's right," came the chorus.

"So we must be on our best behavior. Cautious. Aware of our every move lest the pigs bring false charges against us. So let us not drink wine or beer today or behave carelessly. We must be models of discipline. For all eyes will be on the Revolution."

"Proud Black People. What do we want?"

"Black Power."

"What do we want?"

"Black Power. Black Power now." Righteous fists swung to the air like a million torches. Hands clapped. I felt the march momentum. Two boys no older than I sprang from their seats, jumped in the aisle, and started stepping toward the front. Feet stomped. "Your left. Your left. Your left. Right. Left."

"Please be seated, my little brothers," Ronnie instructed. "We will march another time." Ronnie was wise, I could tell.

Before settling in his seat again, he imparted one final word of wisdom: "And sistahs, you support your brothers. You hear me."

The bus pulled on down the highway. Geauga Lake, here we come! The militants played bid whist, spades, and go fish. They drank orange Sun Crest soda and ate orange-flavored, cream-filled Hostess cupcakes. Stupid jokes broke their stoic revolutionary cool, collapsing them into crazy, uncalled-for laughter. Today, the militants just wanted to have fun.

Halfway to Geauga Lake, I dozed off and then woke up worried. Was it safe to trust the white man at Geauga Lake for a whole day, just to have some fun? But DoeDoe said everything would be all right.

To the Geauga Lake turnstile gate Ronnie led us single file, a long paper doll cut from black construction paper. As we approached, a white woman in a pink uniform looked momentarily dazed. After a brief exchange with her, Ronnie sent word down the line: Take out your entry fare, exact change. Ronnie knew how to talk right to those white people. He really was wise.

We fanned out through the park, patches of sleek black birds. I was a misfit magpie in yellow checked shorts, white sleeveless tie blouse, and red sneakers with white rubber-toed soles from Marshall's drugstore.

At the cotton candy stand, a winsome white girl in hip-hugger bell bottoms and a skimpy top came up to DoeDoe and me. "You know," she said, "I'm for Black. Power." As the furry pink candy fizzled in my mouth, I listened. The girl held her head to one side as if her stringy red hair weighed a ton. "I really believe you guys are right. We need a revolution. The pigs are oppressing everybody." She seemed sincere.

DoeDoe nodded and pointed toward the carny games where Ronnie was holding a giant yellow teddy bear. "See. That's Ronnie over there, the minister-in-charge. He can give you information about the Revolution."

Other white people walked half-circles around us. Some stood several feet behind, leaving a big gap in the Ferris wheel line.

On the roller coaster, Ronnie took the first car. DoeDoe and I jumped in the next. Other militants dropped into seats behind us, one to a car. Cautious, two white girls opted at the last minute to take the next train. The tall, skinny blond ride operator locked us down in our seats, kicked a brake bar, and we were off. Rumbling and jerking on a narrow track, the train began to climb. Up we went. The motor roared, drowning out sounds as we rose above the park. Ronnie's head and shoulders swayed as the train inched heavenward. My stomach dropped. I wanted King-Kennedy, my mother. "DoeDoe." I panicked. "I want to get off."

"Shuuuush," she consoled. "Ain't nothing goin' to happen to us. Ronnie's on here. He'll protect us. He's our leader."

We reached the apex, the moment of no return. The motor's battering ceased for a single second. Then down we plunged. I could hear Ronnie laughing, howling defiance as he rode furiously into the white man's wind. Or was Ronnie, who spoke so passionately, at times full of fury, reduced to childish whoops and screams on the white man's roller coaster? The gale lifted his black beret like a toy top whirling, whirling away.

The militants marched straight through the summer of 1971. Come Saturday morning, the black, red, and green banner rippled in the breeze as the militants rounded the corner at Woodland Avenue and Bundy Drive. *Your left. Your left. Your left. Right. Left.* Then the cadre froze at attention. From the ranks stepped Ronnie, slender and agile. He took to the playground bench and passionately praised our black skins. Each time, he left us loving ourselves more than before. The Panthers' pride made us invincible. Not even death could kill us. For we felt no fear.

In an August rain, my pigtails puffed into a defiant halo. Girlfriends teased that my new Afro made me look like Angela Davis, our black militant heroine, whom we had all seen on TV. She was the only black woman we knew who would get right up in the white man's face. And her Afro was a globe to behold. On the hallway stairs, I played to the crowd, pretending to be Davis haranguing about how rotten white people really were (except for the ones like the Hedwicks). "Tell it like it is," my playmates egged me on.

I found more freedom that summer while learning to swim in the Portland-Outhwaite Recreation Center (PORC) pool. The chlorinated blue-green water lifted me, buoyant and light. A sprite, I left my body and blackness behind on the concrete poolside to envy my having set myself free. Maybe all black people would be free if they could swim in the waters of the PORC pool.

Chapter Nine

COME SATURDAY MORNING, I waited at the curb. My Afro buoyant, freshly greased and picked out. My rump tucked into a pair of dungarees, a red, green, and black Black Power patch sewn on the rear. Their Afros stunning and adorned with Afro picks planted in the back, L'il Joe-Joe and Dee-Dee waited with me. Bugs Bunny, Road Runner, Tweetie Bird, Scooby-Doo, the Archies—no Saturday morning cartoon could keep us away. It was time for the black militants to march.

We stood ready to raise our fists to the sky in a Black Power salute. Any minute now, the militants would round the corner of Woodland Avenue and Bundy Drive. We listened for that righteous cadence to come, thundering softly at first like the beating of bird wings, then stronger, stronger. *Your left. Your left. Your left. Right. Left. . . .* We waited, knowing now that the Revolution meant more than marching. But the cadence never came.

Two, three Saturdays went by. My Panthers or Afro Sets and their pride were nowhere to be found.

The angry shoulders and backs moving in marching formation were gone. Now who would march through the project, defying the white man in broad daylight? Who would guide us against "them"? Who would proclaim our black beauty in the streets?

Now there would be no black militant to marry me when I grew up. No one to appreciate my Afro's sheen and embrace me in my dreams. I missed them, their black militant mystique, their pride and protection.

Rumors said that the black militants, Panthers, Afro Set, whoever they were, had "bugged out," taken a wrong turn. Something about guns, shootings, police, and prison. It had happened years ago to militants in faraway places like New York and Los Angeles, too, according to some big boys who looked like they knew what they were talking about. And in Connecticut, the Panthers had even killed somebody, one man said.

"I heard that one of them militant boys got caught breaking into a store over on Quincy Avenue," said a wizened man who sometimes hobbled through the project on his way up Woodland Avenue.

"Seem like them militants is madder at each other than they is with the white man." He leaned on his battered aluminum cane and looked up at the sky. "Any time we start piling up guns and carrying on like the white folks, you know we in trouble. Lord have mercy on the colored people."

Prison? Guns? Breaking into stores on Quincy? Not my militants. Not the men who had laughed so merrily while winning carny games and teddy bears for girlfriends at Geauga Lake amusement park.

To get to the bottom of the matter, DoeDoe and I went on a research mission to the Woodland Branch Public Library. "Excuse me, miss. Do you have any pictures of the Black Panthers?"

"We'll have to go to the adult reading room for the periodicals," said the librarian, a bespectacled woman with a curly Afro who seemed amused at our curiosity. She gave us a quick how-to on using the *Reader's Guide to Periodical Literature*. Then she disappeared into a room and returned quickly. "Be sure to return all the magazines to the counter when you're done," she said firmly as she placed a dusty stack of yellowed *Time*, *Life*, and *Newsweek* magazines in front of us.

"F'get chu," DoeDoe whispered, flicking her wrist once the librarian had turned her back. "Ain't like we was goin' to steal them 'r nothin.'"

Then we turned to our research. "May 1967?" DoeDoe read the dates on the covers and practically gasped. "I was just nine years old in 1967." Could King Kennedy's Afro Sets possibly be that old?

Thumbing through page after dry page, gawking at picture after fading picture of black men in black leather jackets and berets, we came to understand that the militants had been marching left, right, left long before we had ever seen their gleaming black brogans step down Bundy Drive in the King-Kennedy Estates. Left, right, left in California, Connecticut, Chicago, and a dozen other places that we had never been. Surely, our local militants were genuine apostles of these original Panthers.

"'Bobby Hutton, Panther Party member, and Bobby Seale, party chairman, storming the California State Capitol at Sacramento,'" DoeDoe read the photo captions aloud.

We flipped through more pages. Then our eyes fell upon him for the first time. Tall, tammed, leather-jacketed, Afroed, fair-skinned, and intrepid, gripping a submachine gun to his chest, was Huey P. Newton, cofounder and defense minister of the Black Panther Party. Just for a minute, he was our hero, 4-ever.

Nearly twenty years later, our hero would fall on a street in Oakland, California, not far from where his militant forces had once moved. *Your left. Your left. Your left. Right. Left.* Found around the corner from a dope house. Shot three times, once in the back of the head. No suspects and no clear motive. The Revolution gunned down, gagging, coughing up its own blood. *Your left. Your left.* There lay Huey P. Newton, a man of ideals, dying, his agenda gone awry, his direction unclear: Whether we as a people should go left, right, or straight ahead.

And locally, Harllel Jones, prime minister of the Afro Sets, would be framed for murder and serve six years of a 10-year sentence in Lucasville Prison, before being released on appeal.

But in the mind of a girl growing up Afro-American in 1971, the black militants and their ideals marched triumphantly ever onward, dark and defiant, immortal as myth. *You left. Your left. Your left. Right. Left.*

In the King-Kennedy Estates, Black Power and pride disappeared in the retreating steps of the militant marchers. We were left with an angry sense of us and them-ness, our collective poverty overwhelming, our immobility staggering. Three thousand tenants warehoused, tight-packed, into six city blocks where no whites were to be found, we had no target and no outlet for fighting the oppression the Afro Sets had urged us to fight. We turned on ourselves. It happened fast, like insects sealed in an airtight jar: frantic buzzing, frantic flight, colliding and dying.

Barely three years after its auspicious opening, King-Kennedy began to take a dark and desperate turn from which it would never recover. Soon, we rivaled one another in acts of cruelty and self-degradation. People stopped throwing garbage in the incinerators. It piled up in colorful, glittering, foul-smelling mounds, lavish playgrounds for fat, wobbly rats. Boys with rocks busted out the tall glass windows on either side of the steel hallway doors. They were replaced with thick, blurry Plexiglas that obscured the view. Anyone approaching looked like a shadow.

Pissing in the hallway was elevated from accident to achievement. In the middle of a kickball game, Keith ducked under the stairs, spread his feet apart and unzipped. Presently, a steaming, yellowish green stream flowed through the walkway. Then Keith pimp-strutted back to the ball game, smiling like he had brought in a home run. Other boys followed his lead.

My playmates and I got mean. And we played mean name-calling games that seared self-esteem we didn't even know we had. "You're a dick-sucking bitch dog and y'r mama is too." Suddenly, we wanted each other to feel bad. And if name-calling wouldn't do it, then we were willing to fight.

Teeth marks were common scars from habitual battles. Dee-Dee kicked ass regularly, and I tried to stay out of her way. Her big sister Bee-Bee had gone to the detention home for beating up a girl real bad. A boy named Davis Red got sliced with a razor blade till he bled. Grown-ups joined in. A man in Building B-6 beat his wife till her ear bled. Everyone saw her moaning in the dirt. Nearly everyone laughed. And the lady who was supposed to be her best friend said, "That bitch got what she deserved."

Boys who should have been men and men who should have been boys began to gather late at night in the hallway telling lies, flashing switchblades, and smoking. The cinder block reeked of marijuana mingled with roach spray. Boys who used to talk nice took to drinking beer. Their anger flared up in unpredictable rages over a cigarette, a bottle of liquor, a toothpick. In the wee hours, police lights spun across rooms, walls, and faces, quickening heartbeats, sending feet running.

This is when Cookie Parker's mother declared that the project "begets evil and all therein is doomed to a fiery hell, especially those little niggahs in the hallway who were always starting trouble."

Cookie Parker's mother was a tall, hefty woman with a bull's torso and tiny black-framed glasses perched on a little bubble of a nose. They magnified the word of the Lord so Mrs. Parker could read her Bible all day and night. ("Cookie, I want you to cook your brothers' and sisters' dinner tonight. I've got to read the Revelations. That's what the Lord wants me to do tonight.")

Each day, Mrs. Parker stuck her head out her apartment door to deliver a sermon to us "niggahs in the hallway." When boys began to scribble "pussy" and "Dick in Jane" on the cinder block, she called it "the handwriting on the wall." "*Mene, mene, tekle upharsin,*" Mrs. Parker quoted her Bible. "You have been weighed on the scales and found wanting. And you have a lot to atone for, my children, a lot."

One day, the Lord spoke to Mrs. Parker and told her that the fruit of her womb should have nothing to do with the project trash. "If you're living in shit, shit gets on you," Mrs. Parker said in a blunt departure from her usual proverbs. After that, Cookie Parker could not come outside to play anymore. She could not have any company either.

I felt sorry for Cookie, just as I felt sorry for Priscilla, a pretty girl with long black braids who was smart in school. She lived in Building B-6, which had five-bedroom apartments for the people "who had way too many children," according to my mother. Priscilla could never come out to play because she had to take care of her many brothers and sisters. Like a grown woman who had birthed babies, Priscilla's bony, twelve-year-old hip always held an infant. Wherever she went, to the incinerator, the store, three or four toddlers with runny noses waddled behind her. Nobody ever knew where Priscilla's mother was, unless she was bringing home a new baby from the hospital. Dee-Dee, Antoine, Stacey, and me Krazy-Klacked, Hula-Hooped, and double-dutched our days away while Priscilla looked out on childhood from the window of apartment Number 269. Then one of those babies would wail and Priscilla would be gone to soothe it.

Now Cookie was confined as well. That was one less playmate to play jacks with. Out of pity for Cookie, I looped my Hula Hoop on my shoulder, tucked a *Right On!* magazine (Michael Jackson was on the cover) under my arm, and loaded my pockets down with SweeTarts, Pixie Stix, green apple Now and Later candies, Krazy Klackers, and tiny cups from a toy tea set. Around Building A-11 to Cookie's first-floor bedroom window I sneaked, not caring one bit that she had been imprisoned by her mother's god. Forget him, Cookie deserved to have some fun.

Tap, tap, tap on the pane. Like a hyperactive puppy, Cookie's face popped up in the window, eager with an open-mouthed smile. She darted to close the bedroom door, looked, then looked again— Mrs. Parker might be on recess from Bible reading. Cookie dashed back and gleefully opened the window and screen.

A hot draft of urine burned my nostrils. (Mrs. Parker's Bible reading sometimes distracted her from the unpleasant chores of child-rearing. And she loved to keep the heat up Jamaica-high.) But a little whiff of piss was a small price to pay for the grand imagination Cookie brought to our play.

Before her confinement, Cookie once had me undulating, wallowing in dirt, and leaping through the Hula Hoop. "We are dolphins in Lake Erie," Cookie fantasized. Another time, we had climbed the three-story fire escape to the old Dike Elementary School and slid down the furnace smoke stack. "Pretend you are in a parachute floating and landing on a cloud," Cookie yelled as my butt sped toward the concrete.

At the window, Cookie and I played out the final games of our childhood. We sucked the sweet and sour from green apple Now and Laters till our tongues turned chartreuse. We poured red Pixie Stix powder into the tiny teacups and sipped as if it were an exquisite cherry blend.

Under house arrest, Cookie was at my mercy. I could bring tears to her eyes with a threat of departure. After being oppressed by Dee-Dee, the bully queen, I found such control exhilarating. And on occasion, I abused it. But I believed that Reverend Berry's God would probably bless me anyway, just for being nice enough to come and play with Cookie.

We immediately critiqued the color pin-ups of the Jackson Five in *Right On!* "I heard that they wear wigs," I told Cookie, knowing it would upset her.

"They don't wear no wigs. Who told you that lie?"

"This boy named Wendell Wilson. He got a brother named Edwin Starr and he made a record called "War, Hunh. What Is It Good For? Absolutely Nothing." And he works for Motown Records, the same company that the Jackson Five sing for. He said his brother sees the Jackson Five all the time when they are making records. And one time he saw Marlon and Tito taking off their wigs. Yep, that's what he said. I'm not lying."

Cookie was quiet. This was too much for her in voluntary detention and now her heroes found to be ungenuine.

On another page, we ooohed and ahhhed over color photos of the *Soul Train* gang: their dance moves, their clothes, their hairstyles. "Oooh. I wish I could wear my hair like that," Cookie said, pulling a twiggle in a coarse cap of hair that hadn't grown one full inch in the twelve years she had been living.

Cookie Parker's mother never caught us playing at the window. Surely, if she had, we would have been damned to a hell worse than the final chapters of the Revelations.

Meanwhile, her hallway sermons were unceasing. Each day, she poked her head out the doorway and preached. "It's evil in this hallway. It's evil I can feel." Then she snapped the deadbolt to lock out iniquity. We hallway kids leaned against the cinder block and howled. We had no reverence for Mrs. Parker's god. Next day, she was there again. "If you're living in shit," she intoned, "shit gets on you."

Cookie Parker grew up to be a pickpocket and a wig thief. Pageboy, flip, shag, curlicue, rainbow Afro—she stole them all from Kresge's five-and-dime, downtown. She did time in the women's workhouse, got out, birthed a baby boy, and was shot to death by a man whose pockets she tried to pick.

Some kids, including my siblings, went into self-imposed detention to avoid fistfights and savage name-calling.

"Tank head." "Bullet head." "Water head." "Peanut-headed niggah" were the daily taunts that drove my baby brother John inside Number 129 for weeks.

There he parked himself at the living room window and pressed his face to the pane, a patch of his forehead shining as if he had been glued there. If only he could have removed his big head from his shoulders, surely John would have been a happy boy.

Still clutched in one hand was the crumpled paper bag of oddball objects, a portable playground for a boy who could not go outside to play, kick dirt, and find nice friends.

Nothing could keep my baby sister in the house for very long. Tinky was highly sociable. Still, a name-calling attack or scuffle and skinned knee could send her into hiding for a week. At least once a month, she staged a bogus runaway attempt, which she later admitted was inspired by Peter Brady on *The Brady Bunch*. Tinky stuffed clothing into a brown paper bag and ran down Bundy Drive fast as her bony legs could carry her. "I can't stand this place no more. I'm running away and I ain't playing," she cried. Dee-Dee, Darryl, Antoine, Keith, Stacey, and L'il Joe-Joe, creaking up the rear, took off after her with me. By the time she reached Scovill Avenue, two blocks from Building A-11, we caught her and hauled her by wrists and feet back to Number 129.

"Stupid fool," Dee-Dee scolded Tinky along the way. "If you goin' to run away, you 'posed to take some pork 'n' beans, potted meat, Vienna sausage, crackers, and a can opener with you. Not no bag full of clothes."

Dynamite had also retreated after that wild-haired girl (she had a dried-up Afro that flaked like a rusted Brillo pad) named FeeFee pulled a pearl-handled switchblade knife on him one night and threatened to slice. We all suspected that FeeFee had a crush on Dynamite, and had gotten just a little flustered trying to show her affection. Or maybe she had it out for the whole family. Once during a softball game, she threatened to beat me with the bat after I made an oblique reference to her mother and family lineage. Scared as I was, I stood up to FeeFee, and her hair. She backed down, probably figuring that anybody stupid enough to stand up to a wild woman wielding a baseball bat must be carrying a switchblade, razor blade, or worse. I didn't have either. I was just sick and tired of her trying to be so bad.

But FeeFee had succeeded in scaring my brother away. Tall, thick, and wearing an unpicked Afro that came to a nappy point, Dynamite looked like a giant frozen chicken most of the time. On frequent trips to the refrigerator he remained unkempt. But he

picked his matted locks and put on his balloon-sleeved shirt for
trips to Little Acres, the closet-size corner store where he bought
Kool cigarettes. Upon returning, Dynamite locked himself inside
his one-room "psychedelic shack." All day it shook with the rude,
rambunctious rock of the Parliament Funkadelic and George Clinton, the unopposed president of funk. Clinton sang his nonesuch
lyrics with a background chorus that sounded like googobs of people were singing in my brother's room. Or the Ohio Players sang
through their noses, sounding out their rubbery, raucous preludes
to rap. Other times when I walked by Dynamite's door, I heard Sly
and the Family Stone singing a simple song.

But I was beginning to understand that, for my brother, there
were no simple songs. Inside his psychedelic shack, Dynamite was
trying to process the colors of a very complicated, confusing reality,
a kaleidoscope of quicksand. Inside the tube, he was sinking so fast
and so silently. Outside, there were no more gifts of goldfish from
him to me. I missed my big brother.

L'il Joe-Joe, the blues boy, also went into isolation. One day in
the hallway, a big boy in a leather coat—he looked like a man—
purposely tripped L'il Joe-Joe into a puddle of pee. From my perch
on the stairs, I saw the whole thing. But I didn't say a word. I was a
punk and I knew it, letting L'il Joe-Joe get his butt kicked and not
even saying anything.

"Go on, boy, I ain't playing with you now,' L'il Joe-Joe threatened
the big boy like he could actually kick somebody's butt.

I felt L'il Joe-Joe wanting to fight back. His face had grown into
a man's, thick and slightly whiskered. But his body was still a sickly
little boy's, puny and frail.

"Who you callin' boy? Huh?" asked the leather coat, looking
down on L'il Joe-Joe in the puddle of pee. "Who you callin' boy?
I'll kick your butt all the way across that parkin' lot out there. I was
just playin' wit chu, niggah. That's all. To see if you could take it like
a man. And you gon' go act like a punk. See there."

L'il Joe-Joe pulled himself up from the pee. The bar on one leg brace had broken, and was poking up inside his pants leg like a dislocated bone.

After that, L'il Joe-Joe didn't come outside much.

But sometimes late in the evening, daring L'il Joe-Joe took back the hallway from big mean boys. And he beat his bongos into the night, singing his sad songs.

Nothing was going to stop me from going outside to play. Nothing.

By now, Dee-Dee was addicted to fights, her own and others'. At times, she herself would threaten to duke you out, point-blank. Or round and round the contenders she went, skipping and twirling her dance of instigation. "Go on and hit him," she taunted. "I ain't got all day to wait for you to kick his butt."

Somehow, I found Dee-Dee's abuses of me irresistible. After each episode, I returned to her side, hoping against hope for forgiveness, fondness, friendship, only to be socked, kicked, set up, or robbed of my Now and Laters.

"Girl, I'm not in the mood to kick your butt today," Dee-Dee informed me after school one day. "I'm gonna get somebody else to kick it." Then she danced out of the hallway door, leaving me worried about getting another undeserved ass-kicking.

In less than a minute, she poked her head back inside the door. "Come on, girl, the Williams brothers and them want to play some hide-n-go-get-it."

"I don't want to play no hide-n-go-get-it," I told her. Dee-Dee swore that everybody in her old neighborhood loved to play hide-n-go-get-it. But I believed that Dee-Dee had invented the game as another sadistic fix. The rules were simple: On the count of ten, all the girls hid; then the boys came looking for them. The first girl to be found was felt on all over, up and down—breasts, booty, everything. I felt like we were rehearsing to be raped, which was something awful that grown men did to girls that made them nasty. I did not wish to play.

"Girl, what I tell you? I'm gonna get somebody to kick your butt if you don't come on," Dee-Dee warned.

"One . . . two . . . three . . . four . . ." Outside, Darryl counted out loud, facing the comer of a brick wall where he wasn't supposed to be able to see where we were hiding. I ran as fast and as far as I could. I hated playing hide-n-go-get-it. It was nasty. Plus, if boys felt on you too much, you might end up becoming a ho' and getting pregnant.

According to some people, this is what had happened to Dee-Dee's big sister. Avis let so many men feel on her that she became pregnant and gave birth to a baby boy named Booboo. That was his real name, the only one he had. I swear. Now, boys who sometimes hung out in the hallway called Avis a ho' behind her back. Grown women called her an "'unwed mother."

"Least I did get married 'fo I had these children," other young mothers said with regard to Avis and her boy without a father. This made me glad that Charles Lyles was my father even if he was not around.

Rumors hissed that Avis worked for the poontang peddlers down on East Fifty-fifth Street, shaking her money maker into the night. Decked out in sandals that laced up her legs like a Trojan goddess, hot pants, halter top, and shag wigs from Kresge's, Avis had a hard beauty about her. Men could sense her sexiness seconds before she arrived on the scene. She was always out there, crushing hearts with her heels like pieces of broken glass ground into the concrete. For, just like Dee-Dee, she could be mean, a Negress not to be messed with.

But sometimes Avis stood in the hallway by herself, quiet, looking out those blurry Plexiglas windows at Bundy Drive. Maybe she was waiting for a man to pick her up so he could feel all over her. Those times, Avis had a certain serenity about her. When I came upon her there, she was nice to me, tossing me a Tootsie Roll or a crisp piece of Wrigley's Spearmint gum from her big leather patchwork purse. I thought about asking her how much money she charged those men to feel on her. I thought better of it. That might hurt her feelings, if she had any. Maybe bad women like Avis didn't have any feelings. I kept my mouth shut. Even if the rumors about Avis were true, those times in the hallway, her soft touch and tough grace transcended her tramping.

Just the same, I did not want to end up a ho' like her. "Five . . . six . . ." Darryl counted impatiently. I ran toward the parking lot. Where could I hide? Behind a rear fender? Inside an old junked Ford whose door might let out a rusty grunt and betray me?

"Seven . . . eight . . . nine . . . ten. Ready or not, here we come." Darryl turned and took his hands from his eyes.

"Oh yeah, we gon' get us some now," said a zealous Antoine, squeezing a pair of invisible titties in the air.

On the count of nine, I had dodged behind the fender. My bright green bell-bottom pants gave me away.

"I see you under there, girl," Antoine yelled, running toward me from the curb. Darryl, Maurice, and two other boys followed. "We gon' get us some now." I sat still, bearing down, trying to squeeze myself out of existence, anything to avoid the humiliation to come.

When Darryl reached for my arm I yanked away. "Go on, boy. Leave me alone. Y'all ain't feeling all over me. Go feel on Dee-Dee. She's the one that wanted to play."

"What' the matter for you, girl? Think you too good to get felt on with your yellow butt?" Darryl yelled.

"Don't chu wish your ass was yellow too, you prune-black nig-gah," I shot back, knowing instantly that I had gone beyond the point of no return. We worked our way back to the building, yelling at the top of our lungs.

"Your mama's a white bitch. And that's how you got that way." In nearly every confrontation, my mother's skin, white as canned, condensed milk, became the ultimate object of attack.

"Your mama's a big fat bitch from eating up all the food at that restaurant where she works." I had gone way too far now. The Williamses would not tolerate a "your mama," plus an assault on her fabulous waitressing job. No way.

Bamm. Blamm. My skull rebounded off the corrugated brick wall of A-11. Darryl's brown fist recoiled. Stars. I saw stars, up close. Dazzling, bursting bullets of white light inside my head.

"Say something about my mother again and you gon' get more than that." I heard Darryl's voice in the darkness that was quickly blocking out the stars in my head.

Two sympathizers managed to maneuver my body, suddenly weak and swaying, to the door of apartment Number 133. When it opened, they displayed my slightly swollen left eye to Mrs. Williams. She stared coolly, as if knocking the hell out of me was the only natural thing for her son to do.

My flesh did not bruise. But my heart did. Up till now, Darryl and Antoine had been my friends. But this sultry summer, when the project seemed like a boiling cauldron, something was changing in them. A brute meanness got hold of them and would not let go.

Just the summer before, we had caught lightning bugs in mayonnaise jars. At dusk, when our mothers called us in, we set them free to twinkle over the project like little living stars. This year, when I turned the jar upside down, Darryl commanded: "Kill them som bitches." In a frenzied dance, I stomped and ground them into the dirt, stamping out every light.

At night in my bed, curled under the sheets, I felt bad for killing the beautiful little flying lanterns, for they were harmless. The meanness had gotten hold of me too.

But I didn't dare jump bad with Dee-Dee or my pugnacious playmates anymore. They would kick my butt. Instead, come fall, I got tough at Kennard Junior High School. I chose my victims carefully. Old Mr. Salo, a white social studies teacher with big baleful eyes, was my favorite person to mess with.

Actually, Mr. Salo was young, but he looked old. Bluish purple bags ringed his eyes, partially hidden by shiny blond bangs. When I peeked in the teacher's lounge, there he sat, chain-smoking Camels. In class, Mr. Salo told us slavery was a terrible thing. "I'm not ashamed to say it. The white man's got a lot to atone for." Week after week it seemed, regardless of the subject matter, Mr. Salo detoured the discussion to slavery and racism. "If there is a heaven," Mr. Salo said, "you can be pretty sure there won't be any white men up there. No, sirree."

I, for one, was sick of Mr. Salo and his sadness about being white. It wasn't my fault. White people were strange, with their shaggy hair and pale bluish gray skin, and they had definitely done some things wrong, the Afro Set had convinced me of that. But Momma always said it was "ugly" to complain too much. Still, I showed Mr. Salo no mercy, fidgeting and passing vulgar notes to my classmates about him.

He caught me and assigned me to stand in a corner holding two fat textbooks (that we never used anyway) over my head until the bell rang. "Old white honkie," I sassed under my breath.

But inside I felt bad for poor old Mr. Salo. He seemed to be saying he was sorry for every rotten thing the whites had ever done wrong. Every day, it seemed, he would stand before the class as if naked in his loosened tie and rolled shirtsleeves baring pale, hairy, moley arms, and renounce his whiteness once and for all. Poor Mr. Salo, feeling sad and chain-smoking away the guilt and anxieties of the whole white world. He just couldn't shake those worries long enough to see that we liked him just the way he was, white and all, teaching us the painful truth of history.

Fall was kickball season and on Fridays after school we played in the parking lot till dark. One evening, Dee-Dee's team was out. Mine was up, ready to kick in some home runs. I relished winning a game against Dee-Dee. Most of the time, it bruised her ego so bad that she declared her team the winner anyway, damn the facts.

"Hey y'all," came a voice that was not part of our kickball game. "Somebody got shot over there in the parking lot behind C-5. He still over there in his car. They waitin' for the police to come get him."

We paused for a minute, eyeing each other to determine whether this mishap merited interruption of our game.

"Let's go see," said Keith on a whim, hoping his teammates would agree. We ran, skipped, and leaped to our new adventure. A dozen men, whom I had seen in our hallway at different times, surrounded a dark green Buick, shaking their heads and staring at oil spots on the ground.

"Do you know who it is?" asked Keith, suddenly very bold.

"Naw. But I think he lived in C-5," one of the men answered.

"He dead?" Keith asked in disbelief. No one had said that it was a real live corpse.

"Yeah. They got him good. Y'all can go 'head and look if you want to," another man said, as if he was granting us privilege in matters only he controlled. We eyed each other for the coward among us. We were pulled in by the intrigue of death and violence, yet repelled by the fear and closeness of it.

It was too late to back out now and hold on to a shred of dignity. We had no excuse. The police would be a while. Lately, they took their time getting to King-Kennedy.

We lined up at the driver's side window. One by one by one, we stepped up to peep in at the corpse. I brought up the rear, hoping for sirens, that the police, the ambulance, the fire department would arrive before my turn. Maybe the man could be revived, resurrected, just like Jesus, the son of Reverend Berry's God. Maybe he could live happily ever after.

I had never seen a freshly dead body, only ones that had been meticulously prepared for viewing by Mr. Wills, Cleveland's most famous black undertaker. My hands grew cold and damp, probably just like the corpse's. Kickball was calling. But trying to get everyone to turn and run back to the game might rouse Dee-Dee's wrath. She had probably set up this whole shooting thing just because her team was losing. It was her fault that everyone always wanted to fight to prove how bad they were. The muscles in my neck quivered and constricted, like a rope being rigged. Hatred for Dee-Dee locked my jaws and joints. I wanted to smack her, punch her, stomp her, bite her, dig my nails into her flesh until her whole body was covered with bleeding half moons.

Antoine was next. He stepped up, looked back at the rest of us in line behind him. His big lips were slanted in a smirk. He poked his head in the window. After a beat he stepped back with one wide swaying step. "Aw, that wasn't nothing," he told us. "Any chump could handle that."

Next Keith. Then me. Keith boldly stuck his head in. He knew this was a test of his badness. He must have stood there three minutes, though I suspect his eyes were shut tight and he held his breath the whole time.

"You next, Sugarbabe. Go 'head," somebody said. I looked in askance and saw the head slumped on the steering wheel as if it were a pillow. The mouth was frozen wide open like he was saying "ouch" when the gun blast peeled the skin from his forehead. Two teeth were missing from the man who lived in C-5.

I squinted my eyes just enough to see the space in his pink gums. Then I squeezed them shut and decided: Reverend Berry's God was clearly useless in the King-Kennedy project. He worked just fine in nice neighborhoods like Mount Pleasant where we used to live, where men had jobs at the steel mill. But in the projects, Reverend Berry's God seemed to have no power. I had prayed for the meanness to go away, to blow over like a bad storm. Instead, Dee-Dee, Darryl, Antoine, Keith, even L'il Joe-Joe and me, even our parents, only grew angrier, till the light of everyday smiles had left our faces.

Now, right on our playground, someone had killed the man who lived in C-5. He was the first. Who would be next? And who was responsible? The black militants who had gone bad? Or was it one of "the oppressors" who were against us like the Afro Sets said, sneaking into the project trying to kill us off?

Two minutes must have passed. I kept studying the colorful inside of my eyelids as I swallowed hot vomit rising in my throat. The iron-like mustiness of the dead man's blood filled my nostrils. Suppressing a shiver, in one motion, I swiveled from the corpse in the car to face my peers, determined to show no fear.

"That ain't nothing," I said, dismissing with a flick of my smart-aleck wrist the bits of skullbone and blood that I had seen on the dashboard.

By now, police sirens were howling closer and closer.

"It sho ain't," Dee-Dee agreed, regrouping quickly from the fear I saw flash in her eyes: She knew she was a bully and couldn't afford to be scared. "That ain't nothing to be scared of," she said, kicking a rock. "'Let's go finish our game before it gets dark. We're goin' to win." As a crowd gathered, we skipped, skipped, skipped away to resume our play.

Chapter Ten

A FEW DAYS LATER, while we were playing jacks in the hallway, little lying Keith tried to tell one of his tales on the dead man.

"Hey, Sugarbabe. You know that man that got killed the other night when we was playing kickball? They put his body in the incinerator and burned him up. Last night when that real black smoke was coming from the incinerator, that was him, burning up. And this morning when my mother told me to take out the garbage, I looked in there and I saw one of his bones sticking right out of the fire."

"You lying niggah," Dee-Dee nearly shouted at the horror of it. "I saw them when they put his body in that big old black bag with the zipper and drove it away. Now this niggah gon' say they burned him in the incinerator. You know you lyin.'"

Keith insisted. "But when they saw he was dead and they couldn't do nothing about it, that's when they put him in the incinerator."

I wasn't going to stand for Keith's big old lie. "No, they didn't," I butted in. "They can't just put you in no incinerator when you die. You have to go to the House of Wills Funeral Home first. And they have to put you in a coffin and a suit and you have to have a funeral first. That's what the law says." (I wasn't really sure about that last part, but it sounded good. Plus, there seemed to be some kind of rules on handling death.)

"Y'all don't know what you talkin' about," said Keith, looking like he was going to cry if we kept challenging his lie. "Then whose bone was that I saw in the incinerator ashes?"

"Show us the bone since you said it's still in there." Dee-Dee demanded evidence, regardless of how gruesome.

Keith got quiet, like he always did when he wasn't quite telling the truth. "I ain't going back over there. I'm scared. Plus, I saw a big old rat over there. It was in one of those big old piles of garbage. And it had a tail like a long piece of pink bubble gum."

"Eeeew. Boy, why don't you shut up?" I said.

"Them things is back again." Dee-Dee was in a state of disbelief. "I thought we got rid of them that time."

"That time" referred to the dead heat of summer months gone by. A boy from Building B-9 had started the whole thing.

We didn't even know his name. He was gangly, his hair shaved close on a lumpy brown scalp. We were hanging out in front of Building A-11 when he walked right up to us. In one hand, he swung a baseball bat gently back and forth like a pendulum. The other propped a shovel on his shoulder. Four rough looking, shiny-faced boys in striped shirts and shorts flanked him like bodyguards. I knew right away: They were coming to kick somebody's butt real bad.

As the boy with the bat drew near, we got real quiet. "Y'all wanta come?" he asked, swinging the bat back and forth.

"Where?" Keith wolfed out like he was bad or something.

"We're going to kill some of them rats livin' at the incinerator," the boy said. "They 'bout to take over 'round here." Out the comers of our eyes, we checked one another's reactions to this most unusual proposition.

"'Come on," the boy from B-9 urged. "They getting so fat they 'bout to run us out of here. Other night, my sister was taking the garbage out to the 'cinerator and one of 'em with big old yellow teeth crawled right up on her little sock 'n' almost bit her."

It was true. The rats were getting real bad. But that piddling sock tale wasn't enough to convince us to mount an all-out assault on them. Besides, he should have been taking out the garbage instead of his little sister. He was probably a lazy punk.

"My momma talked to the people at Cleveland Metropolitan Housing Authority and they told her that they were going to send a whole bunch of exterminators out here to set traps to kill those rats," I said.

"It's up to us," the boy said impatiently. "'We can't be waitin' on no CMHA to do nothin' for us. We either get these mothafuckahs under control 'r they gon' overrun this mothafuckah. What if they bite one of these little kids 'r somethin'?"

"What if they bite one of us?" Keith asked. That's what I wanted to know too.

"They won't if enough of us go after 'em," the boy said with the confidence of an exterminating company executive. "They so fat they can't even run all that fast."

The boy from B-9 was right and we knew it. King-Kennedy wasn't a clean place anymore. The walls moved with roaches. Some were interesting, fat, shiny brown ovals like the stones on display in Mrs. Adam's science class. Some were creepy. When the hallway reeked and streams of pee ran through the tile like a map, I took it upon myself to clean. My hands turned pink, raw, and wrinkly from wringing a gray river from the mop. But as soon as I was done, I knew, some boy would come piss again. Once, some boys who were mad at my big brother deposited a leaky plastic bag of rancid chitterlings right in front of Number 129. I went to get my mop, but I couldn't wipe that odor away.

Another time in the triangle of darkness under the hallway stairs, Maria, the retarded girl who lived on the third floor, did "number two." My mother called the maintenance man from CMHA to come clean it up. He never came. I got my mop, a dustpan, and a bottle of bleach and doused those turds till they turned gray and crumbled like incinerator ash. Grown people who lived in A-11 complimented me for my diligence in keeping the hallway clean. Sometimes they tossed me a quarter. Or Hattie rewarded me with a free "deluxe freeze cup" made from grape and green-lime Kool-Aid.

At the incinerators, rats had grown fat and fruitful. In broad daylight, they waddled right past you as if you weren't even there, their bellies wet and hanging so low they left trails like giant, squishy snails. The incinerator door was completely out of bounds. From a distance believed to be safe, residents tossed tin cans, ribbons of potato peels, dollops of solidified fat on already high piles outside the inferno door. Others poured garbage straight out second-floor windows. The rats grew even bolder.

His shovel slung over one shoulder and bat at the ready, the boy from B-9 seemed wise and resolute like a leader. He knew what he was talking about. It was the rats or us. CMHA didn't give a damn as far as we could tell. We couldn't count on them to do our dirty work for us. We would take this matter into our own hands.

"Wait right here," said Antoine, raring to go. "My Mama's got an axe that she keeps under her bed. I'm going to get it."

One by one, we disappeared into our apartments then returned armed with boards, bats, one axe, two shovels, one ten-pound end of a barbell, and an old skate with metal wheels. (I had considered arming myself with my big sister Linda's old baton, but decided it just wasn't built for this task.)

"Whose skate is that?"

"My brother's," said Stacey, who was considered to be stuck-up and seditty. Even she had been roused by the boy from B-9's passion and reason. "He don't use it anymore."

We moved toward the first incinerator—the one where the rat had threatened the little sister of the boy from B-9. Along the way, we rallied and recruited others to join our cause.

Some balked at our audacity: "Who them niggahs think they are, going after rats?"

Others were concerned: "Y'all gonnna catch the rabie, get sick, go to the hospital, and die," a boy yelled from Building B-6 after turning down our invitation to extermination.

"You just chicken," Dee-Dee spat back. "I ain't scared of no rats."

"Yeah. We're going to get those motherfuckahs." By the time we reached the first incinerator, about fifteen warriors had joined our rat-killing expedition.

"There go one. Get him. Get him."

A slick furry head poked out of a pile of trash. *Frack!* With the shovel back, the boy from B-9 smashed down on it. Out they came, six or seven at once scurrying every which way.

The bloated, disoriented rats were no match for us. They could barely scamper fast enough to escape a board or bat coming down.

Like crazy we swung. *Frack! Bam! Ughh!* Even L'il Joe-Joe managed to down a chubby, slimy-looking one. We chased. We cornered. Then we slammed down with the skate or bat. Next, the backup crew with a purloined garden hose and a two-by-four moved in for the final kill. Then *frack!* again. B-9 bashed his bat down on another. Innards every shade of pink spurted every which way, like balloons bursting into pieces. Rat blood spattered our play clothes. Before dying, the squishy creatures let go a high, final squeal like a bad blues singer wailing at the end of a recording destined to be a flop. Neither the screeching nor the stench unnerved us. For a moment, we recoiled, then kept on killing.

The rodents could have turned, clawed, and sunk their yellow fangs into our flesh. Deep down inside we knew this. But we were children and our injured dignity overrode reason and fear. We were full of retaliation for the rats. How dare they enter the place where we lived and try to take over? Us or them. We united against the rats like the Panthers against the whites. And we would be victorious.

With each strike, we grunted and moaned because the killing hurt so good. "Take that," said Keith, "You som bitch." Stacey was too slow. I grabbed her skate and swung until my arms ached, till I was dizzy, thirsty, and wholly exhilarated by our sudden daring and the power of conquest.

In the middle of one battle, out the corner of my eye, I saw Dee-Dee frozen in horror at the whole scene. Dee-Dee, my sister, my nemesis. O warrior who taught me how to fight every enemy, every battle, real or imagined. There she cowered, quivering, afraid. I never feared her again.

On the sidelines, tenants gathered. Women held their children's hands, cheering us on a safe distance from the carnage. We sucked in the air of triumph and puffed out our chests like a matador on a winning streak.

Onward. We moved to the next incinerator. The crowd followed. Then the next. When it was all over, L'il Joe-Joe, who had trailed behind to count, reported the kill: thirty-seven rats, possibly thirty-eight. No human casualties.

"The Rat-killing Crew." We were baaaaad. Our reputation spread quickly through the project. We were heroes. Grown men who were rumored to carry pistols and switchblade knives summoned our services. "Did you hear about them kids that live in A-11 and B-9?" Younger kids boasted on our behalf. "They went after those rats at the incinerator and killed every one." Whenever rats got out of hand, we were called in to do the job. With our bats, broomsticks, two-by-fours, an occasional brick, and that roller skate, we arrived, ready, willing, able to exterminate.

Some days after getting the job done, we were rewarded with freeze cups by ladies who lived in the buildings where rats had attempted a takeover. "Come on in my apartment and wash your hands first. You know those rats are full of germs," said Mrs. Stallings in Building C-5.

One day we were interrupted from our play and dispatched to the Building B-6 incinerator. Rats were just about ready to take over there, a whiny-voiced woman had said. Just as a dozen of us rounded the corner with bats, boards, and the skate (with a rope as shoestring now), a nice lady in a suit and high heels called to us. She wore pretty, shiny lipstick too.

"May I talk to you all for just a second?" She talked real proper, straight through her nose like some of my teachers at school. "We heard what a good job you kids are doing keeping the rats under control here in the King-Kennedy Estates. And we would like to put you all on the six o'clock evening news broadcast so the people of the city of Cleveland can see the fine work you youngsters are doing here."

"For real?" asked B-9, our official leader.

"For real," said the nice lady. "This is George. He's my photographer." An older man with a big square movie camera on his shoulder said, "Hi. I'm George."

"How did you know we was killing rats?" B-9 wanted more info first. He sure was smart.

"Oh, word has gotten around," Miss Reporter answered.

For once, we were doing something good, not something evil, like Cookie Parker's mother always said we were. Now the whole world was going to be able to see us in action.

"Momma! Turn on the TV. We're going to be on the six o'clock evening news," I reported as soon as I walked in the door. "This lady—she had on a nice suit—and her photographer said they were going to put us on the six o'clock evening news."

"What in the world are you going to be on the six o'clock news for?"

"Killing the rats."

"Killing rats?"

The Rat-killing Crew's reputation had spread to just about everyone in the project, except Lillian Lyles. I had not exactly mentioned it to her.

"Killing rats?" Disbelief shaded Momma's face. "I heard about some kids around here killing rats. But I just knew my children weren't stupid enough to join them."

"It was all of us, Ma. We had to do something. Them rats was 'bout to take over the King-Kennedy Estates."

"Killing rats. Girl, are you crazy? Don't you know you can get rabies and end up having convulsions? I—"

In the middle of our dispute, the nicely dressed lady appeared on the TV screen. Her report went something like this: "'Today, young residents today in the King-Kennedy Estates public housing project on the east side took maintenance matters into their own hands. Fed up with rats and unfulfilled promises of extermination, these very brave youngsters did a little exterminating of their own.'"

There was something funny in her tone—like she really wasn't on our side, like she might be against us or something. Then we popped on the screen, slamming, swinging, running after the rats. The camera was up close right in B-9's face as he swung the board down hard. His eyes looked huge, bulging. His mouth was open, his tongue wagging. In the background, our battle moans could be heard: "There go one. Get him. Get him. Don't let that mother-*bleep-bleep* get away."

Then the screen blinked to Miss Reporter. CMHA officials could not be reached for comment, she said.

The report had been aimed at making CMHA look bad. But it made us look worse. The pretty TV reporter in her nice suit and heels had stripped all the dignity out of our enterprise. There we were in living color, a rat-killing mob, swinging clubs, cussing, and hollering at the top of our lungs. On the TV screen, we were a screaming band of heathens, lunatic enough to do hand-to-hand combat with an army of rats. Surely, people would think we were natural-born savages, capable of any subhuman act.

In my heart, I knew that we were just kids trying to keep our community clean, trying to show that we didn't have to ask CMHA to do anything for us. The rat killing had been our most dignified stand: us against them.

Momma was embarrassed down to the tingly roots of her teeth: The King-Kennedy Estates had not turned out to be the promised land she had envisioned. But this was too much. Her child out killing rats with her bare hands, practically. Then on television, telling the whole damn world that Lillian Lyles couldn't provide a decent place for her children to live.

.   .   .

The year 1972 found Lillian Lyles a woman without a savior. By then, Mayor Carl B. Stokes was gone. On April 16, 1971, when Carl B. Stokes announced on TV that he would not run for mayor again, Momma had cried out just as she had when Martin Luther King was shot. The mayor's announcement came about seven months after a black man had killed a white man on East 110th Street and Woodland Avenue. Angry whites had surrounded Carl B. Stokes's nice home with his kids and pregnant wife inside. After that, Momma said, whites and blacks always at each other had gotten to be too much for Carl B. Stokes. "He ain't but one man," she said. "How much can he stand?"

When her savior stepped down, Momma had faithfully "endorsed," as she called it, Arnold Pinkney, a black school board president who was Carl B. Stokes's first choice. "Pinkney ain't Carl B. Stokes, and never will be. But he's a good man," was Momma's campaign slogan. When Pinkney lost, Momma campaigned for James Carney. Every evening after work, she headed to his storefront headquarters to call people and ask them to vote for Carney, even though he wasn't black like Carl B. Stokes.

After hours of talking politics, munching batter-dipped fried chicken, and sipping grape, Momma came home clear-eyed and energized in the wee hours of the morning. When Carney lost, Momma didn't talk so much about politics anymore.

On trips downtown, we passed by once bright orange-lidded trash cans that had been the trademark of Carl B. Stokes's "Cleveland: NOW!" That was the "urban uplift" program that Momma had bragged about the most. Now the orange cans were battered, and foul-smelling like rotten pumpkins. The city Momma loved was still dirty and deeply divided.

Whenever she detected the daydreamy glaze of fantasy in her children's deep-set brown eyes, statements full of fanciful thinking, or any other sign that we were off somewhere in the stars like

Charles Lyles, Lillian Lyles brought us back to earth with a crude clarion: "You better wake up and see Cleveland."

She grew disenchanted with government, then downright cynical. The project was just part of "the system" designed to keep her down, she complained while tossing clothes into the compact washer she had bought from Sears and hooked up to the sink in the tiny kitchen of Number 129. "The King-Kennedy Estates show just how stupid Uncle Sam is. If the federal government built it, nine times out of ten, you know it ain't no good. Even the way this damn place is built is all wrong."

Momma was right. The hallway was dark and scary, its lone light bulb busted out. Inside Number 129 was crowded and uncomfortable. Outside, every day, incinerators blew fine black ash in our eyes.

"Now who would want to live in a place like this?" Lillian Lyles wanted to know. So did I.

As Momma's disgust and disappointment in the project deepened, so did her anger at the forces that had brought us there, mainly Charles Lyles.

"Other people get married and work hard and put their money together so they can buy a nice home. But you couldn't do that with Charles Lyles, no sirree."

Was Momma being fair to Charles Lyles? I believed that he would have come back home long ago, if only he had found a job in the steel mill. I didn't know Charles Lyles well enough to be mad at him the way Momma was. But I had spent some time wondering if he was really looking all that hard to find a job in a steel mill. He had stopped calling us even back before the riots. And we hadn't heard from him at all since moving to King-Kennedy. I missed him, though I wasn't quite sure who it was that I missed.

I knew that the No. 14 bus could take me up Kinsman Road to the bar and grill where I might have found Charles Lyles. He would be sitting on a barstool sipping beer, acting crazy, and making everybody in the place laugh real hard. Getting fifty cents for bus fare wasn't the problem. My freeze cup business was booming (I had jacked up prices from five cents to seven). Plus, on some Saturdays, I cleaned at my Aunt Cora's, splashing and scrubbing pungent vinegar water on the sticky clear plastic covers on her precious French provincial furniture. (Aunt Cora still had a lot of the South in her from growing up in Aberdeen, Mississippi. She liked the idea of having a girl come to clean her house weekly.) I wanted to go, but something in me wouldn't take that ride.

One Saturday evening, our new turquoise Trimline telephone rang. Momma, always full of energy, picked it up quick.

"Hi, Skeeter. How you?" Her voice was low and surprised.

At last, Charles Lyles was calling for us. He had found a job at a steel mill. He was coming back. He was coming to give us some money. We would buy hamburgers and egg-yellow buns. With the change left over, we would buy German chocolate brownies from Hough Bakeries, downtown. We would make fresh lemonade and stir in a pack of grape Kool-Aid. While we gorged, Charles Lyles would break the news: We would be moving out of the project, back to East 123rd Street where the steel people lived. Yippeeeee.

I didn't dare speak. Words might curse my dream from coming true.

"We been fine." Lillian Lyles was terse. She jumped to the point. "You workin'?"

"Naw." I could hear his voice small inside the phone. "Listen, Lil'yan" (that's the way he pronounced Momma's name), "can you lend me 'bout fifty dollars for two weeks?"

Momma answered in her sweetest voice, "Naw. I'm sorry, Skeeter. I ain't got it. I've got so many bills to pay. Linda is in the Upward Bound Program and trying to go on to college. So I've had to help her with that. And Tinky been havin' those asthma attacks, keeping me running to the hospital."

The other end was silent. Tinky was my father's favorite. Wasn't he going to ask to speak to me? Like a race car referee, I signaled crazily to Momma, hoping. She ignored me.

Fi-nal-ly. "Shorty's right here. She wants to speak to you." She handed my father's voice to me.

"Hi, Skeeter." There was so much to tell. "We live in the King-Kennedy Estates now. And we have—useta have, Afro Sets and the Black Panthers here. They are fighting for the liberation of all black people. And I learned how to swim at the PORC." There was more. "And Skeeter, one day we was playing kickball in the parking lot and this man got killed and we saw him in his car, waiting for the police to come. And we was on the six o'clock evening news for killing the—"

"Ain't that something, Sugarbabe. You really know what's goin' on now, don't chu?"

"But I don't like it here because these kids be beatin' us up all the time. When I go back to school in the fall I'll be in the eighth grade. Have you been able to find a job yet?"

"Naw, Sugarbabe, I'm still lookin' around," Charles Lyles said. "Been doin' a few odd jobs here and there. But I'll be down there to see you all in a couple of weeks."

"Hey, Skeeter, guess what? I been workin' over at Aunt Cora's, cleanin' up and dustin' on Saturdays. And she paid me fifteen dollars last week for scrubbing her ceiling. My neck was hur-tin' when I got finished." I overemphasized the "hurtin'" part so he would know how hard I had worked.

The other end was quiet. In the seconds that passed, maybe Charles Lyles was contemplating asking for that fifteen dollars. (It was my whole life savings, two stiff cardboard-smelling five- and ten-dollar bills tucked away in the Kotex belt box that Momma had given me. But I wasn't going to tell Charles Lyles all of that.) A father's pride must have kept him from asking for my life savings.

"Sugarbabe, can you put your mother back on the phone?"

Disappointed that he wasn't more interested in my activities and adventures, I gave the phone back to Momma. After a few minutes, she hung up.

"Callin' here, askin' me to loan him fifty dollars when we haven't heard from him in almost seven years. He got the nerve of a brass-assed monkey," was her only comment.

"Tinky," I whispered to my younger sister that night when we were in bed. "Skeeter called today. He is coming to see us in two weeks."

"That no-good niggah ain't coming to see us." She was brutally realistic for a six-year-old. "He ain't no good."

"Uh-hunn. He said he was coming," I protested. "And he said he might take us downtown to the Hippodrome to see a movie." So badly did I want to believe it that I added details to make the possibility of a visit seem more real.

"He ain't gon' take us nowhere," Tinky yawned. "Now go to sleep."

If I had known Charles Lyles just a little, Tinky, who was two years old when he left, knew him not at all. He had been fond of her curly hair and puffy red lips. In front of her crib just to make her coo, he had posed me on his shoulders. I cooperated reluctantly, jealous that I was no longer the brightest star in his universe. But Tinky held no memory of those times. She retained only negative sound bites picked up from conversations overheard between Linda and Momma.

Two weeks came and went. Working at Aunt Cora's earned me fifteen more dollars. That brought my savings to four crisp ten- and five-dollar bills. I folded them four times over and tucked them in the Kotex belt box (I still didn't need to use that belt yet). If Charles Lyles came, I planned to lend it all to him, if he still needed it. My sister Linda said I was "a stupid fool with no common sense" because Charles Lyles never paid nobody back. I never got a chance to be a fool because Charles Lyles never showed up.

I could feel Momma's faith in the project dying and begged her to move someplace, anyplace else. Tinky and John joined my pleas.

We couldn't take any more: the pissy hallway, Mrs. Parker's daily damnations, our hostile, moody playmates, the rats, the chance that there might be another killing in the middle of our kickball game. We lived in constant fear of a sudden, unprovoked attack: schoolbooks kicked to the curb, spit, fists, a baseball bat.

"We're not moving anywhere and that's that," Momma said. We thought her heartless, mean, evil. We did not understand that with five children, a job that paid $2,000 a year, and a meager welfare check, Lillian Lyles had nowhere else to go.

But like Cookie Parker's mother, Lillian Lyles didn't want the project trash to sully her children.

"Where's your damn pride?" Momma would scold and curl her lower lip in contempt when I brought home bad habits picked up in the streets of the project. I was proud: of peeing in the hallway without getting caught; of calling Mrs. Parker a bitch to her face; of cutting up in class till my teacher nearly cried; of accompanying my playmates on missions to Marshall's Drugstore to steal candy necklaces, though I never, ever stole anything myself, for I knew that would bring down the wrath of Reverend Berry's God, not to mention Momma; of playing the "dozens" so deftly and brutishly that tears of humiliation welled up in my opponent's eyes. Yes, I had pride.

But in Number 129, nasty curses, rudeness, and name-calling weren't valued. "Why can't you get good grades? Why can't you be like your big sister Linda?" was all I ever heard.

Linda was Momma's point of pride. Unlike Dee-Dee's sister Avis, and some other grown-up girls in the project, Linda had not become a ho' or pregnant. Linda was a star. She was now president of her class at East Tech and took great pride in her school. The crumbling sixty-year-old building with the Gothic façade had had an on-and-off history as a co-ed school attended mostly by immigrant kids. It became home to the district's first experiment with teaching technical trades and an extended school day. When blacks moved into the Outhwaite area, East Tech became an athletic powerhouse, producing Olympic track and field medalists Jesse Owens and Harrison Dillard.

When the East Technical High School Scarabs won the 1972 State Basketball Championship, Linda, the chief drum majorette, led the way through the project streets. From the curb, Momma beamed powerful as a police searchlight at her daughter.

Down East Fifty-fifth Street the victory parade came, the band decked out in uniforms, brown and gold, the school colors, and chanting: "East Tech. Tech. Tech. Tech. East Tech. Tech. Tech. Tech."

Linda kept the cadence. In the frost-biting February wind, her feet never missed a step. Brown and gold tassels swayed in time on mid-calf marching boots polished white so many times they looked dingy as the dirty snow. A brown and gold pleated miniskirt bobbed over her ample behind. Thick-boned, Linda marched with husky grace, one hand on her hip, her pelvis tilted toward the skies.

At the band's cue, she paused with poise and precision, shook her behind to the east, uptown, then to the west, downtown. Then she twirled and whirled her baton up, up, up, up into the heavens, high above the dome of the Shiloh Baptist Church, high as the dormers atop the House of Wills Funeral Home. Streaking like a comet, the silver scepter returned to earth. Linda's fat fingers stopped its descent. With aplomb and flair, she spun it back into orbit.

All the while, Linda smiled hard as a beauty pageant contestant in the swimsuit competition. The whole world was watching: cameras from all three television stations, both newspapers, parents, teachers, friends, potential boyfriends. The parade moved past the Carver Homes, the Longwood Apartments, and back to the site of the new East Technical High School. Up ahead Linda high-stepped, her baton one with the moving skies.

Nobody had to ask. I volunteered the information. "That's my big sister, Linda. That's her right there. Out in front."

"East Tech. Tech. Tech. Tech. East Tech. Tech. Tech. Tech." The drumbeat picked up. Trombones blared loud enough to stir the unburied dead at the House of Wills. "Make Me Smile," the band played on. Feet stomped. And we felt the freedom of dancing in the streets.

East Technical High School was king of Cleveland that day. The Scarabs basketball team stood on the school steps, grinned, and held the gleaming trophy aloft. Cameras clicked. Bulbs flashed.

The lineup included co-captains James Abrams and Larry Bolden, Van Glenn Neil as starting guard, Michael Sinclair (who later played for the Cleveland Browns) as forward, and Nate Washington as center. Willie Colquit, another phenomenal player, was from Detroit. (He died of Luekemia shortly after graduation.) The head coach was John Chavers (who managed to send the whole team on to colleges from which they graduated).

The Scarabs had gone down to Columbus, the capital, and "put a hurtin'" on those other teams. That's what everyone was saying. Their trophy was our trophy. Their victory, ours. It was more triumphant than the Black Panthers, Afro Set, or whoever. It wasn't just rhetoric. They had done something real. Nobody could deny it. Nobody could take it away. This was real victory. All the people of the project were exalted. And my big sister Linda, with the high forehead just like Charles Lyles's, had been the princess who led the victory procession.

Linda marched on to other victories. There was the rhinestone-belted, halter-top prom dress, revealing her bare shoulders, at once awkward and proud. There was her shimmering face on the cold gray June graduation day at East Technical High School. From my seat in the bleachers, I caught the glint of her beloved baton, hidden in the flutings of her dark robe and held tightly in her hand.

And there was the proper-talking, long-winded principal who proudly announced Linda's crowning achievement: "Because of Miss Lyles's participation in the Upward Bound Program, she has received a scholarship to attend Case Western Reserve University at University Circle in the city of Cleveland, Ohio. She is an outstanding young lady."

Linda was pretty, determined, independent, smart, popular, and now she had become the first person in our family to go to college. My once chubby, chicken-butt-nosed sister had waved her baton like a magic wand and become a woman.

At night on my knees in the dark, I prayed to God that some day I could be, would be just as outstanding.

"Did you see it when the ice-cream men got killed?" My friend Kim was always the first to bring up the subject.

"Nope. I didn't see it. Did you see it?" came the usual and expected response, just as Kim had hoped. With that, she launched into a graphic recounting of the robbery and murder of the two ice-cream vendors.

Kim was a knobby-kneed girl of eleven with chalk-white buck teeth (she always had those white flakes around the comers of her mouth as if she had just finished eating a bowl of Rice Krispies). Two Afro-puff ponytails held a buoyant orbit on her head. In the weeks following the killing of the ice-cream men, she became a near-celebrity throughout the project for her detailed eyewitness account. Even the police had talked to her and written down what she said in their little notebooks.

It had been the ice-cream men who rescued us from boredom and the cloying heat rising from the black asphalt on those hot, sticky summer evenings. Every day at about nine P.M., the white truck appeared—Freeze Pops, strawberry Krunch Bars, Nutty Drumsticks for sale. Moving slowly down Bundy Drive, it tinkled a gentle nursery rhyme like a giant music box on wheels. A pied piper, it called kids who ran from all directions, begging mothers, big sisters, brothers, anybody for a quarter to buy a sugary, creamy, cold treat. We lined up fifteen and twenty deep. Astro Pops for fifty cents. Popsicles, fifteen. A Reese's Cup, Blow-Pop, or grape-flavored jawbreaker, a nickel.

The ice-cream men were cute, with oval faces, sweet smiles and curly Afros, just a trace of a mustache and maybe dimples. On top of that, they were kind, sometimes giving us kids a free ice-cream sandwich or two, when we stood in front of the truck staring wistfully because we had been unsuccessful at wringing a nickel or dime out of our mothers.

On the evening news the anchorman, Doug Adair, reported that the ice-cream men were William (Billy) Isom, 22, and Daniel (Danny) Isom, 15, two brothers trying to earn a little extra money when they were gunned down by two ruthless robbers in the King-Kennedy Estates public housing project. "They shot Danny in the right temple from less than six inches away. Billy was shot in the head and then twice in the chest," Doug Adair reported. Then, with that tone that newscasters have sometimes, he added, "A 'Saturday Night Special' handgun was used in the murder."

Dee-Dee, Antoine, Keith, and I had missed the murder on the night of July 3, 1972. We were busy selling our own homemade Kool-Aid "freeze-cups" all that day at the senior citizens' building. By the time evening rolled around, I was exhausted and had gone inside Number 129 to watch TV. The next day, the Fourth of July, we saw the sidewalk across from my window spattered with dried blood brown as fudge.

The newspaper reported that the police couldn't find any witnesses, but our playmate Kim swore she had seen "the whole thing." And as if to keep the killings indelible inside her mind, Kim kept retelling it again, again, and over again. When she wore out one audience, she wandered over to other buildings—A-18, B-12, A-20—in search of another.

"Did you see it when the ice-cream men got killed?" she asked, hoping for a fresh audience.

"Nope. Did you see it?"

"Yep. I saw the whole thing," she said, ready to replay it all yet again. "I was standing right there in the line at the side of the ice-cream truck. It was playing 'Twinkle, twinkle little star, how I wonder what you are.' And I was trying to decide whether to get me a Krunch Bar for a quarter or a Drumstick for fifteen cents . . ."

After wowing the crowd at Building A-18 with her account, Kim skipped on over to a bunch of kids at Building B-12. This time she told it with more flair, gestures, voice inflection.

"Did you see it when the ice-cream men got killed?"

"Naw. I didn't see it. Did you?

"Yep. These two men were pushing everybody in line like they were trying to sponge. And they was saying, "Brother man, brother man, I want you to give it up. I want you to give it up right now, brother man." At first, I thought they might be in the Afro Set or the Panthers or something because they useta say 'brother man' all the time too . . . "

The next day, Kim visited the playgrounds and basketball courts.

"Hey, y'all. I saw the whole thing when the ice-cream men got killed."

"You did!"

"Yep. At first, the ice-cream men thought them robbers was playing. Then one of 'em pulled out a gun. It was silvery and shiny like a mashed-up soda-pop can. He pointed it right at one of the ice-cream men. He was trying to give them the money. But the robbers started gettin' real scared like they thought the police was comin'. They said, "Hurry up, my brother man. Hurry up." That's when they shot one of the ice-cream men. He fell over on that little counter. 'N' his arm hit the button that made the truck music stop playing 'Twinkle, Twinkle Little Star'. Yep. I saw the whole thing."

Kim's need to tell it over and over and over again was unending. She was a parrot gone berserk: "Did you see it when the ice-cream men got killed?" She went up to perfect strangers who lived in the project. "I saw the whole thing . . ."

Eventually, she ran out of strangers. That left Kim no choice but to repeat the account, with slight embellishments and more histrionics, to those of us who had already heard it.

One day, months after the killing, after two men had been arrested and charged with the crime, Dee-Dee couldn't take it any more. "Shut up, girl. We're tired of hearing you talk about those ice-cream men getting killed," she erupted. "You act like they're still getting killed. Like they're getting killed every day. Why don't you just shut up 'r I'm gonna kick your ass 'n' I ain't playin' with you, either. Get sick of you sayin' the same thing over and over, driving it into the ground."

Kim fell silent and looked forlorn, like she had been mistreated profoundly.

Under threat of ostracism and an ass-kicking, Kim's storytelling ceased. The forced silence must have confined the killing to images and sounds inside her head that replayed again and again, like "Twinkle, Twinkle Little Star." It wasn't long before Kim quit coming outside to play. And in the fall after the first few days of school, Kim stopped attending. Sometimes, from her living room window on the second floor of one of the B buildings, Kim smiled and waved down at us.

In October, once again, Dee-Dee and I knocked on Kim's door to ask if she could come out to play. Her little brother Birmingham poked his head outside the apartment door and whispered: "Kim is real sick. She scratched out all her hair. They had to put her in the hospital on the West Side and tape up her fingers. The doctor said she has to stay in there for a long time till she stop scratching her hair out. Shuush. Don't tell nobody," Birmingham said, pressing a baby finger to his lips. "My mama told me not to tell nobody or she going to whip my ass."

"Twinkle, twinkle, little star, how I wonder what you are." In King-Kennedy, death could play out as simply as a Mother Goose tune. Somebody could just walk up and shoot you, even if you were not messing with them, and you would bleed until you died. Kim knew. What happened to the ice-cream men could happen to her.

To Birmingham. To her secretive mother. To any of my playmates. To my brothers and sisters. To me.

The fear was enough to drive Kim's hands like some kind of crazy electric pick, digging up every strand of her hair from the roots till her scalp was a bed of sores.

"I want to move. I want to move. I want to move away from this place." I wept into my pillow late at night, grieving for Kim, the ice-cream men, the scattered strawberry Krunch Bars melting down the sewer.

Chapter Eleven

I BROUGHT ONE OF the ice-cream men back to life.

He was cute, with a deep voice like the Temptations singing background on "Just My Imagination."

"I'm sorry you got shot trying to sell us some ice cream, Popsicles, 'n' stuff," I said.

"That's okay, baby. I know you didn't mean for it to happen to me." He knew I was sincere.

Then we got married in a big ceremony. I wore a curly Afro and a halter dress like Diana Ross wore in *Lady Sings the Blues*. He found a good job at a steel mill. We bought a long, blue Ninety-eight, brand-new. On Sundays, after Reverend Berry's sermon at Mount Olive Baptist Church, we drove around my old Mount Pleasant neighborhood in the Ninety-eight and everybody envied us.

Oh, what a delicious healer my imagination could be! Suffering. Pain. Melancholy. My mind's enchantment could cure it, albeit temporarily. Fantasy made me sole owner of a special reality. Only I could create it and only I could destroy it. Never had I known such power.

After the ice-cream killings, I retreated on frequent binges of fantasy. I returned with my mind and emotions refreshed, ready to deal with the next round of survival in the project. Fantasizing became a natural reflex: Give me one, even slightly unpleasant real-

ity and within seconds my mind transformed it to another more
fragrant, more gentle, more splendid.

Momma sent my body to Kennard Junior High School every day
for eighth grade. But my mind never showed up. It was AWOL, out
fantasizing. So it was that I landed in the slow class.

The top sections one through three were for smart kids who
might get to go to college. Average students went to sections four
and five. Next came the "retardo" sections.

"Hey, Sugarbabe? What section you in? At the beginning of
each high school year, everyone compared.

"Six." That was several steps down from the year before. Now
even Dee-Dee was in a higher section.

Whispers and snickers. Then they just came right out and said it:
"Gheeyawd. I thought you was smarter than that. Section six is for
them retardos. Gheeyawd. I'm glad I'm not in there with you."

"What section you in?" I inquired.

"Four."

"Oh. Okay then." At least they weren't *that* much smarter than
I was—like those stuck-up kids in sections one through three.

All the supposed misfits—the short attention spans, the hyper-
actives, the just plain dumb, and the chronic daydreamers like me
were piled into the slow class. We were slow, and we accepted our
label. Sometimes in the corridors we hitched our narrow hips and
walked cripple, just to look even more retarded than we were supposed to be.

I enjoyed the slow class. Nothing was expected of me and I delivered. Freed from academic expectation, reading and fantasizing
became my basic curriculum. Should the thought enter my head
of getting shot like the ice-cream men on a sultry summer night,
my mind took off to some place where people could fly, or where
birds that didn't doo-doo adorned my Afro with turquoise-colored
feathers and all the people appreciated my plumage.

"Pay attention, Miss Lyles," teachers scolded, intruding on my
interludes. I resented being called back to a world where I could be

killed, beaten up, called ugly names, or forced to breathe in the foul odors of a people turning against itself.

In home economics class, while Mrs. Mills lectured on how to hem a pleated skirt and put in a zipper, I drifted out the window on a magical bolt of cloth, high up over buildings A-18, A-20, B-9, and A-11. I floated to faraway tropical islands where snow fell without winter and icy winds off Lake Erie. Trees grew sweet blue fruit that had no name. Bobby Sherman, alias Jeremy from *Here Come the Brides*, and Tito from the Jackson Five escorted me. Even though Jeremy was white and Tito black, they got along just fine around me. There was no need for Black Panthers or Friendly Town in my fantasies. We went ice skating, swimming, and rode wild horses. My Afro puffed in the wind like a giant dandelion. Gliding through the window on the enchanted fabric, I returned to class just as the bell rang.

My fantasies so preoccupied that no one suspected in the least that I could read. In remedial reading, Mrs. Harper burped vowels. But from the hiding place on my lap, books beckoned: Phileas Fogg was flying around the world in eighty days. I flew along in his beautiful balloon. My head resting on my desk, I read, racing away to England and Bombay, returning only to grunt out a syllable or two to satisfy Mrs. Harper's phonetic hunger. Then off again.

Miss Smith, the lady with the curly Afro at the Woodland Branch Library who had helped DoeDoe and me research the Black Panthers, had become my friend. She now supplied me with one great work of fiction per week. Of course, I had not informed Miss Smith that I was in the slow class for fear she might stop the good books and give me boring ones like Mrs. Harper read.

Poor Mrs. Harper. Mr. Fogg was so much more exciting than the silly books that she wanted to teach us. Once, I raised my hand to tell her so.

"Miss Lyles, I don't want to hear from you a peep / till you have your homework complete."

"But Mizz Harpa, I—"

"Miss Lyles, if you do your work late / you cannot—what, class?"

"Participate" came the chorus. Mrs. Harper always talked in rhyme and had trained the whole class to join in call and response.

"But Mizz Harpa—" I tried to rejoin but Renaldo Johnson in the desk next to mine sniggered loud and kept right on digging at a big wax ball in his ear. If anybody was a retardo, Renaldo was.

"Miss Lyles, I want you to act like talking is out of style," said Mrs. Harper. "And get your work done. Then she can—do what class?—join in the . . ."

"Fun."

Well, if Mrs. Harper wanted to read dull, boring books and do stupid rhymes, I wasn't going to try and stop her with Mr. Fogg. She probably had never heard of Jules Verne anyway. Too busy reading *Understanding Phonics*.

I sank deeper and deeper into the academic dungeon. If I was intelligent, I wasn't quite sure how to go about making that known. Risking further humiliations like those of Mrs. Harper just wasn't worth it.

My brigade of slow, misfit classmates disrupted classes into supervised chaos. We hung out the windows, playing our colored ball transistor radios, snapped back at teachers, mean and nasty, rotated our necks like snapping turtles and flicked our wrists in rebellion: "F'get chu." Bored with lessons that failed to challenge us, the slowest of the slow, we skipped classes.

That is when my "slow-mate" Noella Coles and I stole away to the House of Wills Funeral Home. It was a perfectly intriguing and respectable place to go to cut school on a sunny afternoon. Up we climbed those steep and final stairs. A three-story Victorian-style mansion painted pale pink, the House of Wills rose like a huge wedding cake in the center of East Fifty-fifth Street. In Cleveland, anybody black who had been somebody was memorialized by the House of Wills. Throughout the city, Undertaker Wills and his

1. Me, my mother, and my baby brother John in the old house on East 123rd Street in the Mt. Pleasant neighborhood, about 1967. A year later, we had to let our dog Homer go because we moved into the projects, where dogs were not allowed.

2. My father, Charles Lyles, working as a painter in the early 1960s. He had hoped to work in a steel mill.

3. I was seven when riots erupted nearby in the Hough neighborhood in 1966. Smoke eclipsed the noonday sun. For three days straight, my mother watched the riot reports on our secondhand TV. In 1968, we saw the Glenville neighborhood in flames after the murder of Martin Luther King, Jr. *(Cleveland Press Collection, Cleveland State University Library)*

4. When the King-Kennedy Estates public housing project opened in November 1968, the Lyles family was one of the first to move in. Little more than a warehouse for the poor, in less than four years it would be crime-ridden and filthy. *(Cleveland Press Collection, Cleveland State University Library)*

5. The Afro Set, a so-called black militant group, brought a message of hope, pride, power to the streets of our neighborhood. When they disappeared from the scene, King-Kennedy deteriorated rapidly. *(Cleveland Press Collection, Cleveland State University Library)*

6. My beloved Kennard Junior High on East 46th Street in the Carver Projects was torn down in the early 1980s. Only after arriving at Hawken School did I realize how poorly equipped my old school was. *(Cleveland Press Collection, Cleveland State University Library)*

7. Charles Lyles shining after one of his spectacular living-room performances, sometime around 1964.

8. That's me during a field trip to southern Ohio with the Woodland Branch Public Library summer reading club. I'm in the eighth grade and apparently invincible.

9. My best friend and reading-contest partner, Desiree Kincaid. We read until our eyes ached, trying to win tickets to an Al Green concert.

10. In eighth grade my body went to school but my mind never showed up— it was out fantasizing. By the end of ninth grade, though, I was winning academic awards.

11. The Kennard Junior High School National Junior Honor Society. That's Desiree (front row, first from left), Priscilla Gray, who was just too smart (center), and me in the back row (fourth from the right) with the big smile.

12. Like many families, we fled King-Kennedy's violence. In the mid-1970s, we moved to a smaller housing project on Mt. Auburn Avenue that was safer.

13. Momma in the background and my sister Tinky on the steps with a neighbor. Mt. Auburn allowed us the dignity of a backyard and a flower garden. But many of the residents there, like my family, were just as poor as people in the projects.

14. The summer before I entered Hawken in 1974, the A Better Chance, Inc. scholarship program sponsored a three-day orientation in Philadelphia to help prepare us kids for prep school.

15. The White House mansion, where Hawken students ate lunch, was a jewel left over from the days when the White Motors family owned the land as part of the Circle W Farm. *(Courtesy of Hawken School Archives)*

16. Hawken's sprawling main academic building backed up to glorious woods, where a brook and ancient trees and vines provided a setting for adventure and after-school mischief. *(Courtesy of Hawken School Archives)*

17. Me in front of the main academic building at Hawken. Sometimes I could be rather in-your-face about matters of race and equity.

18. Me in front of Mr. and Mrs. Moore's house on Seville Road in the Lee-Miles neighborhood. Mrs. Moore, my biology teacher from Kennard, offered to let me stay with her while I was attending Hawken.

19. Hawken's historic barn burned to the ground two months before I graduated. Newspapers reported that the smoke could be seen from downtown Cleveland. We students scrounged for buckets, canteens, anything that would hold water, and tried to quell the flames, but to no avail. *(Cleveland Press Collection, Cleveland State University Library)*

20. My senior portrait, taken by Mrs. Moore in her basement. Momma, more practical than poetic, did not care for the Sylvia Plath quotation that accompanied the photo on my yearbook page. But I felt the words aptly expressed my bitter triumph.

21. A Lyles family photo taken in the mid-1990s. Left to right: Scharlton (Dynamite), Lillian Lyles, Beverly (Tinky), me, my brother-in-law, Ingram Lloyd, Wallace (my grandfather), and my niece Maya Lloyd (Linda's daughter). Maya graduated from Duke University in 2007, becoming the second generation of our family to attend college.

apprentices were renowned as masters of death's protocol. They knew how to escort one from this life to the next. In death, it was said, Mr. Wills had found his mission in life.

Once inside, we tiptoed on the thick, velvety maroon carpet. Before entering each viewing room (empty of visitors), we signed the guest books as if we had known personally the dearly departed. Next, we stood coffin side, inspecting Mr. Wills's fine craftsmanship. Just as we had heard our elders do, we marveled at his embalming skill and the stylish but sturdy casket.

"He sure did a good job on her, didn't he now? She looks just like herself," said Noella.

"Mr. Wills really knows how to put you away with panache," I said, in my best impersonation of my Aunt Cora, who collected fancy vocabulary words. Other people whipped out their best clothes on public occasions; Aunt Cora whipped out words that turned heads and made people think she was educated.

"And that sho is a nice box they got her in."

"You know it costs a pretty penny if it came from Wills. But that's alright, 'cause you only go down once in this world. And you ought to be able to go down good."

After several viewings, we parted from the dearly departed, down the steep stairs out into a dull afternoon that seemed bright after the dim parlor.

"Hic. Hic. Hic." Noella broke out into dry spasms of laughter like she was having a hiccup attack. We giggled away our shivers. We had literally looked death in the face and laughed.

"Go on, look up," Noella teased.

"Go on, girl. You want somebody to look up there then you better do it yourself," I replied.

Cleveland's mortuary lore, and there was lots, had it that Mr. Wills had embalmed some bodies so artfully that burying them would have been an affront to the ancient Egyptian mummies, to King Tutankhamen himself. Legend had it, the corpses were entombed in the dormer rooms atop "the House." For years, children had walked by, their eyes practically glued to the sidewalk, fearful that if they looked up someone might wave back from the dead.

Defying fear, our heads turned at the same time to steal a peek at the dormer windows. No one waved. We saw only the pale pink funeral parlor against the gray backdrop of a factory town, looming and surreal as a James Van Der Zee photograph.

I never met or even saw the famous Mr. Wills. But the presence of his pale pink funeral parlor comforted me like a soft lace-shammed pillow. Should death come to me as it had come to the ice-cream men, random and sudden, I would be all right. For Mr. Wills would be there to take me under, dress me gently in my Easter clothes, pick my Afro and lay me out in a magnificent casket for all to see and weep over me.

Despite my fantasizing and flight, I yearned to be smart in school, to be considered an outstanding young lady. It would be a thrill to please teachers at Kennard Junior High School, to blurt out the correct answer from the back of the class, to ace the exam, to win red, green, and blue achievement ribbons.

Teachers were eager to spot and cultivate "good minds," as they called students who seemed to know all the answers and stay out of trouble. There was a near desperation about their efforts and energy. Even the white teachers were in a frenzy, overzealous about achievement. The teachers all buzzed with talk of funding, grants, programs, promises.

At beginning-of-the-school-year assembly, they tried to whet appetites for opportunity. Lots of programs were coming our way, they said: Upward Bound, Job Corps, Work Study, college scholarships. "If you do well, you might be able to get into this or that program," they cajoled. "It might make all the difference in your future."

Sometimes they went on and on and on. Silver-haired Mr. Sampson, the principal of Kennard Junior High, was big on one in particular. "The ABC/A Better Chance program sends especially outstanding, talented young ladies and gentlemen to private school," he said, his gravely voice full of dignity. Dogged teachers proselytized many a malcontent and misbehaver into notebook-carrying, pencil-sharpening achievers.

But not daydreamers like me. I was "slow," "dim," "dumb." No matter how I tried, I simply could not pay attention for very long. Energy would whirl up from my feet and before I knew it I would be up out of my seat starting mischief. I accepted my limitations. And I felt bad that I wouldn't be able to show off for my race and prove that the blacks are as smart as the whites, just like teachers said we ought to be able to do. And that Martin Luther King Jr. did not die in vain.

Why couldn't my teachers like me as I was, toting my colored ball transistor radio, spitting spitballs, picking out my Afro, reading *The Three Musketeers*, and whipping up fantastic stories right out of my own head? Old Mrs. Rooten with her false teeth that kept on moving after she stopped talking; Mrs. Dell with her funny-colored wig and pointy glasses; Miss Nelson, tall, thick, and stern—they all made me sick, always talking about what achievers the students in higher sections were.

I did not understand that all their lives my teachers had ached for the opportunities we were about to receive. Many had been raised tough as a cotton boll in the segregated South. Somehow they managed to educate themselves, only to find that careers available to Negroes were limited to teaching and social work. Now, at last, opportunity was coming down like sweet manna. They would see to it that this new generation would go further than any Negroes before them—with grants, programs, and all the promises from presidents. But these precious black children had to be ready. And these teachers were determined to get us ready. They would scout for the brightest and the best. Even the average would be prepared. They would teach us to beat those standardized tests that so often held their children back. They would groom and refine. Whatever it took.

At the end-of-the-school-year assembly, the chosen were paraded before the entire school. They filed to the stage to accept certificates of achievement, scholarship awards, ribbons. "Mine eyes have seen the glory/Of the coming of the Lord . . ." the ninth grade chorus sang. Mrs. Dot, the music teacher, pounded out the "The Battle Hymn of the Republic" on piano. Swept away in an emotional civil rights moment, she segued into a plucky rendition of "We Shall Overcome," then returned to "The Battle Hymn."

Leading the procession of ninth-graders was Lonnie Hudspeth, a moody looking boy in thick glasses, linty turtleneck (in June), plaid bell-bottoms, and two-toned platform shoes with soles thicker than two books stacked on top of each other. I had to hand it to old Lonnie. Everybody knew he was a brainiac, so smart that he could factor algebra problems in seconds. I didn't even really understand what algebra was.

"These young ladies and gentleman have received very special scholarships through ABC, the A Better Chance program, to attend private school," announced Mr. Sampson, speaking with his usual warm dignity. "In the fall they will be going to New England to attend the most press-stee-gee-ous boarding schools in the United States of America. And they will all go on to very fine colleges and universities. Let's give them a round of vigorous applause. These are outstanding young ladies and gentlemen from Kennard Junior High School in the city of Cleveland, Ohio." (As if we didn't know what city we were in.) Mr. Sampson continued, "I'm so proud of each and every one of you. Congratulations!"

Mr. Sampson's desire for us kids to succeed seemed real. Tan-skinned and thick, he was said by some to be a Native American. Lots of his people lived on reservations, we had learned in Mr. Salo's social studies class. So I guessed Mr. Sampson know what it was like for us Afro American kids, warehoused in the brown and yellow buildings of the King-Kennedy Estates. The more I got to know old Mr. Sampson, the more his pride seemed genuine as a ruby. His kids from Kennard Junior High School in the City of Cleveland were going to show the world something.

But I would never be among the chosen.

At Kennard Junior High School there was no Miss Collins of the creative bosom to bail me out. Plus, I knew that even if I tried harder, my permanent record would still show that I had flunked third grade at Lafayette Elementary School in 1966.

At home, Lillian Lyles was coming to accept that her middle child was not only not so bright, but downright below average. Linda had gone to college. Tinky was in the "major work" class for "gifted" students. John was showing good mechanical sense and know-how.

It looked as if all the programs, all the promises would pass me by. I scrunched up inside, wanting to disappear. The only person who could see me was Mrs. Tierce, my English teacher. . . .

She was a white, hippie-turned-teacher type with long stringy hair and aviator glasses. She twinkled with 1960s idealism that, at the time, I mistook for flakiness. She was tough, but serious about us slow kids. Try as we might, we could not scare Mrs. Tierce away from giving us homework and quizzes.

"Miss Lyles, would you please come up to my desk?" She summoned me one day while we were supposed to be taking a quiz in her English class.

Dag gone. The fresh, sugary wad of grape gum just popped in my mouth would have to go to waste. I retrieved it, spitty, sticky, oozing purple, and stuck it under my desk top.

"Yes, Mizz Tierce." I walked up slowly. I hoped she wasn't going to try and start something with me about chewing gum. Everybody else was chewing it too. She was a new white teacher and basically we students planned to "run over her." But so far Mrs. Tierce hadn't scared quite as easily as we had thought she would.

"Miss Lyles, did you write this?" she inquired sternly, holding up one of my rarely-turned-in homework assignments.

"Yep," I answered and turned to go back to my desk.

"Just a minute, Miss Lyles. You didn't copy it from a book, did you?"

"Nope. I didn't." Mrs. Tierce was trying to call me a liar on the sly. But I wasn't going to get into it with her. You could end up getting suspended for telling off teachers.

"Are you sure, Miss Lyles?" she pressed.

"Yeah. I told you, I didn't copy nothin'. I made it up."

It was a short story about a man who knew the names of every star—my father in disguise. The title was "Assistant King of Heaven." From an encyclopedia in the school library, I had copied the correct spellings of the constellations that Charles Lyles had shown me years ago in the sky above the backyard on East 123rd Street.

"How did you know how to spell all these names? Some of them have Greek origins," asked Mrs. Tierce.

"I looked them up in the 'cyclopedia in the library. You can ask Mizz Mims, the librarian, 'cause she helped me find the astronomy 'cyclopedia."

"En-cyclopedia," Mrs. Tierce corrected.

"Encyclopedia."

"How did you become interested in the stars, Miss Lyles?"

Didn't I have a right to be interested in the stars? They belonged to everybody didn't they? "My father, Charles Lyles—I'm named after him—told me about them and the clouds 'n' stuff." On the surface, I kept my cool.

"Oh, I see. Does your father live with you, Miss Lyles?"

Why was she getting all in my business? "No. He stay up on Kinsman. I think. But he is real smart and knows a lot of things about the sky 'n' stuff."

After what seemed like enough time to write a twenty-page term paper, Mrs. Tierce finally said, "This is a very good story, Miss Lyles." Then she turned to the whole class. "Miss Lyles has written an outstanding story."

My face went red hot like I was eating firecracker candy. "Outstanding." I had done something "outstanding"!

"You may return to your seat now, Miss Lyles."

It kind of hurt my feelings that Mrs. Tierce had implied that I had done something dishonest. But since she liked my story and told the whole class, I let her slide. Next time, I planned to tell her about herself.

Several days went by. Mrs. Tierce told me to report to the guidance office with two well-sharpened No. 2 pencils. There I took a battery of reading and math tests. My fingers gripping the pencil tight, I filled in tiny grids till my hand cramped.

A week later, I was abruptly removed from the slow class, my books collected and a different set issued, including French and algebra texts. Mrs. Tierce informed me that I was going to "three, a higher section," where I would take classes that might help me to go to college.

Sadly, I bade my slow-mates farewell. Renaldo Johnson just sat there digging with his nasty finger and wiping it on the desk. And from the look in Noella Coles's eyes, I could tell that she knew we wouldn't be going together to the House of Wills funeral parlor anymore. Mrs. Tierce and I never really crossed paths much after that, just "hi" and "'bye" in the hallway.

In those days of opportunity, Mrs. Tierce and others were always on the lookout to salvage any child mistakenly discarded into the pile of academic rejects. And there were many. Mrs. Tierce and others like her found us, the children whose intelligence shone through despite traumas and terrors that kept us silent, numbed dumb.

In the smart section, teachers wanted work, lots of it. But I still needed my daily fantasy fix.

I found it at the Wednesday afternoon "Ladies'" dollar matinees in the Hippodrome and Embassy theaters downtown. They were grandiloquent movie houses from another era, with tiled walls, velvety seats, and proscenium arches. My new friend in the smart classes was Desiree Kincaid. We believed we were inside a castle till gooey gum, soda pop, and candy glued our shoe soles to the floor.

Once settled in our plasticky seats, we could see black people seven feet tall. And they were nothing like the boring people in the TV movies that made Momma cry, like *Stormy Weather* and *Imitation of Life*. These movies were rated R. This meant that there would be a scene with people doing it and we were supposed to be too young to see it. But it didn't take much of a lie or disguise to get past the ticket booth.

There was *Sweet Sweetback's Baadasssss Song*, *Super Fly* and *The Mack*. The Mack was a pimp. (This meant he hired hoes to work for him like Dee-Dee's big sister Avis.) In his long white fur coat and wide-brimmed hat, which he wore even in the summertime, he collected money from the hoes. If they got smart, he beat them up. And sometimes he did it to women, sliding slippery over them in bathtub suds or satiny sheets right up there on the screen for everybody to see. The cheap audio magnified the sounds of lovemaking. Desiree and I simmered in our seats, excited, but uncomfortable about the whole idea of doing it.

Coffee, which starred Pam Grier, was about a woman whose breasts were huge, bigger even than Miss Collins's at Lafayette Elementary School so long ago, but not nearly as friendly. Coffee's breasts were tough, heavy, hard, downright mean, not buoyant and merry like Miss Collins's. Coffee's breasts were criminals. They carried guns. They were not kind and encouraging like Miss Collins's. They were rude, bare. Plus, most disturbing of all was the fact that men sucked on Coffee's breasts.

"See. That's what they like to do to them," Desiree whispered in the darkness of the balcony.

My own breasts were budding nicely. But after seeing Coffee allow men to suck her breasts like big Baggies of chocolate milk, I was not so sure anymore that I wanted lively, pointy bosoms.

Besides, my body was doing other things that were far more amazing to me. I now received my own lavender box each month when Momma did her "big" grocery shopping. On it, the nice white lady smiled, serene and mild. She seemed to like having her period. So did I.

There it flowed every month from the magical triangle in the middle of me, now thatched with sparse nappy hair. I didn't have to do anything to make it appear. It was automatic, every time. "Womens and the moods, they goes in cycles but they're still unpredictable." Had I heard Charles Lyles say that once while studying his skies?

When the first flow began, I removed my savings from the Kotex belt box Momma had given me. Out fell a buckled elastic contraption with silver hooks and teeth. "Now, don't be messing around with none of these little mannish boys," Momma firmly warned me. She said not a word more about the matter of menses. Lillian Lyles was more comfortable talking about politics than periods. Still, toward the end of each month, Momma gave me a certain look, checking to make sure that my mysterious red river had begun to rise. She was really checking to see if I had done it, trying to make sure that I was not going to have a baby like Avis the ho'.

I suspected that Lillian Lyles lived in unspoken fear of the day that somebody on a comer down on East Fifty-fifth Street (where hoes commonly congregated) would say to her, "Miss Lyles, your daughter is a sho-nuff nasty old ho'." Or that she would see scrawled on the hallway cinder block, "Sugarbabe Lyles is the biggest ho' in the project."

"No," she would think to herself. "This cannot be. Lillian Wardean Lyles from Aberdeen, Mississippi, did not raise any hoes."

To hold back those bad dreams, I knew that the hallway had to be avoided at all costs. No longer our happy-go-lucky kids' playground, the hallway had become an initiation ground for hoes. It was a place that could steal girlhood and ruin my chances of becoming an outstanding young woman in the world.

In the hallway, an evil inertia had settled. Boys and would-be men who had abandoned school and pursuit of work made it their den. Day come, day go, they took their idle positions. In morning, eyes bloodshot and absent from Boone's Farm apple wine, mouths dry and sour from sleep, they rose and walked toward the hallway. Against the cinder block wall slouched shadows of shoulders weighted down by stolen leather jackets. Kool cigarette butts littered the floor at their feet. "Yeah, man. Did you see that shit?" echoed their empty, aimless exchanges.

"Yeah. Wasn't that some shit?"

Jobless, unable to read, unable to negotiate their own place in the world, they remained in the hallway, time-warped between boyhood and manhood. The cinder block hollow could have been their passageway to the future, a world beyond the project. But they never made it to the necessary threshold of dreams. They stopped inside those walls, walls that were an eerie omen of the prison cinder block that would sooner or later confine too many of their lives.

By the time school let out at three P.M., they had been there in the hallway all day, craving power, dominion over something.

"Go on, Antoine. Y'all better leave me alone," I protested daintily, making my way through the hallway one day after school. Swish. I moved my butt to the left away from his open palm. Then swish, I moved it to the right. Nervous, but nonetheless flattered by this touching, I giggled.

The first times it happened, it was still a game like hide-n-go-get-it.

"Go on, I ain't playing wit you." I skipped, skipped, skipped away.

Then Antoine grabbed my wrist, not like he used to grab it when we played hide-n-go, but different, like I had better not try to pull away. He twisted my arm, turning my back to him, then rammed his hips into my backside. Then his fingers crawled under my skirt and kneaded half of my behind like it was fresh bread dough.

"You better stop it, boy. I told you, I wasn't playing with you."

"Aw shut up, girl. You know you like it."

Did I? Safe inside Number 129, alone in the room shared with Tinky, I could ask myself and hear my answer. Did I like it when boys felt on me? No. No, I did not. Would a boy like having his wee-wee squeezed like a roll of peanut-butter cookie dough?

All through eighth grade, each day when I returned from school to Building A-11, they were there waiting, eighteen-, nineteen-, twenty-year-old boys-turned-bogeymen. At the ready were the hands that used to be nice to me when we played games on the steps: Pick which hand the candy is in and you can have it. Want to play jacks? Krazy Klackers?

"Stop it, Antoine. I ain't playin' wit chu now," I bucked. "Go on. Leave me alone. I'm gonna get my big brother Dynamite to kick your butt."

"You can't hardly get that niggah to come outside, now how you going to get him to kick somebody's butt?"

Dynamite was a recluse; no one feared him. But that was the best threat I could muster. I started to tell them that if they didn't leave me alone, Charles Lyles himself was going to come and duke their asses up. But that would have been a big old lie because I didn't know where in the world Charles Lyles had gone.

Two, four, six, eight dirty hands squeezed and twisted at my brand new bosoms. My nipples stood up, betraying me. The book that I carried, *Daddy Was a Number Runner*, fell in a puddle of stale pee. I stumbled to the gritty tile after it. And I sobbed in shame because between my legs was swollen and soft, slippery and wet against my will.

"You better get on away from me, Antoine. You useta be a Black Panther but now you ain't shit, niggah."

"Come on, Sugarbabe, girl, you know you want it. I give you twenty dollars if you let me suck that thing."

"Get away from me, you ol' dog. Don't chu touch me. Stop it. Stop it." My swinging fists met eyes that threatened to snap my arm like a Popsicle stick.

At first, fantasy failed me in defense against this daily abuse.

There was no special amulet to shrivel fingers, rot wrists, or zap off their "ding-a-lings." No steel Wonder Woman bracelets to repel this evil.

Finally I conjured a real defense. Each day as I drew near Building A-11, Desiree disappeared around a corner and headed to the Carver Estates. (I didn't dare tell her about the hallway boys.) Then their whispers: "Hey, here she comes." I made my face immovable as the lady mannequins' in the May Company Department Store window downtown: Eyes painted, unblinking; mouth drawn, unflinching; cheekbones still as stone.

And I felt nothing. No marijuana-smelling fingertips trying to twist my breasts from me. No coarse palms grazing over my crotch. No forced fist full of my ass.

Once inside Number 129, all was calm, including Momma. In the kitchen, she cooked fried hamburgers with onions and sang, "Stag-o-Lee shot Billy. Shot that poor boy bad."

"Hi, Sugarbabe. How was school?"

"Fine," I answered every day.

Lillian Lyles must never know about the boys in the hallway, I decided. She might misunderstand, think that somehow I had made the boys feel on me. Worse, she might think I was "fast," that I liked having boys feel on me. If that was the case, then there would be no saving me. Lillian Wardean Lyles's daughter would be a stone sho 'nuff ho'.

At night, I prayed fierce prayers. "Dear God: This is Charlise Lyles (sometimes they call me Sugarbabe for short) at 2530 Bundy Drive, Building A-11, apartment Number 129 in the King-Kennedy Estates project. Please stop Antoine and them from feeling on me when I go through the hallway. And please let me not become a ho' because of them. In Jesus' name, Amen."

Reverend Berry's God did not respond. He was probably busy taking care of white people's prayers that weren't nearly as serious.

Maybe it was all my fault: I had been too proud of my budding breasts, had walked with my chest puffed too far forward. Maybe my plaid skirts from Petries were too short. Plus, I had been wearing the "plumberry" Ultra Sheen lipstick that I bought from Marshall's drugstore, trying to look cute. Now see what it had gotten me.

Plus, I was probably making too much of it. Didn't all girls everywhere get felt on in the schoolyard by stupid boys who were just trying to say, "Hey, I like you," "Hey, I wanta go with you, girl"? This touching that boys wanted to do to me was just a funny kind of flattery, cute and harmless like toddlers playing house or kiss tag. It was really something good. And I was twisting it all up, making it bad, something evil.

My breasts had developed larger than I had hoped. Along with my bushy reddish Afro, my bosoms arrived everywhere a few inches before the rest of me—just like Miss Collins's. It all rested atop legs skinny as sausage sacks, unsuitable for stockings and heels; still, the overall effect could make boys get hot if there weren't a whole lot of other pretty girls around. Maybe an average looking, high-yellow girl who wasn't really all that smart (even if I was in a higher section at school) should be happy to get all the play she could. Right?

Maybe that's why God was not even worried about answering my prayers.

For many a girl growing up in a project, the boys in the hallway are the original "gauntlet." Boys without power beget misogyny. I tried to welcome their abuse as a rite of womanhood for which I should have been grateful. I told myself I had no right to be traumatized. There had been no breaking. No entering. No blood. No semen. A respect for *real* violation forbade me to moan.

One night before bed, I decided to send my prayers elsewhere, not to Reverend Berry's God. Instead of sending them out and up to him, I pressed them deep inside my heart, deeper with every word.

Some days on the playground, Antoine apologized. "You know the other day in the hallway? We were just playin' with you, Sugarbabe. We didn't mean nothin'. We cool, ain't we?" asked Antoine. Then he pushed me in the tire swing, way up into clouds. As a peace offering, I shared my sweet and sour green apple Now and Laters. I hoped he would remember my generosity next time in the hallway. But the sweet exchange dissolved in his memory like sugar on the tongue.

"Don't you hate living down here? I wish we could move someplace else. Don't chu?" I asked my little sister Tinky one night as we settled in bed.

"Yep," came her tiny voice in the dark between slurps on her two fingers. "All anybody likes to do around here is fight. They always wanta beat somebody up."

"Let's ask Momma again if we can move," I pressed.

"Where you think we gonna move to?" came her scolding reply. Tinky remained rational beyond her years. "You know Momma's trying to save up some money to help Linda while she's in college."

That was right. How could I think of moving when my sister's education was at stake—everything that she had ever worked for? I shut my mouth and went to sleep.

On the way to my dreams, I heard L'il Joe-Joe take back the hallway. His imperfect hands beat out a perfect poem. His lonely, sad song slipped into all the sleeping souls in Building A-11. Then the melody rose in the midnight sky, going back to where blues come from.

Chapter Twelve

HORSES. A GIRL ON a horse. Her hair bushy, her skin autumn-leaf brown and yellow, like mine. The horse was shiny black as the playground tar top in July. Its belly was a cauldron, its thighs naked cords of strength. I wanted to ride.

Pillars. A brown boy sat with his head in a book on steps beneath huge pillars like the ones on the courthouse downtown that sent my brother to the detention home. I could tell this boy was in an important place.

A dormitory. A smiling boy, browner than the others, sat on top of a bunk bed reading a fat, interesting book.

Boarding school. The bright pictures on the brochure said it all. One day, shortly after I had started ninth grade, Mr. White, the school guidance counselor, placed it in my hands. Tall and wiry, with an Adam's apple that looked like he had gulped down a walnut whole, Mr. White was another opportunity scout.

"ABC is the name of the program," he explained. Mr. White had gathered Carmela Lincoln, Kim Davies, Gary Byrd, Roosevelt Jefferson, Ronnie Jackson, and me in his office because we were considered smart and made good grades. I still had some doubts about how smart I was. Nonetheless, I had come along to hear what Mr. White had to say.

"ABC stands for A Better Chance, Inc.," Mr. White went on. "If you get good grades, really good grades, like straight A's, A Better Chance might award you a special scholarship to go to a private boarding school in the New England area. If you study hard and keep getting good grades while you're there, you'll probably be able to get into an excellent college." Mr. White seemed delighted to be telling us this, happy to be the harbinger of opportunity.

We all nodded, faking like we knew what a boarding school was.

"What does boarding mean?" I broke the stupid silence. "Does that mean you have to leave home to go to school?"

"Yes, Miss Lyles," Mr. White answered. "It means you live at the school in a dormitory room that you share with another student. You have to stay there until the end of the semester. Then you come home for the summer."

"Is boarding school mostly for white kids?" Roosevelt inquired. First things first. We weren't about to go to a school with all white kids. No doubt, they would try to oppress us, just like the Panthers had said.

"Yes. They enroll mostly white students." That was one good thing about Mr. White, you could always count on him to tell the truth. We were ready to leave now.

"However," Mr. White went on, "it will be good for you to experience a different environment. You shouldn't worry about that, Mr. Jefferson. Besides, there will be other Afro-American students there."

"How many?" I wanted to know.

"Maybe twenty or so."

"Out of how many?"

"Well, these are very small schools. That's part of what makes them so good. Maybe about four hundred or so. Some have more students."

It didn't sound good: a school far away full of white people. No, thank you.

"How would we get up to New England?" Carmela asked.

"Who's going to pay for us to get back home?" Roosevelt wanted vital information.

"Where do you eat dinner if you live in a dormitory?" Ronnie asked. Even though he had a skinny butt, Ronnie was always thinking about food.

"In a cafeteria, fool." Even I knew that.

"Miss Lyles," our good guidance counselor scolded. "Watch your tongue."

"I'm sorry, Ronnie," I apologized. But sometimes that boy asked some stupid questions.

"Are the kids at those boarding schools real smart?" I always liked to check the competition. "Do you think they are going to be smarter than us?"

"No, Miss Lyles. They are not smarter than you. There are few people in the world who are smarter than you." (Mr. White wasn't fooling me. He said that to everybody.) "But you'll have to work hard. And you can't be a smart-aleck with people all the time or they can send you back home."

Ronnie didn't like the idea. "Why do we have to leave home just to go to school? I'd rather just go to East Tech and play B-ball with the Scarabs and go to the state championships in Columbus."

Then stay your butt here, stupid, I thought, but held back. I was ready to go to boarding school. Ready to work or do whatever I had to do to get out of King-Kennedy, out of the hallway. Shoot, white people didn't seem so bad—some of them. If they were like the Hedwicks at Friendly Town, maybe I could get along with them. This boarding school business sounded like my chance, my ticket.

I intended to take it. For the next two semesters: No cutting class to visit the House of Wills. No dancing to Al "Let's Stay Together" Green in the rec room after lunch. No acting a fool in study hall. No roaming the halls on outrageous detours to the lavatory. No trading Now and Laters or Jackson Five cards in class. No peddling potato chips from my locker for a nickel profit and ending up late for class. No calling Mr. Spooner, the French teacher, names—"*Monsieur Spooner, l'nstructeur avec la tête grande.*"

All trips to fantasy land were canceled. All roads and detours blocked, the main gate locked. When I reached out to touch it, a trumpet blasted "PAY ATTENTION."

In Miss Nelson's English class, the eight parts of speech became my mantra. I bowed before the wide oak of a woman whose mere presence demanded that one speak correct grammar, punctuate properly, and distinguish a linking verb from a regular verb.

Extra credit meant extra reading, report writing, calculating, scrubbing test tubes, and some general kissing up. I had no shame. Extra credit meant running for class president. I whipped up a plan for an end-of-the-school-year good citizenship dance and won. I forced my skinny legs to run for track.

Mr. Blakeman, the music teacher with spooky deep-set eyes and wiry blond hair, wrote an original Christmas play. I was the star. The title was *We May Never Pass This Way Again*. All the songs were written by Seals and Crofts, two whites who played the guitar. Mr. Blakeman pointed to the cover of their album, showing us that either Seals or Crofts had married a black woman. The Panthers probably wouldn't have had too much to say to her, I thought. In the play, my monologue talked about the special stars in the universe that people could count on to guide them in life, just like the three wise men did. The play reminded me of Charles Lyles and the way he used to think about the universe all the time. Nearly four years had passed since we had moved to the project, and Charles Lyles still hadn't shown his face. And he wasn't about to show up to see me play my part in the Christmas play. That didn't stop me from wishing.

I starred opposite Oswald Stuard who—I swear—had what was probably his first erection while we were right up there on stage. I think he had been staring too hard at my breasts as he recited lines from memory. His face went blank and bewildered. And he sort of tottered on his stack-heeled shoes. I whispered the forgotten line:

"We may never pass this way again."

Mrs. Moore, the science teacher, must have seen my efforts to excel. She took a liking to me. This required much forgiving on her part, for the dollop of white hair that sat upon her head like whipped cream was an endless source of amusement to me. Mrs. Moore's shiny paper bag–brown face was youthful, but her hair must have been a thousand years old. Her pointy, rhinestone cat glasses tickled me too. At the sight of them, there was no holding back crude jokes mumbled just loud enough for her to hear in class. She never seemed to mind.

"I heard you like to read," she said one day after class as I scrubbed the Bunsen burner table for extra credit.

"Yep. I'm in Mr. Jarvey's English class now. And he always gives us something good to read, like we just finished reading *A Teacup Full of Roses*. That book was good."

"Well, next week, Mrs. Royals [the soft-spoken algebra teacher] and I are going downtown to Higbee's Department Store to have lunch and to see a black woman who wrote a wonderful book that's out in paperback now. Would you like to come along, Miss Lyles?"

"How we gon' get there?" Transportation was no easy matter in my life. Without a car, "How we gon' get there?" had to be answered before anything else could be considered.

"We're going to ride in my car," said Mrs. Moore.

It was as simple as that. Cool! Next question: "How much is it going to cost?" It didn't make any sense for me to say I could go if it was going to cost a lot of money. Pride kept me from asking Momma for money, even though she would have scraped and figured out some way to tie a few dollars in a handkerchief and place it under my pillow.

"Don't worry. We'll treat you to lunch," Mrs. Moore said.

"Okay then. I can go."

Come Friday, Vaseline sheened my face like a brand-new doll baby's. Dime-store earrings glittered beneath my donut hairdo. The creases pressed into my best plaid cuffed bell-bottoms could have cut somebody. My patent leather bubble-toe, two-toned oxfords were buffed bright. Looking my best, I was ready to go downtown to Higbee's to meet this black lady who had written "such a wonderful book."

Up the escalators we moved. Rising above mannequins who wore pretty two-toned, bell-bottom suits with vests. Passing beautiful dishes and curio cabinets like in magazines. Lingerie 5. Furniture/Luggage 6. Finally, Books 7.

And there she stood, a tall, dark, commanding woman. She could be seen—and felt—from across the aisles of a big, busy department store. A crown of colorful rags wrapped high around her head. Her eyes were far apart, wide and exotic, yet wise like Mrs. Moore's. Her gap-toothed smile was endless. And she gave it to each of the strangers who approached her, a book outstretched in their hands as if seeking the queen's seal.

Mrs. Moore pushed me into the receiving line. First an old woman in a shaggy fur hat. Then a lady who looked something like my mother. Next a younger white woman. Then me.

When Maya Angelou spoke, I knew God was a woman: Her voice rich as a mineral mine, deep as a river, rising up out of the earth.

"And what is your name, young lady?" She bent her huge body to look right in my face.

"Charlise Lillianne Lyles." I felt someone so regal would want to know my full title.

I stood rapt in Ms. Angelou's majesty. Meanwhile, Mrs.

Moore had picked up a copy of the book and gotten in line to have Ms. Angelou sign it.

"Charlise? How do you spell that?" she inquired with elegant curiosity, not like clumsy old teachers who had puzzled and stumbled over the spelling and pronunciation of such an unusual name.

"C-H-A-R-L-I-S-E," I enunciated each letter perfectly. "It's pronounced Charlise like Charles. I'm named after my father. His name is Charles Lyles. He invented my name so it would sound like his. My middle name is after my mother, Lillian, except it has a *n* and an *e* on the end."

"Miss Lyles is an outstanding young lady," Mrs. Moore declared to Ms. Angelou. I winced with embarrassment even though I now believed this statement to be true.

She signed the book: "Joy to Miss Charlise Lillianne Lyles. Maya Angelou."

"Thank you, Ms. Angelou. I hope you can come back to Cleveland again. It probably looks real boring, but it's not. Plus, we used to have a black mayor here named Carl B. Stokes. But we don't anymore." For some reason, I thought Ms. Angelou would want to know this about Cleveland.

"Thank you, Miss Lyles."

"Thank you."

The name of her book was strange: *I Know Why the Caged Bird Sings*. Hopefully it was not some science book about birds that Mrs. Moore had gotten her mind set on me reading. I planned to give her an oral book report in exchange for the book. But that would be hard if it was boring.

Then Mrs. Moore, who walked at the speed of a high-powered robot and who knew we had to be back at school for sixth period class, swept the book up, extended a gracious thank you to Ms. Angelou, and headed to the cash register.

From her wallet she pulled a shiny blue plastic card that looked like the IDs that students displayed to be admitted into the school cafeteria.

"What's that?" I asked, realizing too late that maybe it was none of my business, that maybe Mrs. Moore didn't have any money. "It's a credit card," said Mrs. Moore.

"Oh." I still didn't quite get it. But I knew that it had value like money when the cashier took it, pressed it in a thing that looked like a long, skinny waffle iron, and handed Mrs. Moore the book in a nice bag.

In spite of Tinky's complaints, I kept the light on nearly all night, reading the story of a girl gone mute after being raped. In the deep, deep South, a place where all the whites were as mean as the Panthers said, she fought for the dignity of her life.

The caged bird's song lifted me. I studied harder than ever.

"Day school?!"

Mr. White, the guidance counselor, had promised us that we would receive scholarships to *boarding school*, not "day school." I had never even heard of a day school. Wasn't every school a day school?

But after a year of hard work, I had received a letter from Hawken, a day school in Gates Mills, Ohio, about thirty-five miles from where I lived. They were interested in meeting and interviewing me, it said. No fair. I wanted—needed—to go to boarding school, far away in the place called New England, which I would have to fly on a plane to get to, something I had never done. Not no day school. How was I supposed to get way out to that school in the suburbs? We didn't have a car. Was there a bus like the No. 14/Kinsman Road that could take me way out there every day? I would have to get up at four A.M. and walk in the dark to catch it. And when I returned home the hallway boys would still be waiting to feel on me.

Didn't the people at the stupid Hawken School know that we did not have a car to get me way out there to their special school?

There was no choice. I would have to tell old tall, skinny Mr. White off. I should have known not to believe that old white punk in the first place.

"Mr. White." I stalked him down in the school corridor.

"How are you today, Miss Lyles?"

"Mr. White. I want to get a scholarship to a boarding school in New England like the ones you told us about. That's what I want.

Boarding school, not no day school. Didn't any of the boarding schools like my application?"

"Well, Miss Lyles, the teachers at the Hawken School told me they were impressed with your application, and really wanted to meet and talk with you."

"But Mr. White. I don't have no way—excuse me—any way, to get way out to that school. My mother does not have a car. How can I get there? Why couldn't you just tell them that I have to go to boarding school in New England? That's what I put on my application. Remember?"

His happy face went pitifully blank. As much as Mr. White wanted to help me and my classmates take the prep school ticket, he had no solutions for the cumbersome quirks of poverty that could trip up opportunity.

Momma was delighted that I had gone from the slow class to showing remarkable promise: Her prayers had been answered. We wracked our brains trying to figure a way to get me to a school thirty-five miles from Building A-11. Catching the rapid transit at four A.M. in the dark was too risky. And we knew no one who worked in the suburbs who could give me a ride. After two weeks, Momma, the master opportunity scout herself, gave up.

"Well, Sugarbabe," she sighed. "That Hawken is probably a good school. But school is what you make it. You can go to East Tech or John Adams and do just as good. You can still take the college classes and probably get a scholarship to go to Case Western Reserve like your sister did."

Hawken wasn't the boarding school I had hoped for. But the prospect of going there had begun to excite me, especially with all my teachers calling it "the opportunity of a lifetime" and stopping in the school hallway to congratulate me right in front of everybody as if I had already been accepted.

"We're all really quite proud of you, Miss Lyles. You've certainly come a long way here at Kennard Junior High School," Mr. Salo, the social studies teacher announced, as if I had won the Miss Black America pageant.

"Miss Lyles, you're certainly going to get an *exxxcelent education* at the Hawken School. There's no doubt in my mind," said Mrs. Bowden, who spoke so proper I couldn't stand it.

And Mrs. Tierce, who had rescued me from the slow class, she winked and smiled whenever our paths crossed in the corridor.

The scholarship would be in vain, I told Mr. White again and again. That didn't stop him from taking me on a spring visit to Hawken School. In his long white Oldsmobile, we rode out of Cleveland's bald gray light into the lush, dark greenness of Shaker Heights, where trees seemed to grow taller and arch higher, like the vaulted ceiling of a cathedral. Stone mansions with gates and gargoyles slid by. A funny-looking yellow train on a track rode alongside us. Through the windows, I saw white men reading newspapers and yawning. With the moving of the train, their heads wobbled gently like the toy puppy dogs that people put in the rear windows of Fords and Chevrolets. When the train stopped, an old lady, black as blue, stepped off carrying a shopping bag. She was probably on her way to clean up somebody's house for twenty dollars a day and rapid transit fare back home, just like my Momma used to.

Mr. White drove on past a green sign that said Beachwood. Along the road, bright white houses with colorful shutters and big garage doors popped up like daisies in a field. Surely these were the same neighborhoods where the families on *Bewitched* and *The Brady Bunch* lived.

Green shutters gave way to green fields. I rolled down the window to breathe in the air. It was clean and pure, different from city air. I was just a little bit annoyed with Mr. White. He hadn't told me that this school was way out in the country with no buildings or anything.

Then Mr. White turned onto the foot of a steep hill and shifted into fourth gear. We began the long climb up a magic mountain of opulence where big houses, mansions to me, stood in silence.

At the top, glorious trees bowed their branches in prayer over the Hawken School

I saw the big red barn first. Quite possibly, horses were inside, Mr. White said.

Horses, with their moody nostrils, were the stuff of my special blend of comic-book, super-heroine, early-adolescent erotic fantasy: Naked, I mounted, my pelvis an arc of triumph. Uphill into misty morning I rode, my eyes flashing like chips of starlight. Dew drops settled silver on my nipples. And morning glories opened in envy. Yes, I wanted to ride horses at Hawken School. There was a wonderful freedom about this place. I could feel it.

The students were mostly white, though some of them were brown like Fritos with very dark hair. Some had teeth enmeshed in silver wire. "What happened to their teeth?" I whispered to Mr. White.

"Those are braces. They help to straighten out your teeth. My son has some."

"Do you get to take them off?"

"Yes. Once your teeth are all straight."

I felt sorry for them. They had not gotten perfectly straight teeth naturally like I had gotten from Charles Lyles.

Other students wore jackets that seemed to float them a foot above the earth like astronauts in orbit. There were a few black students. They dressed way too plain, but had the nerve to look at me funny. It didn't bother me; I knew I was looking good with my bushy blow-out Afro and two-toned bell-bottom jeans. Also, they talked way too proper for me. Maybe it was a good thing that I wouldn't be coming to the Hawken School after all.

The teachers seemed nice enough, but there were no black ones. Their smiles at me seemed frozen and awkward, but somehow sincere, like Mr. Hedwick's Friendly Town smile.

"We definitely want you to come to our school," said Mr. Wheeler, the director of admissions, shaking my hand and smiling the broadest Friendly Town smile of all.

I didn't want to hurt his feelings by telling him that I had no way to get to his nice school. Mr. White didn't mention it either. After sitting in on an English class where a misty-eyed man read poetry much too passionately, Mr. White and I slid into the Oldsmobile and rode down the magic mountain, back into the dull gray city.

Maybe Mr. White thought that seeing the Hawken School would motivate me to find transportation. But we simply had no "resources," Momma said, using her newfound social work vocabulary.

A few weeks after our visit, a letter arrived congratulating me for "being accepted to the Hawken School." It also said I was now bound by the school motto: "That the better self shall prevail, and each generation introduce its successor to a higher plane of life." Well, that made me nervous. Then I remembered there was no need to worry. I would not be attending the Hawken School because there was no way for me to get there. So much for "a higher plane of life."

I promptly reported to Mr. White one last time—maybe he would get it through his head—that I would not be able to accept the scholarship to Hawken School. Instead I would go to East Tech and march through the streets in great glory when the Scarabs won the state basketball championship once again. I would get into the Upward Bound program and go to college from there. It was a perfectly good plan. Even Momma said so. Mr. White pursed his lips. Without a word, he went back to his cubicle in the guidance office.

"I heard you won a scholarship to go to the Hawken School," Mrs. Moore remarked one afternoon as she drove me home after school. Staying late to clean labs for extra credit had become a habit.

"Yep." I gazed out the window at the playground sliding by. "But I don't have a way to get there. We don't have no car or nothing. So I told Mr. White the other day that I wouldn't be able to go."

Mrs. Moore was quiet. The breeze blowing through the window fluffed up her hair like cockatoo feathers. I suppressed a giggle.

"Well, maybe you could live at my house and go to school from there," she said. "I live not far from where the Hawken School bus stops on South Woodland Road. I see it on my way to work some mornings. I could drop you off there in the morning and pick you up in the evening. Ask your mother tonight and see what she says."

Surely, surely this lady with the crazy white hair was joking! I went home, ate dinner, did homework, and went to sleep without a word to Momma.

"Well, did you ask your mother?" Mrs. Moore asked the next day as I filed out of her biology class.

"Naw. Are you really for real? I thought you might just be kiddin' or something."

That night I did ask. Momma, always preoccupied with paying bills, was immediately suspicious. "How much would I have to pay her to keep you?" Stupid me had forgotten to ask about that part.

"Nothing," Mrs. Moore said the next day when I inquired. "You just study hard and make good grades. That'll be enough."

Momma was ecstatic, though still slightly wary. Tinky, John, and I danced around the living room that night to "Mighty Love" by the Spinners. (Every third Saturday, the eight-track tape man delivered a new tape. The latest songs for just five dollars.) It looked like I was going to the Hawken School after all.

Momma's suspicion lingered. And I had my own. I had heard Mrs. Moore say that she had no children. Perhaps this was a Cinderella setup: Mrs. Moore would require me to pay my keep by polishing windows and scrubbing floors. The endless chores would leave me too exhausted to study. I would flunk out and end up back in the project. Or my big mouth would get the best of me. I would tell Mrs. Moore off for trying to work me to death and she would kick me out, back to the hallway.

But a visit to Mrs. Moore's warm, comfortable home erased all concern about ulterior motives. A wallpapered room all to myself awaited. Plus, an electric typewriter and Time/Life books about every country.

"Are you sure there won't be any charge?" asked Momma, who had come to investigate the goodness and decency of the home that would hold her daughter.

"Oh no, not at all," said Mrs. Moore. "We'll be delighted to have her." Mrs. Moore and Mr. Moore, a huge, friendly Hershey bar–brown man with pointy ears, nodded agreement. Welcome.

It was settled. I would live with Mrs. Moore during the week and catch the bus home to my family for weekends.

Guilt paddled me for all the times I had giggled and cracked jokes at Mrs. Moore's whipped meringue hairdo and cat glasses.

At last the ticket arrived in the mail with my name on it. At last. My destination: Philadelphia, Haverford College, and the A Better Chance summer orientation program, designed to prepare me for prep school. The plane would depart the next week at nine in the morning. My sister Linda was responsible for getting me to the airport. She was now proud owner of the first and only car in the Lyles family, a red secondhand MG Midget bought with summer job earnings.

My summer job cleaning playgrounds for the City of Cleveland had paid for a halter and cardigan set, a peach colored miniskirt, and wedge-heeled sandals to wear on the plane. My Afro had grown way too long and could no longer be trusted to stay in one place, so Momma pressed my hair and rolled it on sponge rollers. I didn't mind wearing pressed curls for my first flight.

Plucked from public housing projects, big-city tenements, backwoods, and barrios, we assembled. All sixty of us, the chosen children of the program.

Freida, a girl with freckles, an Afro, and round glasses, was our group leader. We could and would succeed at our new schools, Freida instilled in us. We were representing our people. We were there to prove that Afro-Americans were the best, the brightest. We had to work hard and deliver. It was okay to have fun, but we had to be about our work. Not every kid, black or white, had the chance that we had. Expectation was heavy in the air.

For five days we were drilled on the keys to success: grammar quizzes, mathematics brush-ups, lectures on history, time management, organization, good manners, neatness. Graduates of the ABC program who had gone on to schools like Harvard, Yale, and Princeton advised us on the fine and painful points of prep school.

At seven o'clock every evening we gathered in a musty college dormitory lounge with a giant moon and big yellow stars painted on the wall. It was time for our rap session.

Mikey was our "facilitator." He was a skinny Haverford student with sallow skin, a tame Afro (nothing like the ones we wore in the project), and a Mickey Mouse laugh. He was a graduate of the ABC program who had supposedly mastered the feared "transition," the test that was to make or break us. He whipped out new terms on us like "culture shock" and "adjustment period."

Mikey tried his best to get us to talk about just how scared we all really were about going away to these nice white schools. What made us nervous? What worried us?

A loud-talking girl from Camden, New Jersey, who wore funny hair ornaments, was deeply troubled. She swore that dead babies dumped in trash cans were turning up all over Camden. The perpetrators were known to her. They were girls just like us, she said. Only they would never be awarded scholarships.

"Now how am I supposed to tell these white kids with calculators that I know people who offed their own babies?" the girl from Camden asked Mikey.

He didn't touch that one. But he babbled on warmly about how we were all in this together, and nobody at those schools knew what it was like to be poor and black, and that he would be on our side all the way, even though we would probably never see him again. We were all part of the great ABC oversoul.

"Are those people at that school going to be thinking I'm dumb?" asked Sheerie Davis from Washington, D.C.

"Well," said Mikey, "some of them may think that, but you've got to prove them wrong."

The next rap session brought our women worries to the surface. "Are there going to be any black boys at that school for me to go out with?" Debra, a girl from Wilmington, Delaware, finally broke out about the real deal—what all the girls had been thinking about all along. "What if those white girls start trying to take all the black dudes? Then what am I supposed to do?"

"Now these are all very good questions," Mikey answered nervously. "I'm glad you asked them. That's what this orientation is all about. There will be more than enough dudes to go around." Mikey seemed to think that answer would satisfy us. He simply did not understand how much we needed to be affirmed by our black brothers, especially the ones who were smart and going somewhere. We needed them to praise our Afros, our budding figures, and the outfits we wore—even if they didn't care too much for our brains. For if they defected, we would have no soul mates.

"What do—does—'orientation' mean, Mikey?" I asked. I had faked it all along. Orientation was a word I really didn't understand.

"This program is called orientation because it's designed to keep you from getting lost," Mikey explained. "Oriented means that you know where you are and you know where you're going."

Escaping the boys in the hallway had been my only goal when I had first heard about the A Better Chance program. Representing the entire race of Afro-Americans, "culture shock," "adjustment periods," white kids who couldn't understand my world and who might think I was dumb, and worrying about white girls stealing my boyfriends had not really crossed my mind until now. Mikey and the evening rap sessions designed to orient me had made one thing painfully dear: I did not know where I was going or why. A hard lesson learned: Trying to escape something is not a goal in and of itself; you've got to know where you want to escape *to*.

Was there still time to back out? I wondered to myself, but didn't dare ask. Time to be afraid and admit it? To say, "Psych. I was just playing. I don't really want to go to no prep school with all those white people. I was just playing. Okay?

Back home in Cleveland, Momma, proud that I hadn't turned out to be slow after all, was bragging about her daughter going to private school to anybody who would listen. Tinky was boasting to people: "My sister is going away to a pry-vette school. One day, I'm going to go to one too." And Mrs. Moore was expecting me to move into my new bedroom in two months. There was no way out.

As orientation week went by, having good old plain fun became more and more important to just about everybody. (Everybody except John Philpotts, a brainiac-looking boy from Patterson, New Jersey. He was always studying over in a corner somewhere.)

We really did want to take this opportunity "to prove ourselves as young Afro-Americans of promise," as program rhetoric went. But it was summertime, summertime, eighty degrees every day, and most of us were just fourteen years old. What we really wanted was to eat strawberry swirl ice cream, go window shopping for school clothes, and to the movies to see *Claudine*, which was about a black lady with lots of kids who met a nice man. While they fell in love, Gladys Knight sang hopeful, soulful songs in the background.

And, of course, we wanted romance. We were the best and the brightest, and we wanted to rap to each other.

At breakfast, lunch, dinner, in English class, and at the movies in the dark. All week long, Darryl Washington, a boy from Trenton, New Jersey, who was going to go to a school in New Canaan, Connecticut, had been trying to talk to me. His skin was cinnamon brown, his Afro clipped close. He wore nice floral print shirts, polyester knit pants, and tan oxford shoes with crepe soles. Ripe as a pomegranate in October, I felt ready to sample real love. Darryl, however, was gentle and timid about touching, unlike the zombie boys back home in the hallway.

The third night of orientation stormed. Lightning flashed the sky lavender. A million raindrops could not stop Darryl Washington from taking his chance. First kiss. First flight. His soft, playful voice whispered from a patch of earth kept dry by a stand of ancient oak trees: "Charlise. Charming Charlise." Warm and thick, his lips bumped then caressed mine. A million more raindrops fell. First kiss. First flight. In the distance, car headlights streaked across a road. First kiss. First flight. And on that summer night in Philadelphia in 1974, there was the possibility of love, sparkling opalescent and disappearing fast like a spider web in the rain. We promised to write.

On the bus ride to the airport, we bounced through the streets of the city of Brotherly Love, saying our good-byes.

We knew that nobody had really dared to tell us the whole truth about this prep school business. What those white people would really be like. And just how much it was going to hurt. We had unwittingly thrust ourselves into the middle of the big battle between whites and blacks, something greater then ourselves. And now we had to leave our homes, get out there, and prove that blacks could take what whites dished out without flinching. And we would have to do it on their turf. When we messed up there would he no one to soothe us. When we advanced there would be no one to cheer us on.

Where would this chance take us?

At the airport, we parted, knowing we would never again be just some kids from the project, spitting spitballs, smacking on purple gum, wearing two-toned socks with high-top tennis shoes, and tippy-toeing artfully over puddles of pee.

June dragged by. I worked hard at my job, cleaning up parks and playgrounds. I bought two pairs of Converse tennis shoes. And I wondered about Charles Lyles, whether he would want to know that I was going to be going to a special school.

The Woodland Branch Public Library posted a sign for the summer teen reading contest. I was glad to have something to do, especially since the grand prize was two tickets to see Al Green live in concert. Desiree was my chosen reading partner.

Almost magically, the men and boys of the hallway stopped feeling on me when they heard I had won a scholarship. They now parted ranks like trained sentries when I walked through the cinder block corridor. I hugged my library books tightly. Their eyes burned envy right through me till I wanted to give them a scholarship, anything to make them leave their post in the hallway forever.

Rumors said that Dee-Dee was going to have a baby. I believed it because she was always in the hallway. She had become a "ho'" like her big sister Avis. Now she was running around telling everybody that I was already acting stuck-up because I was going to "that school." She was telling a lie and she knew it.

Preparing to move, I contemplated the contents of my closet: four pairs of shoes, two pairs of two-toned bellbottoms, six blouses, six skirt sets, a tennis dress stolen or on extended, uninformed loan from my big sister, rocks recovered from a science field trip to Brecksville Park, and three Al Green albums. How best to transport it all to the new room awaiting me at Mrs. Moore's?

Most of the time, apartment number 129 was as quiet as the House of Wills at midday. Momma piddled in her own closets. She brought home a paperback dictionary, thesaurus, and notebooks from Woolworth's. "Don't you think you'll need these out at that school?"

Some of Momma's saviors had panned out. The programs had delivered a solid return for her children. Her oldest son, Dynamite, was having problems. But John was a carefree boy who now rode his bicycle fearlessly through the project. And her girls were doing fine: Linda in college at Case Western Reserve University; Tinky at the top of the "gifted" class; and me on my way to prep school with a big scholarship.

Lillian Lyles was still working on some dreams for herself, but there had been setbacks. As a Head Start counselor she had established a good reputation in the social services. She took courses in early childhood development at Cuyahoga Community College. The job had prestige. Plus, Momma liked helping people and they liked her. But pay remained low. We needed more money, plain and simple. To bring it in, Momma went back to cleaning in the suburbs on Saturdays for a Jewish family. Twenty dollars and bus fare home.

"Do you know that boy out in Cleveland Heights where I go to clean goes to the same school you're going to be going to?" Momma broached one Saturday evening. "Yes, he does. He's supposed to be real smart."

We didn't know whether to be embarrassed or proud. Somehow that said something. We had caught up. And we had to keep on running. We smiled about it, kept a twinkle in our eye about it. From time to time, Momma would muse aloud: "Wonder what he'll think when he sees the cleaning lady's daughter sitting right next to him in class?"

My stomach queased hot and crampy at the mere thought of being with the whites every single day. It made me feel love for Building A-11 for the very first time. Soon I would be leaving the dark, stinky hallways, the odor of urine, Mrs. Parker's sermons, only to return on weekends, Christmas break, and summer vacations, a visitor in Number 129.

One night over a dinner of tuna casserole, broccoli, and orange Kool-Aid, Momma made her feelings known about me going off to the Hawken School. She put down her fork and took a long sip. "I remember when you were just eight years old," she said to me. "You used to clean up the house real good all the time. You have always been very organized, just like your daddy, Charles "Skeeter" Lyles. Even when you were a little girl, you loved to ask questions about every little thing, even the sky, just like he did. Now, I don't want you goin' out to that school with all those white folks and actin' a fool. You hear me?"

It stunned me good that Momma had said something decent about my father. Usually, she said nothing at all or scolded him under her breath because we had ended up in the project. Why had she invoked his name and character to remind me not to behave in an undignified manner at my new school? Why had she chosen to remind me that I had come from a man who took it upon himself to know by name every planet and every star?

That night in the hallway, L'il Joe-Joe sang low and lonely. While he beat those bongos, I sat on the steps thinking. Aunt Cora had called the week before to report a sighting: She had seen my father up on Kinsman Road at the bar and grill. This was my chance. Charles Lyles should know about me leaving home to go to a fancy white school way out in the woods. I would find him and tell him. Maybe he would know something about the whites that might help me prepare for Hawken. Or maybe he didn't like them at all, just like the Panthers, and would instruct me on just how to deal with them if they tried to oppress me.

Linda, who was now in college but occasionally came home to visit, did not think it was a good idea.

"Knowing that Negro," she said, without even taking her eye off her soap opera, "he'll probably try to borrow some money from you. Besides, we haven't seen that niggah in so long we don't even know where he lives or what he looks like."

Tinky, ten years old and still brutally honest and practical, didn't go along with it either. "He don't never come to visit us so why should you go visit him? He probably ain't studyin' you."

What did she know? She had been just a toddler when Charles Lyles left. She had no real memories of him. She did not know that he had access to the stars and knew all the moon's business. But I knew.

My brain may have been on vacation from school, but it told me that my sisters were right. I'd be better off spending fifty cents on an Astro Pop and a pack of Wrigley's Spearmint chewing gum than on bus fare trying to find Charles Lyles.

But on my way home from the Woodland Branch Public Library one lazy late June after-noon, a lark sang sweetly to me. Just a block away, the bus was coming up the avenue. I took off running past Daniel's Supermarket, the men's clothing shop, and Marshall's drugstore, my big red vinyl bag full of books beating at my backside. "Please." All along I was praying not to miss my ride.

PART THREE

Another Beginning

Chapter 13

THE HAWKEN SCHOOL BUS route ran east on South Woodland Road, straight out of the steel heart of Cleveland. It started near Shaker Square, an unofficial border of race and class in Cleveland, where Buckeye Road became the more aristocratic-sounding South Woodland Road. Crossing over the bumpy rapid transit tracks, the bus entered Shaker Heights, one of the nation's most wealthy suburbs. There, oak trees seemed to grow taller, greener, their branches arching high overhead like praying hands.

At 7:30 A.M., Mrs. Moore had promptly deposited me at the bus stop at Lee and South Woodland roads. It was the intersection where several of the few black kids who attended Hawken boarded the bus. Kids like Michael Williams, a fair-skinned boy with a reddish Afro. His family was what my momma called "middle-class," meaning they didn't have to work two or three menial jobs like she did. Middle-class people lived in nice houses, and the fathers lived right there with them. Michael and other black Hawken students were the first I had ever met who lived in Shaker or the Lee-Harvard area, where teachers like Mrs. Moore lived. Still, the Hawken bus did not offer them the nearly door-to-door service it provided to wealthier, white children who lived deep in Shaker, Beachwood, and Hunting Valley. Getting to the South Woodland stop in time to catch the bus required some of us to rise from our warm beds as much as two hours earlier.

"Hi," offered one nerdy-looking boy with a close-cropped Afro. "My name is Darryl Fore." He spoke a little too proper for my taste.

"Hi. My name is Charlise. I used to go to Kennard Junior High School." That was all that I could muster up to say. I offered nothing more, and neither did he.

Soon the yellow school bus zoomed toward us across Lee Road and jerked to a stop. The doors popped open like bread out of a toaster, and we climbed aboard.

I sat down on a cold, vinyl bus seat by myself. The morning was sunny and warm, but my hands were clammy and icy, gripping five notebooks I had bought from Kresge's five and dime downtown. I felt keenly aware of myself—my skinny body topped with a pair of oversized breasts. Just weeks ago I had been proud of them. Now, they felt awkward and annoying. I pulled the front of my thin, blue windbreaker tightly and zipped it up. My Afro seemed too bushy. *Why didn't you braid it and roll it up on curlers the night before?* I scolded myself silently. It would've been curlier, and I would've looked cuter. My thick glasses pressed on my flat nose, tilting slightly to the right. They were octagonal wire frames shaped like STOP signs, just like the ones Don Cornelius wore on the *Soul Train* TV show. I hoped my new Hawken classmates would appreciate just how "bad" they were, the way that my friends at Kennard Junior High School had. ("Oooo Shorty," they'd praised. "You got you some bad glasses. Where you get them from, girl?" "Dr. Frederick's Optical, downtown on Prospect," I'd replied proudly.) Now, they felt crooked on my face, no matter how I poked or prodded. I would've just taken them off, except that would've made the sight of my new Hawken classmates boarding the bus one big blur.

One by one, those classmates stepped on board as Dave, the friendly enough old white guy who drove the bus, pulled up to the corners of the streets where they lived in large colonials with pillars or Tudors surrounded by manicured lawns. Dave's greetings eased my anxious curiosity about them. As each boarded, he delivered a clever, flattering introduction, as if he were hosting *The Ed Sullivan Show.* "Hiya, Aaron, tennis champ. How's that backhand gonna do this year?" "Hey, there, Keith, gonna take the debate team to the state championships this year? Iknowyoukindoit."

At South Woodland and Drummond Road, Seth Boorman stepped briskly on board, one hand tightly holding a black briefcase. He deposited himself into the seat nearest to me and with a flick of his thumbs snapped open the briefcase's brass fasteners. The lid popped up to reveal a neatly organized cache: a stack of notebooks, pencils, pens, a calculator (I had never seen one before), and a few books, including a dictionary. He lifted one book, stuck his nose in it, and began to read. I wondered whether Seth Boorman had read as many books as I had read over the summer, whether his father had made him read about Hirohito and Winston Churchill.

At South Woodland and Falmouth Road, Kathy Hofferberg bounced on board, short and compact, with a bobbed hairdo. Her squinty brown eyes, halved by low-hanging lids, scanned the bus as if seeking targets. My classmates and I would learn that Kathy wielded a saberlike wit without fear or favor. It led us to conclude that the name of the street where she caught the bus sounded quite apropos—Falmouth. Kathy had attitude—and, I would later learn, empathy.

At Warrensville Center Road, the bus turned north for a block or two, then east again, onto Shaker Boulevard and into Beachwood, a suburb of new ranch and modern homes. Wood and brick with large windows and pitched roofs, they looked like the house where the Brady Bunch lived. I had heard my Aunt Cora, who sometimes pretended to be more worldly than her life in an apartment on Superior Avenue, call Beachwood the home of Cleveland's *nouveau riche.* "That means new money, honey," she'd say. "They just earned it."

Next stop, Michael Steinman bounced on board, rosy-cheeked and gangly. With a large black leather briefcase in one hand, a calculator fastened to his belt, and a watch that seemed inordinately large for his bony wrist, Michael looked like an academic Astro Boy, ready to blast off into new frontiers of achievement and excellence. It was as if the white boys on the Hawken bus were pretending to be like their fathers—grown up lawyers, bankers, businessmen.

Most of the black kids who had boarded the bus with me at Lee Road had taken seats in the rear. They seemed to own the last four rows, because none of the new passengers ventured that far. Mostly boys with well-trimmed Afros, they seemed no more or less friendly toward me than my new white schoolmates. Some of them already knew each other because they had attended the Hawken Lower School together. Most of them were toting briefcases, too. Probably urged on by proud fathers who were custodians or dry cleaner operators, the Hawken black boys seemed to be rehearsing to fulfill their fathers' unfulfilled dreams of practicing law or running banks.

More stops: Mandy Stenbeck, giggly with round brown eyes that seemed perpetually amazed; Debbie Zeller, bright, gentle, and soft-spoken; Robin Greene, cheerful, calm, and focused with piercing blue eyes; Delbert Winton, eccentric-seeming with waves of red hair and an intensely furrowed brow.

As bus seats began to fill up, the noise of voices excited about the first day of school—with girls in attendance for the first time in the school's history—began to rise. A starry-eyed kid with dark hair had quietly taken the seat beside me, but I didn't dare open my mouth. As more new classmates boarded at stop after stop, the butterflies swirling in my narrow belly began to flutter up a storm.

After each stop, the bus gears groaned and the engine jerked, yanking me forward, farther away from Cleveland, a city where a river can catch fire and burn, a city where ice-cream vendors are murdered in front of a little girl's bedroom window, a city where fathers filled with shame because they cannot find a job in a steel mill leave their wives, sons, and daughters to fend for themselves.

Finally, the bus turned on to Mayfield Road and began a long uphill climb. The butterfly wings beat faster. Who among these strange, rich, white kids would become my friends? Would those black middle-class kids look down on me, be ashamed of me? Who would understand the world from which I came, a world away from the privilege and prestige of Hawken? Who would accept me as I was, just a girl growing up Afro and American, a girl who had to fend off would-be molesters on her knees in cold puddles of piss in the hallway of a public housing project, a girl who dreamed that someday her jobless father would find work, move back home, and read great books with her?

Up the bus climbed, past a suburban shopping plaza, past tall trees. As Dave shifted, the gears groaned and the engine whined, pulling us to the top of Mayfield Hill. It was a steep climb.

At the top of the hill, the bus turned left onto County Line Road. The aroma of freshly cut grass filled my nostrils, and the rolling lawn that skirted Hawken School, separating it from the road, came into full view. The campus stretched out over sixty-five acres of rolling and flat, marshy, and wooded land acquired in 1960 from the widow of Walter C. White, of the famous White Motor Company. My old guidance counselor at Kennard had told me to look up the history of the school. I learned that back in the 1920s, the White family had made plenty of money as the only major manufacturer of both steam- and gasoline-powered cars. After World War II, the land had been White's Circle W Farm, the site of grand polo competitions.

The gateway to the Hawken Upper School was the great polo horse barn, once the center of the Circle W Farm. It stood defiantly red with a black rooftop, in contrast to its pastel, bucolic surroundings. The year Hawken acquired the land for the campus, a fire had broken out in the barn but was quelled. Now the old barn stood stalwart, seemingly immovable.

It even dwarfed the grand White House mansion, which stood at the opposite end of campus with its pompous pillars and also served as the school dining hall, a far cry from Kennard's brick cafeteria with folding tables. Three full stories of brick and wood, the barn was built in three cavernous wings that spanned more than fifty feet. Erect and invincible, brick silos with dormer windows stood like loyal sentinels.

(Though the barn was foreboding, it served a kinder, gentler mission, too. It was home to Hawken's famed animal husbandry course, where many of my classmates would fall in love with caring for the placid cows. It would give me the chance to learn about animals other than the strays my brother Dynamite brought home and nurtured—rabbits, mutts, gerbils, and an occasional snake. How wondrous that Hawken had real farm animals! I wished everyone from the King-Kennedy rat-killing crew could come see them.)

As students lined up to pile off the bus, I at first remained glued to my seat. Through the window, I watched a parking lot of shiny cars gleaming in the morning sun. Mercedes, Jaguars, BMWs, a Corvette or two, and here and there a Cadillac, the ride I was most familiar with because a pimp named Elrod used to cruise King-Kennedy in a lavender Cadillac El Dorado.

Then, nervous still, I stepped off the bus and took in a gulp of air sweet with straw and pine. Gone was the taste of the choking, black soot that burst from exhaust pipes of the big Regional Transit Authority buses as they lumbered through the streets of Cleveland. A gravelly, dusty road cut through forest, past a rough lawn leading up to the main building.

It was nothing like Kennard Junior High School, the aging, three-story brick building ensconced between the Portland Outhwaite Recreation Center and the Carver Estates housing project. Hawken's main academic building was a long, low, rambling ranch. Only two stories high, it was topped by a cupola with four windows, a single spire reaching toward heaven with a weather vane twirling in the gentle wind.

To my delight, I immediately noticed a scattering of additional black students among the throng of whites moving swiftly toward the main building. They had arrived on the other Hawken School bus, which traveled up the northeast corridor from the suburb of Cleveland Heights. A lot of them carried briefcases, too. Practically limping as he tugged his heavy briefcase was Davin Miles, a petite fellow with the biggest Afro I had ever seen. He moved briskly toward the door as if he just couldn't wait to get to class.

This was the first year of co-education at the Upper School, but the girls appeared to go with the flow as if they had always been a part of the school, despite its fifty-nine-year, all-male history. Dressed for the first day of school in bright print blouses and short skirts, they quickly paired with other girls and some boys, whom they seemed to know already.

My clammy hands gripped tighter my five new notebooks. Head down, I made my way to class by myself, taking in the scene. All about me I heard students' voices, high and chirpy, almost like cartoon characters. Yet the content of their conversation sounded like adults talking. Some snapped out perfectly pronounced words, speaking what my friends at Kennard would be sure to call "proper." Like an interloper, I listened in on exchanges loaded with words I did not recognize, references to unfamiliar activities like lacrosse and places like Israel, which I knew about only because of the murder of Israeli athletes by Palestinian terrorists at the 1972 Olympics in Munich, Germany. In the end, eleven were killed and the image of the masked terrorist on the balcony of the athletes' apartment was etched indelibly in my brain as the first awareness of the age-old conflict between the Arab and Jewish peoples.

My first class was English—"Elements of Poetry" with Mr. Scott. Dreamy-eyed and tall with wavy, nearly shoulder-length hair, he looked like a Roman statue confined to an ancient palladium for eternity. I entered Mr. Scott's classroom in the lower level and sat down quietly amid the empty seats. Only nine or ten other students had arrived so far, though it was already 8:45 A.M. Apparently, Mr. Scott didn't seem to care that the other students hadn't arrived. Laid back and calm, he welcomed us to the first day of class and began to explain a few thoughts on poetry and the class requirements.

206 / Charlise Lyles

That's when it hit me.

The rest of the poetry class *had* already arrived. We eleven or so students were the whole class.

The Hawken School brochure had promised small class sizes, and all my classes would deliver. At Kennard, every classroom had been packed with at least thirty kids, sometimes more—so many that teachers like Mrs. Royal in algebra could not see them talking in the back of the room, passing Now and Later candies, even cigarettes. Nor could she see those who paid attention but were struggling to understand the equation on the board or those of us who had mastered a concept and were ready to move on to more challenging problems.

At first, sitting in a classroom with so few other students, I felt naked and exposed. It didn't help my nervousness one bit. *Sound and Sense* was the textbook. Mr. Scott explained that it was named after a poem by Alexander Pope, an old white poet from the seventeenth century. "True ease in writing comes from art, not chance; as those who move easiest have learned to dance," he recited, dreamily. In a graceful way, he transformed the class into a sweet, thoughtful discourse.

Gently, Mr. Scott pulled me in. "What kind of poetry do you like?" he asked. After stammering a bit, I gathered myself and boldly stated that I enjoyed reading Langston Hughes. "His poems tell stories and even make you laugh," I said. As I spoke, I was keenly aware of how different my voice was from my new classmates. Their sentences pitched at the end as if they were asking for permission to be believed. Mine were awkward, the words thick and ill-pronounced. I wondered if my classmates knew how awkward I suddenly felt at the sound of my own voice.

Mr. Scott said he would to teach us how to listen and "scan" verse for rhyme and meter. To me that sounded like turning poetry into a math problem, draining the fun out of it.

Next, Mr. Scott informed us that we would be required to write "papers" in order to pass his class. Papers were new to me. I had done reports, written essay answers on quizzes, and multiple choice questions on tests, but a paper? My shoulders tightened. My head began to pound as Mr. Scott announced the due date. We were to base our topic on unique analysis of content and genre—whatever that meant. I left Mr. Scott's class in a state of worry and anger, too ashamed to ask for further explanation of this paper I was supposed to write. A paper. What had I gotten myself into? Why hadn't any-one bothered to tell me that at Hawken School, I would be required to write a paper?

Geometry class was equally puzzling: one part frustration and two parts abstract theory. Mr. Brandt, the instructor, was another sparkly-eyed pedagogue with a hardy voice that resonated with his love of teaching and learning. I had never met a grown man so excited about mathematics. Eagerly, he introduced me to the Pythagorean theorem and Isosceles triangle. And I tried in vain, theorem after theorem, to bridge the gap between what is real and what is abstract. Anise Jones, another black scholarship student like me who had come from Rawlings Junior High School, seemed to have no trouble with that gap. Smiling like a gopher beneath the bangs of her bobbed hairdo, she logically and calmly reasoned her way through each theorem in the workbook. While Anise and other students moved swiftly and independently through the work-book series, I lagged behind. Gradually, I recognized that there were many math concepts I had not been taught, and I would have to catch up to my peers.

As the first weeks of school went by, I stayed late after geometry class, well into my one free period, striving to reason angles, degrees, line segments, bisectors, rhombuses, diameters, and circumferences out of space and onto the solid ground of my mind and a piece of graph paper.

Anise went out for the volleyball and basketball teams, practic-ing during the two hours between the end of classes and the arrival of the school bus at five P.M. I didn't dare. Time lost playing ball instead of studying geometry would spell disaster for my report card, I feared. In the long run, I might have been better off focusing my effort on something else—I might have made more friends.

European History class was taught by Mr. Lovell. He was tall, thick, and blond, with a glum face that could turn suddenly bright when a student offered up an intriguing insight about some enlightened despot or ancient political quandary. Mr. Lovell managed to spark my interest in Louis XVI, Napoleon Bonaparte, Catherine of Spain, Henry the VIII, and Peter the Great. But the insights I enthusiastically offered up, in sentences far less polished and eloquent than Steve Boffberg's, never seemed to spark that bright look on Mr. Lovell's face.

His class was my second introduction to philosophy—my father's ruminations on the world's great thinkers had been my first. In addition to the main history text, Mr. Lovell's class required what he called "supplementary text"—I called it "more reading." The fat paperback included assorted readings from *The Prince* by Machiavelli; *The Social Contract* by Jean Jacques Rousseau; *The Leviathan* by Thomas Hobbes; "The Treatises of Government" by John Locke; and writings by Bacon and Descartes. I liked some of their ideas— though, frankly, some of the stuff seemed obvious to me, not anything that would get anybody remembered for over three hundred years. And I liked the way Descartes wore his hat tilted slightly to the left—like Elrod, the pimp in King-Kennedy.

It bothered me, though, that none of these guys was black and that nobody ever mentioned what was going on in Africa, while Europe was fighting wars, guillotining innocents, and philosophizing. But I read *The Worldly Philosophers* anyway. "Be careful not to do to others the bad things they try to do to you," my father had cautioned me.

Thoughts of my father, whom I had not seen in weeks, haunted me in Mr. Lovell's history class and in poetry class, where Mr. Scott hardly ever talked about Langston Hughes. My father would have asked why there weren't any black people in most of the lessons taught at Hawken School. "You have to be careful," he had told me,

" 'cause they'll write us right out of the world if ain't nobody watchin
'em." And because Charles Lyles wasn't there to do it, I took it upon
myself to raise a few questions.

Mr. Lovell also expected students to write papers. At the end
of one class, he handed out a sheet with suggested paper topics. By
the fourth week of school, ashamed and scared, I finally dared to
ask Bruce Hill, one of the cute black boys, what a paper was. He
explained it concisely enough. "It's when you write your ideas and
concepts down about a particular topic," he said. "You try to do
comparisons and contrasts and use examples. You try to use good
vocabulary words and paragraphs to make your point. You try to
analyze." I considered Bruce smart. Before coming to Hawken, he
had attended Cleveland's Alexander Hamilton, where all the smart
kids went. Several of the black, city kids attending Hawken had
come from Hamilton, which was right across the street from the
Shrimp Boat on E. 130th.

I proposed to Mr. Lovell a paper comparing Machiavelli's "ends
justify the means" concept with Malcolm X's "by any means necessary" philosophy. He didn't get it, and I didn't pursue it.

After two months of classes, four paper assignments, and six geometry exams, I felt woefully unprepared for the challenges of Hawken
School. All the glamour and glory of being a scholarship winner—
hunting down my father to break the news of my achievements and
apparent academic prowess—was gone.

The academic hurt hit sudden, hard, and deep. My classmates'
computation skills, quick answers, insights, big vocabulary words,
and eloquent sentences left me reeling. I ached to accept that somehow Mrs. Royal, Miss Lavdis, Mr. Salo—all the Cleveland Schools
teachers I loved so much—had done me a deep wrong. They had
not taught me all the things that my Hawken classmates seemed to
know and do so well. The only instruction that I had received that
came anywhere close were the unofficial lectures from my drunken

father, selected especially for me from his secondhand library of history and astronomy books.

Some of my teachers at Kennard had taught me well, doing their best in our raggedy, sixty-seven-year-old school building: Miss Nelson's lessons on the eight parts of speech and sentence diagramming—subject, verb, direct object—proved invaluable. And despite mischievous antics that often landed me in the rear corner holding two French texts up over my head as punishment, Mr. Spooner's French class had equipped me well enough to compete with Hawken's finest. *Il n'y a pas de quoi.* And, of course, Mrs. Moore, who had so kindly offered to let me live in her home so that I could be nearer to the Hawken School bus route, had done her best to teach me how to think. "Everything is a system and a process," she'd say, when explaining biology. "DNA is a system and a process. Photosynthesis is a system and a process."

Still, my beloved public school proved no match for private Hawken, so overflowing with resources that its students luxuriated in learning. You name it—slide rules, calculators, and a computer (twenty years before it showed up in most public school classrooms); science labs with microscopes and Bunsen burners that worked; an art studio with three potters wheels and a kiln. And a spanking new arts-communication building was under construction. Its star feature: a proscenium theater, which I hoped to some day grace with my acting talents.

While I delighted in all Hawken's paraphernalia, my teachers' thirty-five-page homework reading assignments, puzzling lectures, queries and quizzes, not to mention *papers*, deepened my academic wounds. Instead of rote memorization, their questions probed my ability to analyze and reason, to think critically and creatively. It was a whole new game.

In class and out, my misery over my academic decline was compounded by the realization that, even though Hawken School was now officially co-ed after fifty-nine years, boys were not exactly jumping up and down to have girls in "their" school. Going co-ed was just another way of "integrating" something, I thought to my-self, just like the United States Supreme Court had tried to make black and white kids go to the same public school since 1954, ac-cording to my old Kennard social studies teacher Mr. Salo. And we could all see just how far they had gotten with that. Momma said people in Boston were throwing rocks and about to riot to keep black kids out of their schools. Well, certainly nobody at Hawken was throwing rocks at girls. But you could feel the subtle put-downs in class when girls thrust their hands into the air first and blurted out the correct answer. And you could feel it in the not-so-subtle sneers when girls' sports were mentioned, demanding to be taken seriously. I wondered whether this co-ed experiment would fail, too, with us girls just going back to where we came from—pissed off (as my new white male classmates liked to say), hurt, and exhausted from trying to be accepted by people who really didn't want us around in the first place.

Was integration worth the energy, I wondered?

On some weekends, I continued my search for my father. On Satur-days, when a two-hour slot opened between homework assignments and I had fifty cents for fare on the No. 14 bus up Kinsman Road, I set out to find him. I wanted Charles Lyles to know about some of the things I was learning in Mr. Lovell's European History class. I wanted him to hear about Machiavelli and his attitude toward the ends and the means. I knew my father would have something insightful to say about it and might know about Machiavelli and *The Prince.* And I was going to tell him about the paper I wrote on "enlightened despots" and how they had the nerve to try to keep the people down in order to protect them. I wondered what he thought about that idea. I wasn't sure that I liked it.

There were also some poems from Mr. Scott's Poetry class that I wanted my father to check out, especially "Stopping by Woods on a Snowy Evening" by Robert Frost. The whole class ended up taking sides on it. Betsy Mueler said it was just a simple poem about a man who was tired after working all day. Robin Gilmer said it was about Santa Claus. And quiet, mysterious Michael said it was about death. He seemed to see images of death in every poem.

My first stop on the search was always the Kinsman Bar and Grill. "Have you seen my daddy, Skeeter Lyles?"

"Nope," Mr. Pursey snapped with an air of decisive finality, like he didn't want to have anything to do with my father and his whereabouts—or with me either, and was sick and tired of me showing up there looking for him. So I rolled my eyes and flicked my wrist. "F'get chu." And I was out the door with my own air of finality.

But a few weeks later, the yearning to see my father usurped my pride and I found myself back at the bar stool in the Kinsman Bar and Grill, inquiring once again: "Have you seen Charles Lyles? Have you seen my daddy?"

"Nope," was all Mr. Pursey was willing to disclose.

I began to wonder whether someone had harmed my father, whether Mr. Pursey indeed knew more than he was letting on. Maybe he had gotten cut up in some bar fight. Aunt Cora had said that once he got a few malt liquors in him, my father was prone to a temper like a hot grill and could get all up in people's faces. I chased that thought out of my mind.

Next, I headed back up to the musty-smelling apartment where I had found my father that summer day and discovered his magical, makeshift library.

Miss furry-lipped Mary answered the door, her wig sitting lopsided on her head. With dark, slightly bloodshot eyes round with surprise, she always said the same thing in the same astonished way: "You Charles's girl, ain't you? You look just like him."

"Is he here?" I asked, ignoring her question. (If she hadn't figured it out by now, too bad for her.) "I need to talk with him. I ain't coming trying to get no money or nothin."

"Naw. I done already told you before, Charles don't stay here no more," she said. Then she added, "No, he sho don't." Miss Mary always seemed to feel the need to repeat everything.

"Well, do you know where I can find him?"

"Nope," she said, taking a drag on her Kool cigarette.

I started to ask whether I could come inside, just so I could check the place out to make sure she was telling the truth. But Mary wasn't having it.

I needed to get on my way back home before my mother arrived from her cleaning job in the suburbs anyway. Lillian Lyles would not approve of me wasting precious study time looking for my father.

Fall gave way to winter and winter turned to spring. But for all of tenth grade, I could not find my father. Charles Lyles was, I concluded, like Don Quixote, errant—a new SAT vocabulary word that I had learned in English class. And, like the tortured but inspired hero of Cervantes's novel, my father was quixotic—another SAT vocabulary word—always out there searching for something that he never seemed to find—a cigarette, a drink, a job, a simple job to pay the bills.

In French class, I continued to shine, conjugating verbs, building *la grande vocabulaire avec engagement dans la conversation*, much to the delight of Mademoiselle Murphy. Ever ebullient, she captured my ability to achieve, just like Miss Collins, the big-bosomed teacher who had rescued me after I failed third grade.

In Poetry class, I was beginning to get the hang of writing papers. But I had yet to produce anything that merited more than a C+.

In Mr. Lovell's European History, a C greeted me on most returned exams and papers. Still, I continued to try my best, yearning to get an A.

Geometry was hardest. Exams were returned to me with what seemed like a million red marks, showing I had not grasped the correct concept to solve the theorem.

Each low grade on an essay or exam curdled the sweet joy of going to school that I had known all of my life. Now, I tasted rancid disappointment—in my beloved Kennard Junior High, in my old teachers, and in myself.

By the end of my first year, it was crystal clear to me: at the Hawken Upper School in Gates Mills, Ohio, students were being prepared to lead; at Kennard Junior High, twenty-five miles to the west among Cleveland's public housing projects, students were being prepared to follow. Upon graduation, we would be expected to file into two different worlds: for most Hawkenites, a lifetime of legacy, wealth, and white-collar work; for most Kennard kids, a lifetime of blue-collar labor and earned wages. In which world would I land? Would I be dragged kicking and yelling into one? Or stand up straight like Lillian Lyles had taught me to do and march into it? Perhaps I would find my place somewhere in between the two.

I began to accept that I would probably spend most of my Hawken "career" (as the headmaster liked to call it) struggling to catch up to my classmates—their smart vocabularies and articulate debates, their sharp, critical inquiry, their abstract reasoning. The in-your-face injustice of the world—the haves and the have-nots—slammed hard into my psyche, collapsing my confidence and courage.

At the end of each school day as the bus sped down Mayfield Hill, I sat once again on the cold, vinyl seat, pondering whether this trip back down the magic mountain would be my last. Instead of returning to Hawken School and to the inferior academic status I had there, I would happily rejoin my old Kennard classmates who now attended East Technical High School. East Tech stood on familiar academic and social territory on East Fifty-fifth Street—next door to Shiloh Baptist Church, which was right next door to the House of Wills funeral parlor, my old stomping ground.

Since starting Hawken, I hadn't gotten together much with my Kennard friends because I needed to study almost all the time. But I longed to be back there with them—Desiree Kincaid, Kim Morgan with her sweet, big-toothed smile and pigtails, and Priscilla Gray, who was probably smarter than all the privileged Hawken students—boys and girls—put together. And I missed Regina, whose eyes were always so sad because her mother had died of the Hong Kong flu in the summer of 1968. I yearned to go to rec class after lunch where we listened to R&B songs, and Leonard Ramsey, who looked and dressed like Barry White, would ask me to dance to "I Can't Get Enough of Your Love, Babe" or "Livin' for You" by Al Green or "The Payback" by James Brown.

Back there, I wouldn't have to be confused about whether some rich white boy was snubbing me because I happened to be born a girl or because I happened to be born a black girl. Or worry about middle-class black kids snubbing me because my Afro looked too nappy to them and my colorful outfits too loud. Just like the Jackson Five sang that they were goin' back to Indiana, I'd go back to where my two-toned pants sets, with pockets on the sides and knees, would be praised.

Back there, I could go to basketball games because I wouldn't have to stay home to study all the time just to get Cs on my papers. And I'd see Danny Thomas, with his fine Afro, who was probably on the Scarabs basketball team by now.

Back there, I would have a chance to be an A student again, maybe at the top of my class.

But each time I mustered the nerve and was just about to announce to Mrs. Moore that I would no longer need to stay in the beautiful, lavender wall-papered bedroom in her home because I would be leaving Hawken School to return to East Tech, a steely resolve would appear in her grayish eyes. At once, that look would freeze and melt the words on the tip of my tongue and send them dripping back down my throat as I swallowed hard.

The same resolve showed in my mother's face on the Sunday evenings when I quietly decided that instead of preparing to catch the No. 14 bus up Kinsman and the No. 48 McCracken bus south back to Mrs. Moore's house, I would simply stay put and watch

The Ed Sullivan Show. I imagined myself announcing to my mother that I would not be returning to Hawken School. Her reaction played in my head over and over: "Opportunity don't knock nothin' but once," she'd say humbly but sternly. "And you better answer and open up the door." I considered trying to bribe her. "I can just go to East Tech and then you won't have to work extra to pay for my books." But I knew that wouldn't work with Lillian Lyles. She could not be unconvinced of all that a good education would do for her little girl growing up Afro and American, just six years after the death of Martin Luther King, Jr.

I never got up the nerve to say, "Momma, I'm not going back to that school." So I had no choice but to stay the course I had chosen.

On the next Monday morning, Mrs. Moore deposited me at the Hawken bus stop at South Woodland and Lee roads. When the bus arrived, I stepped on board, melancholy yet hopeful, bracing myself for another climb up the magic mountain. Stumbling, falling, and getting back up again, day after day, I struggled to meet the standards of Hawken School, even though I had been denied by virtue of race and class many of the tools necessary to rise to those standards.

Yes, I went back. But the smart, charming, outstanding young lady who had first departed for Hawken eager to learn, eager to shine, went quietly into hiding. In her place, a shy, diffident girl emerged, unsure of herself, weak in her resolve. I longed for my former self to return, but she was nowhere to be found.

Chapter 14

THE SUMMER OF 1975 sprinted by.

I got a job with the Cleveland youth employment program cleaning up trash in ditches and playgrounds. Each day, along with a hoard of potato-chip-eating, transistor–radio-playing teenagers, I boarded yet another school bus, this one bound for less than higher ground. I swept asphalt, clearing cigarette butts and broken glass till dust caught in my throat and coated my eyebrows. I poked up trash, dragging a large plastic bag in one hand and wielding a long metal spike in the other. I wondered what summer jobs my Hawken classmates had. Were they picking up broken bottles musty sweet with sour liquor? Were they picking up soggy uncoiled condoms and fast food wrappings alive with flies? But come payday, I didn't even care what they did. F'get them. I was happy to collect $2.10 an hour. Come fall, it would buy schoolbooks and maybe some new clothes.

I didn't miss my Hawken classmates at all. They didn't call me to see how my summer was going, and it didn't occur to me to call them. Besides, I didn't even have anybody's telephone number. I was glad to be reading books I liked instead of the ones my Hawken teachers had required during the school year. Along with my co-worker Frieda, who went to Audubon Junior High School, I raced through the local library's summer reading list. It included everything from *Jubilee* to *Manchild in the Promise Land*—and no works of sixteenth-century philosophy. The bus bumped through the streets from one work site to the next, bobbing our heads up and down. But our eyes stayed glued to the pages. Fervently, we chewed whole packs of Juicy Fruit gum to aid our concentration.

In the evenings, I arrived sweaty and smelly to our home in a new neighborhood. Momma had managed to move us out of the King-Kennedy Estates projects. The murder of the Isom brothers ice-cream vendors had sent her and many others who lived in King-Kennedy looking for a new place to live. It was as if the ice-cream vendors' blood kept on dripping down the sewer drain. And the city morgue truck kept on driving away. And little Kim kept on recounting the incident over and over in an effort to purge it from her psyche. Laden with dread, tenants were eager to leave the new apartment buildings, barely five years old. Any place was better— even the old, sagging tenements with bad plumbing on Superior and Hough avenues where they had come from. No one spoke of it, but there was a feeling that all who dared to stay in King-Kennedy were doomed.

Lillian Lyles did not take that dare. She moved her five kids about two miles southeast to another Cleveland Metropolitan Housing Authority property off East 93rd Street between Kinsman and Buckeye roads. Two rows of brick townhouses built in the early 1970s as part of a new experiment in federally subsidized housing, the Mt. Auburn-Manor Estates were small enough to escape the label of being a "project." But many of the residents there, like my family, were just as poor as people in the projects.

Mt. Auburn allowed us the dignity of a backyard and a flower garden—a bouquet of chrysanthemums in autumn and daffodils in spring. I liked the R&B, slow-jam music my new neighbors played in the parking lot at night and into the early morning hours. "Do the hustle," blared into my window as I lay awake reading late at night. (That nasty "Love Won't Let Me Wait" song that Momma turned off whenever she heard it on the radio crooned under the moonlight. And LaBelle was out looking for love, singing "Lady Marmalade." Momma didn't care too much for that song either.)

I didn't much like my teenage cohorts in the new neighborhood, though, with their dull talk of TV shows and jive-time gossip. And they probably thought I was stuck up, walking around carrying books all the time. Plus, my baby sister Tinky opened her big mouth and told them I went to a private school. Maybe they were right; maybe Hawken was turning me into a little snob.

Still, Kevin, a soft-spoken, brawny dude who lived down the street and was two whole years older than me, asked Momma if he could take me to the movies. She said yes. And while the shark in *Jaws* stalked the beachgoers, chomping limbs, Kevin whispered in my ear his plans: *I'm gonna get me a good job at the Goodyear tire store and we gon get married. Then we'll get us a house out in Warrensville Heights. Then have two or three kids.* There was a sweet sincerity about Kevin, a gentle smile with one slightly crooked lower tooth that made him look like a Jack-o-lantern. Still, his plans for our future did not interest me in the least. At Hawken, Mr. Lovell, who doubled as the college counselor, had made it clear that every student was expected to go to college.

Yep. I had other plans. Besides, Kevin seemed to know nothing about Robert Frost, Langston Hughes, T. S. Eliot, or other poets whom I had decided my mate would at least have to be familiar with.

I didn't hear much from Desiree that summer or anybody else from the old Kennard crew. I stayed to myself most of the time, and that was just fine with me. My oldest brother Dynamite, now nineteen, had taken to acting up something terrible, fighting with Momma all the time. Once he beat me up when we clashed over who would fry the last slice of greasy baloney. Baby sister Tinky was still prone to asthma attacks, so I steered clear, even refraining from smacking her upside the head when she got on my nerves. To escape routine household chaos, I hung out alone in my bedroom, reading.

Occasionally, I dashed down to the storefront library on East 93rd Street. For fun, I went swimming by myself at the Woodhill Park pool. In a lot of ways, our new neighborhood wasn't much better than the projects. Once as I waited at the bus stop, a man in a short-sleeved shirt and stingy-brimmed hat said, "I'll give you twenty dollars if you let me suck your pussy." I declined his offer and took off running to the next bus stop in hopes that he would not be on board when the bus arrived.

By the time August evenings grew cooler, I was ready to move back to the stable, quiet of Mrs. Moore's house on Seville Road. But I wasn't all that eager to go back to Hawken.

Somehow, I had lost my place in the world. I no longer fit in with my old King-Kennedy and Kennard friends. I didn't fit in the mini-project where we had moved. I didn't fit in with the kids on the work bus. I didn't fit in with Kevin and his plans. And I didn't fit in at Hawken, either. I didn't want my classmates to ever see the government-subsidized housing that I lived in. I didn't want them to know that I had picked up garbage all summer for minimum wage. I didn't want them to know that to earn an extra twenty dollars on weekends my mother sometimes rode the bus to University Heights to clean the home of a doctor whose son happened to be one of my Hawken classmates. (Thank goodness he was scheduled to graduate next year, so I would no longer have to take great pains to avoid him in the school corridor.) I didn't want them to know that my brother fought with my mother and beat me up over a piece of salty baloney. I didn't want them to know that a stranger on the street offered twenty dollars to have sex with me. I didn't want them to know that the sound of my asthmatic sister's wheezing and gasping for breath paralyzed me with the fear that death was a heartbeat away.

I had entered the paradoxical space between rejection and wishing, rejecting who I was and wishing to be who I was not. It was a dizzying and discomfiting space, nearly impossible to navigate with composure and grace.

I was still stuck in that space when the Hawken School bus climbed back up Mayfield Hill in September of 1975.

Chemistry class threatened to crush what little academic confidence I had left. The concepts wouldn't take hold in my brain: moles, scientific notation, surface area. Avogadro's number was keeping me up at night. I memorized it: *6.022 x 1023, the calculated value of the number of atoms, molecules, etc., in a gram mole of any chemical substance; a universal constant.* But putting Mr. Avogadro and his number to work was another matter entirely.

Even white kids who had gone to Hawken all their lives and were far better prepared than I felt fear and trepidation in frosty Dr. Bernstein's class. Short and balding, he strutted like a soldier before the blackboard, one hand tucked in his pants pocket, the other wielding chalk that scratched out mercilessly incalculable equations. His lecture questions seemed especially designed to embarrass me alone. But when I delivered my lab notebook to display the results of some experiment that I had botched, Dr. Bernstein spoke gently to me: "Charlise, you *can* do this." He likely recognized that I had not been adequately taught the science foundation to master chemistry. He also recognized that I was too proud and too determined to just give up. I had endurance. Dr. Bernstein's kind words were teaching me to count on that when all else failed.

Algebra II was more misery. All Hawken students were required to take it. I envied some of my old pals at East Tech who didn't have to bother with it if they didn't want to. The teacher, Mr. McCahon, was somewhat of a constant, always decked in an olive-green corduroy blazer and hounds tooth slacks. (He was no Super Fly.) Perpetually gripping a stained coffee mug, he drew great amusement from students trying to solve his number conundrums at the chalkboard. Linear equations and functions, polynomials, powers, roots, radicals, quadratic relations, sequences, and series kept me up at night. Once, after waking at three A.M. to study for an exam on quadratic functions, I scored only 68 out of 100—two points below a C. After class, I made my way to the second-floor girls' bathroom and cried for a good ten minutes inside a smelly stall.

Miss Carr, the school secretary, eased the pain of chemistry and algebra. On my first day back at Hawken, I mistook her super perky pleasantness as merely a back-to-school welcome. I was wrong. Miss Carr's high-voltage happiness was just her way—always. Plump in a simple sheath and bursting with an irrepressible cheerfulness, she greeted every student by practically singing. When I approached her desk nestled in a cramped front office, from behind an IBM Selectric typewriter she sang out in an endearing high soprano: "Chaaaaaaaar—leeeeeeeeeeeeeeeeeeeeeese." The double octave bounced off the walls into the corridor, as she punctuated it with an infectious giggle. "May I help you, Miss Lyles?" she offered ever so sincerely, as I stood utterly amazed that she actually remembered my full name!

Sometimes I wondered how Miss Carr summoned up a powerful cheerfulness day after day for children who were not her own, not even her own students. It was clear that she had found her place on the planet. I could rely on her sunny smile in the darkest of times—a low score on a chemistry exam, some quip from a snobby classmate, an administrative snafu, a bad cold, or just a bad day.

I made a few friends who eased my discomfiture. I grew to like witty Kathy Hofferberg. She had a knack for showing up at moments when Hawken overwhelmed me most. "Well, look at it this way," she might say, "Even perfect people buy pencils with erasers." Or, "Yes, we learn from our mistakes, but we'd probably be more happy with less education." Her levity refreshed me. Kathy's sassy repartee was honed, I imagined, at Jewish weddings and bar and bat mitzvahs, where she played the harp. It was certainly nothing like my own, honed on East 55th Street and in the hallway of Building A-11 of King-Kennedy. I knew how to tell people to stay out of my business. I knew how to fend off would-be teenage molesters with a single turn of phrase. "F'get you, boy. I'm gonna get my brother Dynamite to kick your butt."

Jesse Deans also became my friend. She gave me "granola girl" lessons. Replacing my two-tone pants outfits, I copied her simple smock tops with embroidered borders and corduroy pants. Jesse had real Earth Shoes; I wore imitations purchased downtown from Petries at half the price. I even visited Jesse's big house in Chagrin Falls, filled with the aroma of orange marmalade and pine. Jesse was one of only four classmates I visited during my entire three years at Hawken School. She introduced me to her record collection of James Taylor, John Denver, and Bob Dylan. *"The answer, my friend, is blowing in the wind. The answer is blowing in the wind."* I was delighted to know there was a white man who cared enough to write songs with metaphors about black people needing to be free.

Sometimes I dipped into the SWAMP. The acronym stood for the Swedish Women's-Approved Massage Parlor, an invention of a motley crew of Hawken students, and was also a reference to the popular TV show *M*A*S*H*. The SWAMP was an eclectic assortment of Hawken's most outrageous students. They nested in an upstairs corner of the main academic building, outside the girls' bathroom. They were prone to strange antics rooted in a warped fantasy world, such as a disguising themselves as a crew of court jesters dispatched to the woods to find the king's missing prosthetic leg. I watched other classmates from the sidelines, intrigued by how their behavior reflected their wealth.

R. B. Johnston, Jr., showed modesty and shy grace. He carried a walking stick and wore a grungy down jacket, offering few clues that he was the heir to a jewelry store fortune.

Ashley Parks, a black girl who sometimes drove her father's big banana Cadillac to school, was always cool and fun to be with, never boasting that her parents were well-to-do doctors.

Betsy Chalmer's deportment was quite the contrary. Behind the wheel of her powder-blue Mercedes Benz, smoking a cigarette and talking loudly, she was downright ostentatious. Likewise for

Terry Marshall, who frequently reminded all within earshot that her father owned a prominent luxury car dealership in Cleveland. But I tried to cut Betsy and Terry some slack. I guessed maybe it was hard being rich.

Many of my black classmates at Hawken were stars. Derrick Harkins from the Lee-Harvard area proved a skilled debater who led the Forensic team to the state championships in 1976. Dwayne Maynard, Hawken's star basketball player, was featured in the *Plain Dealer* as a paragon of academic and athletic excellence. He was cute, too, with a very deep voice. Cheryl Goodwin was brilliant in math and capable of grand feats of abstract, analytical thinking. Linda Taylor was a quiet, starry-eyed mathematical genius bound for MIT. They were all from families with fathers who had jobs— school custodians, truck drivers, laborers. Some even owned businesses.

What's more, they had a better academic foundation than I had. Hawken had handpicked most of them from Alexander Hamilton, the city's showcase school for gifted students. On the east side, Hamilton was the Cleveland Public School District's academic Goliath. I later learned that all the prep schools in the eastern suburbs recruited at Hamilton, looking for the smartest, best-prepared, and keenly motivated black kids in the region. The new knowledge that Kennard Junior High wasn't typically on the radar didn't help my wilting academic id.

When I was not envying the academic prowess of my black classmates, I was marveling at my Jewish classmates' rich love of learning.

It was as if education was their birthright. They showed off their learning, strutting about—calculators snapped to their belts, portable chess sets tucked in backpacks, ten-inch slide rules—aka "slick picks"—folded in pockets. The Jewish kids bullied one another with learning. They staged showdowns after classes during the two hours before the school bus arrived. In downstairs classrooms, they showed up with shoe boxes full of index cards ready to debate complex subjects: whether Secretary of State Henry Kissinger was really the *de facto* president during the last year of the Nixon Whitehouse when the president was burdened with the Watergate scandal; whether it was a good idea to normalize relations with China; whether the current United Nations reflected the ideals of the League of Nations from which it was derived. To the students' delight, sometimes Derrick Harkins, the school's best debater who just happened to be black, would show up and challenge them to a verbal duel.

Derrick's quick intellect and eloquence reminded me of boys I had heard and seen on street corners in King-Kennedy matching wits over everything from sports statistics to black history facts and urban legends. They were sharp, thinking on their feet with flare, rhyme, and reason. But their aptitude for arguing wouldn't land them in law school, where many of my Hawken classmates were bound.

I listened to Seth Boorman and Michael Steinman point and counterpoint. My eyes darted back and forth between the two as my ears eagerly awaited the next salvo of logic, persuasion, and debate. I was bedazzled by their clear, concise thinking and precise, eloquent arguments. (Little did I know that such topics were the stuff of dinner-table talk for many of my classmates.)

At times the debates exhausted me and I disappeared to the quiet of the girls' bathroom in the new theater building. I stretched out on the beanbag sofa to read *The Bell Jar* by Sylvia Plath or some other nonfiction assignment. I was beginning to read everything with a different kind of mind. Passion for learning was all around me. In my super high-achieving black classmates. In my newfound Jewish friends. And in the ubiquitous presence of my absent father.

I came to understand Hawken as an institution guided by leaders who valued education above all else, though I did not take well to the title "headmaster." I was still learning about slavery, trying to digest its meaning in regard to the human condition. So someone walking around in 1975 holding a position called "master" was just too much for me.

Still, each Hawken headmaster seemed nice and sincerely concerned about each student, so I let them slide. When Headmaster Young spoke to me in the corridor, I always spoke back.

I sometimes wondered what the small, close-knit Hawken faculty thought of me. Were my academic struggles discussed at faculty meetings? Perhaps they would decide that I was not good enough to even apply for college after all. And if I managed to graduate, perhaps they wouldn't let any more girls from the projects come to Hawken because of me.

The new arts-communication building had opened in spring 1975 with the musical *Carnival*. Hawken alumnus Stephen Klein, a bearded, barrel-chested man who looked more like a pirate than a former Broadway musical actor, had returned to direct the theater program and manage the new state-of-the-art facility. He announced the winter production would be *Guys and Dolls*, the famous musical about crapshooters, cops, and street preachers wrapped around two love stories.

"I made it," I squealed when the audition callbacks were posted and I saw my name listed.

"I made it," squealed a high voice right behind me. It was Amy Beal, a smart, popular blonde. She was always nice to me whenever we encountered one another in the hallway or class. But I still had a hard time liking her. I detected, at times, a bit of pity for a poor scholarship kid like me.

Instead of studying for my upcoming chemistry exam, I practiced Miss Adelaide's lullaby. "Give it all you got, girl," I said to myself in the mirror of the girl's bathroom as callbacks approached. Janet David was on my side. Janet was like me, Afro and American. She had come from a Cleveland public school, too. And like me, she didn't quite fit in at Hawken, despite an affable personality.

In the choir room where callbacks were held, Mr. Klein called my name. "You'll do fine, girl," Janice whispered, as I stepped down the blue-carpeted stairs as if walking down a beauty pageant runway. "Show 'em what you can do." The first low chord of the song plucked out on the piano and I piped up a cappella.

"*I love you a bushel and a peck.*" I camped it up.

"*A bushel and a peck and a hug around the neck.*" I cutie-pied it up.

"*I love you a bushel and a peck. You betcha your pretty neck I do.*" I belted it out, shimmied and shook my narrow hips, giving it all I got, just like Janice had said.

But it was to no avail. The part of Miss Adelaide went to Amy Beal. "*Doodle, doodle, doodle doo.*"

All along, I had known it was a long shot. Me, an Afro-American girl playing Miss Adelaide at Hawken School? Truth is, I might have had a better chance but for the other talented black kids. Daryl Boyd, a boy from the Shaker area and one of the best baritones in the whole school—practically famous for singing in Mr. Rosenzweig's choir—had won the lead as Sky Masterson. Pretty Donna Weathers with her lovely soprano voice trained in her church choir, which she talked about all the time, had been selected to play Sarah Brown. Together, they were a dynamic duet. With black students in the lead roles, it was only fair that other students be given the opportunity to play the supporting parts.

Besides, Scott Lindsey, a tall, broad-chested, baritone senior, was a natural for the role of Arvide Abernathy, head of the Save-A-Soul-Mission brigade. It was just my luck that Scott was also black. With three Afro-Americans in lead roles, I knew it wasn't likely that I'd be chosen for the part of Miss Adelaide. But I auditioned anyway, hoping against hope that somehow Mr. Klein and the whole school would be able to imagine me in the part.

That evening on the bus ride down Mayfield Hill, I pondered, *Why did I want so badly to play the part of a dumb blonde?* Truth was, I wanted people to see my thespian talents beyond my light brown skin, beyond my bushy Afro, beyond my round button nose.

Had I gone to East Tech, I would have won the part of Miss

Adelaide hands down. Or would I? After all, East Tech had its share of cutie pies, including majorettes with major pipes trained in church choirs, just like Donna Weathers. Though I bet none of them could act as good as I could.

But I had made different choices. I could hear my old friend Desiree scolding, "*Girl, didn't nobody tell you to go to that school way out there in the damn woods.*" Yep. Desiree was right. I had chosen to go to Hawken. And not getting to play Miss Adelaide at the Hot Box was just one of the consequences of trying to change my destiny.

I ended up playing Arvide Abernathy's female counterpart, a spunky, vocal sidekick on "Sit Down, You're Rocking the Boat." The opening scene was an opportunity to improvise. The setting was New York City streets buzzing with all manner of activities, legal and illegal. I came up with a bag lady.

My costume was an oversized dress that hung on me like a giant potato sack. I rubbed it in the dirt out back of the arts building to give it a soiled, authentic look. Amy Beal's costume was a cute checkered midriff top, mini skirt, and red Mary Jane tap shoes, topped with a country straw hat.

When the lights came up and the orchestra played, I pushed across the stage a rickety grocery cart packed with rags, tin cans, and milk bottles, singing a song wildly off key. I was the crazy colored, homeless lady. The audience swelled with laughter. My thespian talents had stolen what little part of the show I could steal.

I did not know that my own father would someday face homelessness. Or that some of my beloved playmates from King-Kennedy and Kennard would land on the streets, sleeping on grates. Would those in the audience laugh and pass them by as they begged for a dime or two?

The production was a roaring success. It just so happened that year, 1976, an all-black version of *Guys and Dolls* debuted on Broadway starring Robert Guillaume.

.   .   .

"You *can* do this," Dr. Bernstein had said. And my grades *were rising* in chemistry and Algebra II. In both classes, I wavered between a high C and a low B. Sheer endurance.

In his symposium, Mr. Jusseaume detected a spark in me and began to hound me to improve my performance. "You are smarter than this, Lyles," he'd say to me in a haughty tone. "You can do better." Didn't he understand? This was my best.

The class was a discourse on the great thinkers—from Shakespeare to Saint Thomas Aquinas to Martin Luther King, Jr.—on the virtues of love, justice, and truth. Heavy reading assignments (thirty pages three nights a week) included everything from *King Lear* to "Letter from a Birmingham Jail" to important U.S. Supreme Court rulings. The class was sought after by the school's most thoughtful students.

Mr. Jusseaume was a renaissance thinker, eloquent and reflective. Like my father, he knew books. Lots of books. He knew history, too. He was white—like all the teachers at Hawken—but he was what I imagined Charles Lyles would like to have become, instead of aspiring to work in a steel mill that would never hire him.

In the nearly two years since I had started attending Hawken, I'd had no time to go up Kinsman Road searching for my errant father. Instead, I had to study because Mr. Lovell, who doubled as the college counselor, warned us that eleventh grade was the year that colleges paid the most attention to.

Mr. Jusseaume talked of the importance of developing one's "intellect." What did that mean? It was intelligence illuminated with a curiosity for knowledge and a seeking desire to cultivate the mind, he explained.

That evening, as the school bus sped downhill, abuzz with my chattering classmates, I was filled with quiet delight at my newfound insight into my father. Though he had little else in this world—no nice place to live, no nice clothes, no job, and no power over the alcohol that seemed to consume his life, Charles Lyles still had intellect! The thought buoyed me, lifting me high above all the things my Hawken classmates had—better preparation for Algebra II, horses, vacations in Colorado and Europe, nice homes with fathers who had jobs—all the things that I did not have. *Charles Lyles had intellect!*

Each day after the Hawken bus dropped me off at the corner of Lee and South Woodland, I boarded another RTA bus, which carried me south on Lee Road through Shaker Heights. The big mansions of Shaker gave way to quaint shops and the library at Chagrin Boulevard. Next, Scottsdale Avenue, where some of my black Hawken classmates lived. Then it crossed Harvard Avenue, where more classmates like Raymond Pierce and Brian Martin lived in small, wood-framed bungalows. Finally, the bus crossed the tracks at Miles Road into the Lee-Seville area, where Mrs. Moore's house stood. It was a sturdy, red-brick home with a large picture window and African violets blooming in pink glass planters. Like many of the homes built there after World War II, Mr. Moore and his friends had designed and laid every brick themselves, using Mr. Moore's veteran's benefits to buy the brick and mortar.

Mr. and Mrs. Moore were my first experience of a happily married couple. They lived harmoniously. A tall and taciturn man, Mr. Moore spent most of his days toiling in the basement, finishing up this or that building project. Rice-paper wall covering, turquoise trim, gray-paneling for the basement—whatever Mrs. Moore wished, Mr. Moore dutifully carried out her winsome command.

In the evenings, after I paid my keep by washing the dishes, Mrs. Moore required me to study till bedtime. TV was not part of the deal. Meanwhile, she tended to grading science quizzes. She also planned summer trips abroad with her sister-in-law and another friend—to Samoa, Pakistan, Afghanistan, India, Switzerland, Italy. Mrs. Moore sure knew how to get around. From each excursion, she returned with hundreds of slides she had taken. Mr. Moore built a darkroom in the basement.

Mrs. Moore might don a purple Hawaiian muu muu as she narrated slide shows in the basement for her friends. (Mr. Moore installed a screen.) In her stentorian voice, she recounted amusing anecdotes—about "Starr," an American woman who drove tour buses through Nepal; Katmandu at the foot of the Himalayas; of the nomadic Masai people of Kenya; of a beggar at the Ganges River; a Samoan girl on a beach.

Some evenings, dressed in all purple, her favorite color, with her white hair well coiffed, Mrs. Moore and her sister-in-law headed to Severance Hall for the opera. I had never known a black person who went to the opera. She returned once with the story of *Aida*. It seemed she had stayed all night long—four acts, she said the opera was. Plus, it was all in Italian and set in Egypt.

On Saturday mornings, I rode the bus home to Mt. Auburn Avenue. I had decided that Mt. Auburn-Manor Estates was a mini project—a lot like King-Kennedy, only on a smaller scale. Most teenagers who lived there attended John Hay High School in the University Circle neighborhood or John Adams High School on East 116th Street. I hardly got to know them. Each Saturday, I buried my head in an avalanche of homework. It was the only way that I was going to make it through Hawken.

Sometimes I didn't emerge from the house all weekend, until it was time to return to Mrs. Moore's on Sunday evening. There were no dates. No shopping sprees. No girlfriend get-togethers. No parties. No homecoming games. I didn't even go to Hawken Hawks football games. No concerts. No Scarabs basketball games. No cabarets.

From time to time, I heard rumors about kids from East Tech starting to just disappear from school. One day they were there in homeroom class and the next they were gone. I heard some were starting to "mess around" with "that shit."

I knew what "that shit" referred to—dope—though the specific type remained vague. Still, I knew it meant something powdered, with the potential to be crudely boiled into liquid. It meant something illegal, something more evil than an occasional toke on a joint. That shit meant the hard stuff, stuff that would take you down to where you could not get back up again. Turn you into a ho' to pay your way. Reduce you to the lowest acts of survival. That shit at Hawken School might be a sweet, peaceful puff on high-quality "Mexican Gold," a few students tripping out back in the bucolic woods by a babbling brook. At worse, it was outrageous weekend beer parties where kids got puking drunk and came to school on Monday morning bragging about it. That shit in Cleveland's schools and on Cleveland's streets could and would kill you.

When I did sometimes run into old friends who now attended East Tech, I felt uncomfortable. My new wardrobe choices drew snickers. I now sported those frumpy smock tops, corduroy slacks, and imitation Earth Shoes. The Hawken preppie look.

The way I spoke began to change. My words snapped out high and chirpy, like those chipper white kids on the school bus my first day at Hawken. Words like *perspicacious* and *elusive* popped out of my mouth. It was as if every conversation was a drill for the SAT vocabulary exam. I enjoyed using big words to talk about books I had read. But those words drove a wedge. "Girl, what's the matter with you? You sound so white when you talk," some would say. Desiree just gave it to me straight: "Girl, you need to stop."

I became comfortable with being uncomfortable.

At Hawken, I wouldn't ever fit in, and that was that. I seemed to upset that world at every turn with my own still clunky, awkward grammar, my ghetto insights that sometimes made my classmates snicker. Or at least I thought they were snickering at me. But there were students who did not believe a girl like me—Afro-American and from the ghetto—deserved to be at Hawken.

An upcoming U.S. Supreme Court case, Alan Bakke vs. The Uni-

versity of California at Davis, presented some students an opportunity to express that sentiment. The case, which the court would
rule on after I graduated, challenged "affirmative action." Like many
civil rights initiatives that flowed from the blood of Martin Luther
King, affirmative action, as I saw it, was a chance for black people
to catch up after centuries of racist oppression. It was a chance to
fulfill the potential, the dreams that had been deferred.

My classmate Scott Senarsky, a tightly wound kid who was insep-
arable from his large briefcase, disagreed. Much to his annoyance,
I frequently challenged him to impromptu debates on the issue
whenever I could—in U.S. History class, in the hallway. Finally, he
challenged me to an even more public dual: Friday Convocation,
the schoolwide forum for dialogue and debate.

It started off calmly enough: *Resolved that affirmative action
be abolished as policy by the U. S. government, whereas it is unfair
and inappropriate as a means of compensatory justice.* Politely and
meticulously, we each followed customary forensic protocol: cross
and cross-ex. Scott was careful to emphasize the word "qualified"
several times. I responded with appropriate and aggressive reason,
citing four hundred years of systematic oppression and the relative
infancy of the Civil Rights Act of 1964 and Voting Rights Act of
1965. Again, he emphasized the issue of "qualified." On his fifth
reference, I could stand it no more.

"You're a 'nigger,' you're a nigger, and you're a nigger." I heard the
unrehearsed conclusion roll off of my tongue as I pointed randomly
to members of our audience. "We would all be 'unqualified' niggers
without the privileges and legacy that have given so many access
to opportunity, everyone except Afro-Americans, that is. Yes. We
would all be unqualified." I saw dismay wilt the brows of Hawken's
more conservative faculty members seated in the audience. Others
sniggled quietly. One history teacher recoiled in shock at my words.
Scott Senarsky simply sneered at my sudden candor and brought
the debate to a close by offering his remaining arguments in dull,
unremarkable language.

234 / Charlise Lyles

Our showdown was over. In twenty tense minutes, I had matured ten years. Whether we had proved or disproved the merits of affirmative action, I did not know. But I did know that now, more than ever before, I believed I had a right to be at Hawken School. I was deserving of a good education. And I was qualified, if only by my determination and ability to endure. I would get good grades. I would go to college. And once again I would become an outstanding young lady.

I studied more intensely than ever.

In symposium we discussed the long, meandering poem "The Love Song of J. Alfred Prufrock" by T. S. Eliot. I had studied it before, in Mr. Scott's tenth grade Poetry class, but I just didn't get it. The images seemed morbid and un-poetic, nothing like my man Langston Hughes's "The Negro Speaks of Rivers" and "Raisin in the Sun." The King-Kennedy projects had shown me enough ugly images; I wanted poetry to be pretty, to luxuriate in lyrical beauty. Instead, Mr. T. S.'s lines were of stark, cold isolation. "Like a patient etherized upon a table." Too many big words for a poem. And did I care about an aging British gent going to afternoon tea with a group of ladies? Maybe Mr. T.S. and I needed to exchange places so he could see a corpse shot in the head in a project parking lot.

But as Prufrock, feeling old and out of place, climbed the stairs to tea, he uttered miserably, *Do I dare disturb the universe?* That's how it was for me at Hawken School, I thought, always feeling awkward, out of place, as if I was upsetting everyone's orbit. Imagine! Me with my Afro and stop-sign wire-framed glasses relating to an old, dead white guy poet.

We were going to visit colleges!

In May, Mr. Lovell loaded me and eight other black scholarship students onto a van for a tour of east coast colleges: Goucher, St. John's College (The Great Books College), University of Pennsylvania, Johns Hopkins. Me, Anise, Maria Hairston—who had a nervous laugh that revealed both vulnerability and kindness at once. Nor did cute Earnest Lovelace have a clue as to what to expect. Soft-spoken Mr. Lovell quietly explained the merits and the minuses of each college. He was trying his best to teach us to think about a future for which we had few references. Unlike our other classmates, whose own parents had been planning since birth for them to attend the best colleges in the nation, none of our parents had attended college. Despite all that Hawken had attempted to do for us, it was a future we were ill equipped to imagine.

By the middle of the second trimester, my grades had steadily climbed well above B.

I had come to understand right angles and rhombuses, hexagons, pentagons, bisectors, and that the shortest distance between two points is a straight line.

I factored my way out of Algebra II and scored an 88 on one of Mr. McCahon's most difficult tests. And I soaked in the accompanying fifteen minutes of fame when word spread throughout the school that I had scored high.

After many struggles with Avogadro's number, chemistry exams came somewhat easier. Once on the eve of a dreaded exam, the logic of a particular formula eluded me. Quaking with anxiety, I begged Mrs. Moore, who taught biology at Kennard, to help me. But I could barely explain the concept to her. Both of us had gone to bed bewildered. But at about three A.M., I heard Mrs. Moore's determined feet coming up the stairs, then a knock at my bedroom door. "Charlise, wake up. I figured it out," she said with urgency. I tumbled out of bed, and together we reviewed chemical equations until I could work them from several angles and the morning sky had lightened lavender and lemon gold. I scored an 87 on that test, the highest I ever achieved in chemistry.

At the end-of-the-school-year assembly, I received two awards, both books. One was from Mr. Jusseaume—a collection of poems by the poet W. H. Auden called *Thank You, Fog*. I would have preferred Langston Hughes.

Chapter 15

CLEVELAND WAS "GOING DOWN slow," Momma said. She came to that conclusion over and over as she read the *Cleveland Press.* "Lord have mercy. "I don't know what's going to happen to Cleveland."

In the summer of 1976, Randall Park Mall opened next door to Warrensville Heights, a blue-collar suburb where mostly blacks lived. From May Co. to Sears, with Lane Bryant's and even Petries, Randall was a glittering planet of retail, its alien inhabitants possessed by shopping. I liked it a lot, though I could hardly afford to shop—my only income was twenty dollars earned on weekends scrubbing ceilings and carpets for Aunt Cora. But many other people who used to shop downtown exchanged the bus trip west for a bus trip east to Randall Park's dazzling indoor storefronts. The rise of Randall was the beginning of crazed urban sprawl and the beginning of the end for downtown Cleveland.

There were other losses. In 1971, an NBA franchise had come to town. The Cavaliers were an expansion team, but they could still shoot that hoop even better than the East Tech Scarabs. Plus, they were cute and tall—Bingo Smith had an incredible Afro. I liked the Cavs a lot, though I was never able to afford a ticket to a game. Then in 1974 the team moved out of downtown Cleveland to the new Coliseum in rural Richfield, far to the southeast of Cleveland in neighboring Summit County.

It seemed nobody cared enough about Cleveland anymore—me, John, Tinky, Momma, kids at schools like East Tech, kids and families in the projects, all of us who had no choice but to live within its gritty borders. If anybody had asked my opinion, I would've told them to leave the stores and sports arena right where they were—downtown. After all, people in the suburbs had cars to get places. We had to ride the bus. What's more, they had money to do things in life. We didn't. Jobs were drying up.

Momma's beloved Dorothy Fuldheim, the legendary news woman, kept us informed of the decline. The schools were more imperiled than I had ever realized as a student at Kennard. At City Hall, the dignity and strategy of Carl Stokes was long gone. Mayor Ralph Perk—who managed to set his own hair on fire with a welder's torch at a campaign event—was sinking the city deep, deep into debt. Ultimately, Cleveland—the city where the river burned—was forced to declare another dubious distinction—becoming the first since the Great Depression to default on its loans.

Cleveland would not climb out of debt for nearly a decade, years after all of Lillian Lyles's three daughters had graduated from college. Upon accepting each diploma, Momma would sadly, but perceptively, advise each of us: "Don't stay here. There's no opportunity in Cleveland." Lillian Lyles was smart, I thought. But that advice would lead her daughters to move miles and miles away from Cleveland, leaving her feeling deeply alone.

When the Hawken School bus began the climb up Mayfield Hill in September 1976, I was one of only a few seniors still on board. Most of my classmates now drove themselves to school in their own cars. Since my family had no car—Momma still worked two petty jobs to feed us—I continued to rely on the good graces of Mrs. Moore. Now retired from Kennard Junior High, she continued lodging me at her home on Seville Road, but she no longer chauffeured me. Instead, at 6:30 A.M., I had to catch the RTA bus down Lee Road, which carried me to the Hawken bus stop at South Woodland.

On the school bus I felt overgrown and awkward amongst mostly ninth and tenth graders. We were the only passengers, along with a few other black students who did not have cars. Most of the time I kept my head buried in a book. Occasionally, I stuck my nose over the seat and into the business of Maria Hairston.

Maria was from the Mt. Pleasant neighborhood, near East 143rd Street. On occasion we commiserated over our academic and social struggles at Hawken. Maria was known, upon the slightest provocation, to convulse into bouts of nervous, infectious laughter. But on some mornings she was pensive, peering out of the window. In the fall of our senior year, we knew that we had nearly reached the finish line: college applications. College would be our entrée to the equality our impoverished mothers promised Hawken would deliver. Yet at the same time we could no longer keep silent about the angst and pain of the choice we had made to attend Hawken instead of our assigned Cleveland public schools. In a rather mature fashion, Maria and I reflected on our "Hawken experience," as Headmaster Stenberg liked to call it.

"I call it the 'pleasant interlude,'" Maria whispered. She was referring to our daily journey uphill to Hawken, to the lush, green rarefied world far removed from our gritty lives in a city teeming with litter, farting foul air, and corrupt politics. Though Maria's family was considerably better off than my own, both our circumstances paled in comparison to those of our classmates.

"It makes me feel like Prufrock," I confided. "You know who I'm talking about—that dude in the poem. There's the verse where he says, 'Prepare a face to meet the faces that you meet.' That's how I feel—like I have to put on a face to be someone I'm not and ain't never going to be."

Another verse from Prufrock captured perfectly the endless unease of never quite fitting in at Hawken School: "The eyes that fix you in a formulated phrase."

For I knew that everyone could see right through me.

The whites saw my poverty. My academic unpreparedness. My emotional equanimity in the face of polite yet cruel inequity about which I could do nothing. My gritty determination and daring. Terry Marshall, Betsy Chalmer, Amy Beal, Jesse Deans—they all saw. And my middle-class black classmates saw, too. At times, some of them meted out the meanest punishments–condescending stares and stinging remarks.

Attending Hawken, Maria and I agreed, we had begun to rack up quite a tab of social consequences. Well into our senior year, we knew that we would never know the thrill of attending an East Tech or John Adams High School homecoming game, with marching bands, drum lines, and steppers in time. "East Tech, Tech, Tech. East Tech, Tech."

And we would never go out on a high school date. I was ready for a date, but there were no invitations. Hawken simply didn't have enough black boys to go around. And the few available prospects had no interests in us whatsoever. At times they took great pains to remind us that we were nowhere near as cute as we needed to be to merit their attention. Me with my untamable Afro, stop-sign-shaped glasses, and oversized breasts. Maria with her short, straightened hair, shiny with pomade and wheezing with static electricity that sometimes caused a tuft to spike up like Alfalfa's cowlick. The Hawken boys made it clear that we were "dogs." White boys accepted our academic companionship when it came to studying for tests or matching wits on the chess or backgammon boards. And they made excellent platonic friends. But they expressed no romantic interests. And for the most part, the feeling was mutual.

Though one time, affection led me to explore the possibilities.

Dylan Heathrow played the saxophone and keyboard. He was the only white boy in the whole Hawken School who seemed to have any rhythm and any blues. I liked him. A lot. I decided to tell him so on a between-classes stroll to the tennis courts, a potentially romantic spot, shrouded in woods and wisteria. Sweetly, I revealed that I had been thinking about him. A lot. That I thought he was something special. Dylan laughed in my face, guffawing and mean, baring his gums in a way that made him look like a wild hyena.

Maria and I also compared notes on the different standards we witnessed in the two parts of our lives. A small pack of Hawken students notorious for Saturday-night keg parties and smoking marijuana in the woods behind the school went unpunished. Or they were dispatched to counselors to help them deal with emotional issues. But in Cleveland, kids in my neighborhood were arrested for drug possession and held in stark, cold juvenile detention centers for months. One boy named Ronnie, who was only sixteen years old, went to jail for eighteen months.

As I alternated between these two worlds, the reporter in me was born. I became an observer. I positioned myself on the periphery of both Hawken and my life in Cleveland, watching, recording details in my journal (a spiral notebook), collecting data, parsing out perceptions, but always standing apart from either side. There, perched on the edge of the in between, I found some ease.

Still, no matter the social price we were paying, neither Maria nor I could deny this truth: Hawken had promised an excellent education, and it had delivered.

Senior year offered a menu of sophisticated collegelike courses designed and taught by Hawken's most thoughtful instructors. Each aimed to give prospective graduates a potent dose of intellectual rigor—and a leg up on the first and even the second year of college.

A course on the Supreme Court was much coveted, and fortunately I made the cut. So did star scholar Seth Boorman (still practically chained to his voluminous briefcase) and Amy Beal. (I was not yet ready to forgive her for being chosen for the part of Miss Adelaide in *Guys and Dolls*.) Kenyon Cramer, chairman of the history department, taught the class. It was widely known that he did not give A's. Period. His signature trait was a dry, exasperated, highly audible sigh. He assigned each student a Supreme Court justice, whose biography and major opinions were to be analyzed by tracking the evolution of the justice's judicial and political disposition. I was assigned Justice Potter Stewart. *F'get chu*, I thought, flicking my wrist behind old Cramer's back, disappointed that Justice Thurgood Marshall, the only Afro-American to have served on the court, had not been assigned to me—the only Afro-American in the class.

That came the closest of any Hawken class I had taken to centering on the quintessential question of America—race and equity. We studied the justices' opinions in Dred Scott vs. Sanford (1857), Plessy vs. Ferguson (1892), and Shelley vs. Kraemer (1948), which struck down restrictive covenants that prohibited whites from selling property to blacks within certain boundaries. And there was the string of cases leading up to the now-famous school desegregation case: Sweatt vs. Painter (1950), in which the court ruled that the University of Texas had to integrate its law school. Then, finally, Linda Brown vs. the Board of Topeka Kansas, which outlawed legal school segregation in May 1954, followed by Brown vs. Board II in 1955.

Fancying myself a lawyer, I took to memorizing key passages of court decisions:

"The judgments . . . are reversed and the cases are remanded to the District Courts to take such proceedings and enter such orders and decrees consistent with this opinion as are necessary and proper to admit the parties to these cases to public schools on a racially nondiscriminatory basis with all deliberate speed."

"Racial discrimination in public education is unconstitutional, and all provisions of federal, state or local law requiring or permitting such discrimination must yield to this principle," I recited from the opinion I had studied the night before.

At times, my recitations brought the decibel level up even higher on Mr. Cramer's very audible sigh. "Lyles," he scolded, "I'm not trying to get you to memorize. I am trying to get you to think."

And I *was* thinking. I wondered if my friends at East Tech were tracking the evolution of Supreme Court decisions. Were they receiving such rich lessons?

In 1976, Momma—always on top of the news, just like Dorothy Fuldheim—instructed me to sit down at the kitchen table. She shoved the front page of the *Cleveland Press* under my nose and ordered me to read. The story said that the federal court had ruled the Cleveland Board of Education guilty of separating black and white students on purpose to maintain a segregated school system.

"See that?" Momma said, pointing her long index finger at the term "de facto" on the newsprint. "Did they teach you what that means at that school out there?"

"Nope," I bowed my head, slightly ashamed that I did not quite know the answer.

"Well, that word is Latin," Momma said, "and I took Latin when I went to John Adams—John Adams was one of the best schools in Cleveland back then." Oh boy, I had heard Momma's John-Adams-was-a-good-school-back-then lecture before. I shifted in my seat in hopes that this would not be the extended, long-playing version.

"And when I took Latin at John Adams I learned the word 'de facto,'" she said, accenting the "de" hard. "It means 'in actuality.' It means *'In fact this is the way it really is.'* De facto means in reality. And that judge—what's his name?"

"Battisti, Momma. His name is Battisti."

"Well, Mister Judge Battisti has told the truth about Cleveland Schools. But believe me, he'll probably never have another good night's sleep as long as he lives on this earth." Momma was prone to hyperbole (a word that "they" *had* taught me at "that school out there") and I grimaced at her unhappy prediction for the judge.

Reed vs. Rhodes. Anthony Reed represented himself, the local chapter of the NAACP and sundry other groups. They were incensed at the district's unjust crowding of black kids into run-down, beaten-up buildings that were well over fifty years old in order to avoid sending them to the west side, where mostly whites attended less crowded schools. Battisti's ruling pointed to maneuvers by the Board of Education—such as half-day school, building new schools, reassigning students—all designed to avoid transferring black kids to those white west-side schools where there was plenty of space.

"Busing is coming," Momma warned, her voice low and slightly mournful, like a lighthouse flashing danger signals. "Just like they did in Boston. Busing is coming."

A year later after I had graduated from Hawken, Mister Judge Battisti's order for busing would move down from the bench of the Sixth Circuit District Court to wreak all kinds of mayhem on a city that had already begun to crumble around the edges.

My baby sister Tinky escaped the upheaval via the path I had plowed through to Hawken. School recruiters discovered her at Alexander Hamilton Junior High School, where she graduated at the top of her class. The merits of my performance at Hawken also helped to open the gate. She was accepted to the prestigious Choate Rosemary Hall prep school in Connecticut. However, fearful of leaving home, she opted for Hawken, receiving nearly a full scholarship, though slightly less than the generous one I had received four years prior. The financial burden would weigh heavier on my mother's shoulders. Still, Momma, quiet, determined, well-informed, and without complaint, continued to work two and three jobs—cleaning, ringing up retail cash registers, and taking on sundry odd tasks in between—to respectfully pay her bills.

With a more solid academic background than I had, Tinky would emerge as a Hawken academic diamond. Teacher ZoAnn Dusenbury would praise her as "one of the most perceptive students I've encountered in thirty years of teaching." Having outgrown the asthma that had nearly crippled her as a child, Tinky would also shine as captain of the girls' basketball team and a member of the volleyball and track teams.

My baby brother John would not be so fortunate. Indeed, his

schooling got caught in the crosstown maze of animosity, angst, and academic disorientation that was busing for desegregation. Even before busing, the chaos of Cleveland Schools' near bankruptcy in 1978 and other instability had done their damage. Teachers' union strikes in 1978 and 1979 had left John home idle. It hurt me to think of him sitting home alone not learning. I knew that even when he was in school, he was not getting the richness of resources that I had gotten at Hawken. This was lemon and salt on my tongue. Plus, I had heard that the desegregation order had sent many of the east side's finest teachers—such as Mr. Jarvey and Miss Nelson—to the west side. Then in 1982, as some 550 Cleveland school buses continued to transport more than 30,000 students across town, John was on board, assigned to West Technical High School. Only 7.5 miles from our doorstep in the mini projects on Mt. Auburn Avenue, it seemed a hemisphere a way.

That ride would require John to catch the school bus every morning barely before dawn. He made the West Tech basketball team. My mother, still without a car, could not attend games. Had John been assigned to a neighborhood school just a few miles away, Momma might have been able to make it to a game or two. I couldn't make it—by that time I had gone on to college in New England. And Tinky was attending Hawken, half a world away, up the magic mountain. And of course, Charles Lyles was nowhere to be found. John had grown up not knowing his father at all.

My story about my father's makeshift library and love of books didn't seem to do too much for John. He was a boy on the cusp of manhood who needed a father, one present and real enough to attend his son's ballgames. Acclaimed by his teammates as a phenomenal player, John excelled on West Tech's teams from 1983 through 1985. On snowy winter evenings, the long, late-night bus rides home from games were grueling, but John played on, rebounding and dunking. Forward, Number 44, dancing down the court, scoring big, John played on and on.

Many a night John, with the grace of Gazelle, sent a three-pointer arcing into the hoop. Then his dark, hope-filled eyes would dart to the bleachers to find not a single family member there to cheer his glory.

I had never seen so many black people on TV before in my life! So powerful was the spectacle that it seduced me into breaking the rules of the household that had governed my two-and-a-half-year stay at Mrs. Moore's house. In January 1977, for two straight weeks at nine P.M., when I should have been doing my homework, unbeknownst to Mr. or Mrs. Moore, I sneaked down to the basement to watch the miniseries *Roots: The Saga of an American Family.*

Night after night, I roiled in anger and agony as brutal slave masters packed Africans into the filthy hold of a ship, chopped off Kunte Kinte's foot to stop him from running away, raped black women and sold their children off to other plantations. I watched through to the triumphant ending, in which Chicken George cock-fought his way to freedom and came back with gold to buy his family out of postwar sharecropping.

Mrs. Moore let me know just how disappointed she was that I had broken the household rule by watching TV instead of tending to my endless Hawken homework assignments—three to four hours was a typical load. Well, as far as I was concerned, my breaking the rules was all her fault. After all, it was she who had taken me to hear Alex Haley, the author of *Roots*, lecture at the University of Akron the year before when his popular book began to climb the bestsellers list across the country.

The trip to hear Haley was just one of the many excursions Mrs. Moore used to expose me to the world beyond the projects. They dated back to her days as my biology teacher at Kennard when she spirited me to Higbees, a downtown department store, to meet author Maya Angelou. I didn't know it then, but Mrs. Moore's hope was that I would get a glimpse of the world that poverty had forbidden me, and that I would get from it a vision for my future, one far beyond King-Kennedy, perhaps even beyond Cleveland and Ohio.

Seeing and hearing Alex Haley did just that. A short man with high yellow skin like mine, he spoke eloquently of his quest to trace his roots back to Africa. In my eyes, he was Langston Hughes and every other black writer I had ever imagined all rolled into one. And there he stood—real on a stage before me and hundreds of others. From my seat next to Mrs. Moore in the auditorium, I peered down at Alex Haley and thought, *Maybe someday I can be a writer*.

If that was ever going to happen, getting accepted to college was the first big step. I had made it to the middle of the third quintile in class ranking. That meant I was just slightly above average for Hawken. But by my own measure, I was outstanding. I had taken the SAT twice and emerged from the angst and anxiety of the exam with a 680 out of 800 on the verbal and 520 out of 800 on math, my highest scores.

In college counselor Lovell's office, I pored over college catalogues. Fearful that I would not be accepted anywhere, I planned to apply to as many schools as I could. Twenty ought to do it, I thought.

Mr. Lovell solemnly urged me to "reflect"—that was a big senior-year word at Hawken—on my "educational experience" so far. How did I want to shape my education in the future? I knew one thing: I'd had enough of going to school with uppity Hawken boys—black or white—who thought they deserved to have a school all to themselves, who sometimes seemed to have trouble accepting that we girls were just as smart as they. College would be my "big pay back," like James Brown said on his record.

On the college tour the year before, Mr. Lovell had taken us to women's colleges—Goucher in Baltimore, and Bryn Mawr outside of Philadelphia.

"Why would somebody want to go to an all-women's college?" I snapped at what seemed a silly idea at the time.

"Because some say they offer young women a greater opportunity for intellectual freedom," Mr. Lovell replied.

Intellectual freedom. I liked the sound of those words. I had sensed their meaning as I read books like Sylvia Plath's *The Bell Jar*, an autobiographical novel by a poet who walked the edge between scholarly good girl and snippy bitch. She was a white girl with attitude. Lyrical yet in-your-face, Plath and other women poets were new voices to my ears: "I do it so it feels real. /I do it so it feels like hell," Plath wrote in one poem. She was like Maya Angelou, telling it like it was with craft that made it sound pretty and poetic. Plath was a graduate of Smith—a women's college.

I applied to every women's college I could find: Goucher, Vassar, Barnard, Smith, Bryn Mawr. I received an acceptance to Goucher and Smith. But pulled by my love of theater and the joy I found in improvisation and acting, I also applied to the Boston University School of Performing Arts. It required an on-site audition, for which I used a monologue from *Who's Afraid of Virginia Woolf.* Seventeen-year-old me, playing old drunken Martha raging at George. I chose that piece instead of a monologue from a traditional black play because I wanted the auditioners to see my acting talents beyond color, to see my raw versatile potential. On the cold weekend in January when I took the Amtrak train from downtown Cleveland to Boston, I found the competition far more fierce than Amy Beal in *Guys and Dolls*. Plus, all the girls seemed slimmer and cuter than me—and they could sing. But three months later I received an acceptance letter to what was then one of the country's most prestigious performing arts programs. Suddenly, the prospect of attending a women's college was not so appealing. After pondering my decision for two weeks, I quietly sent my acceptance letter to Boston University because I truly wanted to understand the art of drama and what I could bring to it—and because it offered almost a full scholarship.

College! I was going to go to college. Momma was quietly delighted, though concerned that I had not chosen to study something more practical like education or social work. "You sure you're going to be able to make a living, girl?" She asked, almost plaintively.

Senior projects for Hawken students were supposed to be a first foray into the real world of work. They could last three or six weeks. Many Jewish students left to work on *kibbutzim,* collective farms in Israel. Some students worked for the Cleveland Orchestra or in a doctor's office. Some tended plants in greenhouses. We each designed and arranged our own gig.

I headed to Washington, D.C., for my senior project, working in the office of Congressman Charles A. Vanik from the 21st District. My U.S. History teacher, Mr. Banks, suggested that if I planned to pursue government or law as a career, time in Vanik's office would serve me well, as Vanik was on the House Ways and Means Committee.

I needed to tell my father, that incorrigible no-show, that I had made it all the way through Hawken, that I had "developed intellect," that I was going to go to college. And that there was a seat for him at my graduation, if he could get himself together to come. I had not laid eyes on him for the entire three years that I had been at Hawken. I heard he had called the house some months before and Tinky had picked up the telephone. He promised to meet her on the corner of E. 130th Street, near the Shrimp Boat and Alexander Hamilton, where she attended school. She kept her end of the deal, waiting, but he never showed. Momma said Tinky had come home crying.

Still, I hoped that I would be able to find Charles Lyles. On rainy weekends in mid-April, I set out looking for him.

Abandoned storefronts, gray and weathered, stretched on for blocks as I trudged down Kinsman Road. So many businesses had just disappeared in the three short years since I had found my father and his makeshift library living off Kinsman. The cleaners on Abel Street gone. The record mart gone. The Kinsman Bar and Grill gone, its windows boarded up and door chained shut behind a tattered screen that flapped in the wind.

When T. S. Eliot wrote that "April is the cruelest month," he must have been in Cleveland. Out of a gray, unforgiving sky, hard, cold rain beat down on my red, fake down jacket and soaked the insides of my imitation Earth Shoes. Did Miss Mary, the lady with the mustache, still live up on East 147th Street? Maybe if I went to her apartment door and faked crying, she would give up my father's whereabouts. Headed toward 147th Street, I crossed over a tree lawn littered with chicken bones, food drippings, and battered garbage cans. Filthy water squishing through my cheap shoes, my toes ached from the cold. The wind kicked a pop can in my path.

There wasn't even anywhere to leave a message for my father, no one to tell that his daughter, Charlise—the one he named after himself—was looking for him. Maybe I should just go on home. Momma said Charles Lyles was no good. Even my sister Linda had said it. Just like Aunt Cora had said, he probably didn't care nothing about me anyway.

I caught sight of the No. 14 bus coming and waved it down before it could speed past the stop. I ran to catch it, dropped fifty cents in the box, and went home to do my homework.

It was just two months before graduation and I sat in English class with no shoes on, like the white girls, happily heralding the arrival of spring.

"The barn! The barn is on fire!"

A student ran from one classroom to the next in the lower level yelling the alarm. At first I thought it was just another prank by members of the SWAMP, up to their endless antics, this time gone way too far.

But a look out the window revealed dense smoke billowing from the roof of Hawken's big red barn. From the sides of the structure, wooden boards crackling with flames popped like projectiles into the air. I had not seen anything like it since the flames that engulfed Cleveland's east side during the Glenville and Hough riots.

Located just north of the main academic building, the fifty-five-year-old barn was the home of the school's beloved animal husbandry program. Hawken boasted that it was "the largest non-commercial barn" in Ohio. I had spent little time there, though its stalwart red presence had been part of the lure of Hawken for me. It had practically been a second home for my granola friend Jesse Deans. Sometimes, we had sat on the side of the vast red barn, playing her John Denver cassettes, munching on raisin granola, eavesdropping on the animals inside burping, mewling, mooing, and farting. Now the barn was disappearing before our eyes, melting in a raging red furnace.

Run. Run! Get water. Come on. Let's go.

I ran. Seth Boorman ran. Kathy Hofferberg ran. Michael Steinman ran. Amy Beal ran. George Dixon ran. Anise Jones ran. Michael Williams ran. Ashley Parks ran. Fast and hard, with all our might, we ran toward the burning barn, as if pounding down our own growing sense of helplessness in the face of the fire.

We scrounged for buckets, canteens, any vessel that would hold water. Breathless, some of us headed toward the marsh, hoping to dig up mud to throw on the flames. Head of School Robinson and the maintenance chief, Mr. Taylor, tried to hold the flames at bay with a garden hose.

It was to no avail. A twenty-five-mile-per-hour April wind whipped the flames into an unyielding conflagration. A thick, thunderous wave of black smoke rose over the side of the barn. Beneath it, a voluptuous blaze blossomed around the three cavernous, three-story buildings and silos that comprised the majestic barn. Sirens from seven fire engines screamed toward the campus. I could hear the sounds of frightened animals.

Students were everywhere—stamping out fires spreading to the nearby brush, dousing long petals of leaping fire on neighboring houses. Mr. Scott, the poetry teacher, hosed down flames on the roof of a faculty member's house. Mr. Marsee, the country-talking chemistry teacher, rescued the cattle.

The smoke could be seen from the Terminal Tower in downtown Cleveland, fifteen miles way. Could my old friends at East Tech see Hawken burning? Could they imagine me running, hauling buckets, dirt and tears streaking down my face as I tried desperately to save a part of the school I had come to love, a school that would never welcome *them* inside its classrooms?

In the flames, I saw Cleveland—Kennard Junior High, East Tech, the Cuyahoga River burning, a black mayor and his brother glittering like good and gold, riots on the streets of Glenville, the black steel men yearning to be hired in steaming foundries, the green bottles of Thunderbird wine—the thief that would steal Charles Lyles's life—swelling, thinning, and finally bursting into sibilant crystals of heat. I saw the buildings in the King-Kennedy Estates housing project—"the Browns" and "the Yellows"—melting into ribbons of red. I saw the Afro Sets, dark and defiant, marching left-right-left through molten streets. I saw the ice-cream vendors' bloodied truck and the slick, bloated rats scurrying from a skinny girl in pointy glasses wielding a baseball bat.

And from the flames, a new young woman emerged, Afro-American, outstanding, and authentic. It was a daring, new self. A self one who could maneuver in the most alien environments, like a strange astronaut. A self who had grown socially savvy, toning down my ghetto graces when I ventured east, beyond Shaker Square. And leaving perfect grammar behind for the beloved vernacular of my people when it was time to head west, back into the nitty gritty of Cleveland. A self mindful of injustice and the illusions of inferiority that it breeds. A self who could call a convocation of Hawken students "niggers" with impunity and a mischievous sense of irony and pride—and land on her feet, winning the dubious yearbook distinction of Best Impromptu Speaker. It was a confident, wise self who would march off to Boston University and, finding it too large and impersonal for my prep school-trained taste, promptly transfer to Smith after all, "a women's college" that offered me intellectual freedom and creativity.

Hawken had been my crucible, forging me in the fires of rejection rooted in the gross injustices of my native land. Gradually, my confidence and courage had returned. In the end, Hawken had taken my identity and given it back to me, smarter, stronger, bolder. I could now become a voice more powerful.

As the flames receded, I saw a single frightened horse galloping away, "dark-eyed" and panicked. The siren engines descending Mayfield Road waned as silence and ash fell over our hilltop utopia. Ghosts, coated in gray ash, choking on soot, students and teachers stumbled about, stunned and disoriented, as if suddenly awakened from an amnesiac fugue.

In a single hour the barn had been completely destroyed.

"Chaaaaaaaar-leeeeeeeeese," I heard Miss Carr's shrill voice screech through the smoke with urgency. *The bus is coming,* she said. *Go back to the main building and get your books. The buses are coming.*

The Hawken yearbook was low density in contrast to the thumbnail photographs in the East Tech yearbook. Each of my classmates received an entire page on which to express their sentiments upon graduation. Most thanked parents, family, friends, including boyfriends and girlfriends. It was a time to dabble with clever graphics, be mysterious, or just plain silly. The more thoughtful among us waxed poetic or profound.

I chose a portrait Mrs. Moore had taken of me in the basement of her home. My parting words were from a poem by Sylvia Plath, the white girl with attitude: "Out of the ashes I rise with my red hair and I eat men like air." Momma, more practical than poetic, did not care for the passage. But I felt Plath's words aptly expressed my bitter triumph at Hawken.

Many seniors would be heading off to prestigious colleges. Seth Boorman was accepted to Harvard; Michael Steinman to Yale. Black students fared just as well. Cheryl Goodwin was off to Princeton. Bruce Hill to Tufts University. Maria to Barnard. Janet Eatman to Northwestern University. Michael Williams to Boston University.

Among the ninety-six yearbook pages representing the class of 1977, my favorite was Susan Hellerstein's. She quoted Dr. Seuss:

Today you are you.
That is truer than true.
There is no one alive who is you-er than you,
Shout loud I am lucky to be what I am.
Thank goodness I'm not just a ham of a clam,
Or a dusty old jar of sour gooseberry jam.
I am what I am
That's a great thing to be.

At the June 11, 1977, commencement ceremony when my name was called, I stepped onto the stage with aplomb, shook Headmaster Stenberg's hand firmly, accepted my Hawken diploma in my left hand, pivoted, flashed a sassy, Kodak smile at my family, and returned to my seat.

I longed for my father to be there. But he was not. On that day, as I celebrated my first real achievement in life, I did not know that I would see my father only three more times before his death a decade later on April 15, 1988. When death took him from the brink of homelessness, the knowledge that Charles Lyles had intellect, a seeking desire to cultivate his mind, eased my sorrow.

After teacakes and punch, hugs and yearbook signings, no rush of sentimentality took hold of me. It did not occur to me that my relationship with most of my Hawken classmates would survive this last trip down Mayfield hill. As the festivities wound down, Tinky, Momma, and her friend Mr. Medley, all dressed in their Easter best with the sheen of Vaseline on their foreheads and shins, strolled toward the parking lot of Mercedes and BMWs. I wanted my family to enjoy the beauty of the campus before returning to the noisy city. Tinky, Momma, and Mr. Medley admired the rolling green expanse in front of the school. I took my time, not worried one bit that my classmates might see Mr. Medley's rusted out 1968 Ford Gran Torino. Finally, my family was ready to go back to what they knew. We piled in the car; I soaked in one last, long look at the sprawling green campus, the wisteria vines, the dense woods behind the main building, the athletic fields, the White House where students dined for lunch, and the scorched mass of earth where the barn had stood only a few months before.

"Come on, Sugarbabe," Momma called. "It's time for us to go." She was right.

As the rickety green Torino, hesitant and heaving, descended the hill, my former classmates and their families whizzed by in Audis, Jaguars, Volvos. I cast my eyes downward at the peeling vinyl seats, at the poverty we could not afford to hide. And I smiled gently at my mother in the front seat. I felt equal, happy, and at ease. I was me, Charlise Lyles, "truer than true," all because I had taken that uncomfortable, uneven ride, beyond the steel heart of Cleveland.

Epilogue

AND WHO UPSET THE stars, startled the moon, jarred a comet from its path? It was just me, a girl growing up Afro and American at the edge of a new era.

In the context of that time, 1968 to 1977, my destiny was tied up with white America's efforts to right racial wrongs, black America's determination to seize on long-denied opportunity, the dismal failure of public housing, and the beginnings of a steel-belt city's fall from industrial grace.

In the context of my soul, I sought a vision beyond the beguiling boundaries of race, sex, and class. I yearned to see beyond the project incinerator's black, stinging ash. I yearned to see a rainbow on the wet, gritty sidewalk instead of the blood of murdered ice-cream vendors washing down the sewer.

I have told my story in three voices: the voice of an adolescent girl seeking affirmation, the voice of a child losing her innocence to the ugly inequities found in the core of America's cities, and the voice of the woman I have become, a woman who finds herself still sorting out the meaning of the most pivotal experience of my life.

Who is the woman I have become? She is forged out of that summer in 1974 spent in the grand and erudite company of Charles "Skeeter" Lyles. With all his books, his plastic tumbler full of Thunderbird, and his soiled pants pockets sagging with dreams, Charles

Lyles made me understand that to cultivate a fearless love of learning and inquiry was to endlessly disturb the universe, to step out into an uncertain orbit where the center of gravity shifted or even disappeared.

Charles Lyles left this universe in the spring of 1988, just five days after I returned from a pilgrimage in Asia, where I had gone, just as he told me, to find my spiritual path.

And the woman I have become? She was molded from my mother's Mississippi-turned-Midwestern plain-spokenness and resourcefulness, her direct and tough-love way of being. Constantly seeking opportunity for her children, endlessly guiding us to take part in our community, our city—even when promises went unfulfilled, Lillian Lyles dared us to believe that we held the power to shape our own destinies, despite our poverty, poor schools, and the public housing in which we lived.

My brothers and sisters are all part of the woman I have become. Linda doesn't sell crocheted Afro tams and purses anymore. She earned an M.B.A. She's a prize-winning children's photographer and a teacher at a private girls' school outside of Philadelphia. Tinky followed in my footsteps to Hawken, where her wit and perception impressed and disarmed, then went on to Brown and Howard universities, where she studied psychology and statistics. My poetic and insightful brothers, John and Dynamite, honest and hardworking, have struggled hard to find their way in a society that ruthlessly conspires to bring about the destruction of men of brown hues by their own hands.

King-Kennedy is part of the woman I have become. It's in the way I walk fearlessly and foolishly through bad neighborhoods, where folks tell me I shouldn't go. It's in the way I talk—real plain and direct—and in the stony way my face sometimes settles when no one is around.

It's in the emptiness of rarely ever seeing any of my childhood playmates. What became of Dee-Dee, Keith, and DoeDoe? Did they find happiness, health, and prosperity, or did ill fates befall them? Are they in jail or free somewhere fulfilling their potential and their hearts' desires? I lower my eyes and my face flushes with guilt because I know that I just got lucky and a whole lot of other kids from King-Kennedy Estates didn't. Desiree, my old library-reading-contest partner, remains my only friend from Kennard.

And Hawken is part of the woman I have become, in the way that I dared to navigate the treacherous shoals of race and class on a precarious path of upward social mobility, which requires one, almost by default, to cultivate the ability to stand fiercely alone.

It's in the way I can switch from the cadence of urban vernacular to the eloquence of high literary discourse or to "corporate-ese." It's in the way I take risks, a certain daring that compels me to step out, confident in my ability to press on in the face of uncertainty. It's in the way that I have to swallow hard in order to digest the in-your-face inequity of America's apartheid education system fifty-four years after Brown vs. the Board of Education of Topeka, Kansas, and forty years after Great Society–era programs like A Better Chance delivered me to higher educational ground.

Hawken is in me—in the way I can treasure loose ties to my old Jewish classmates just as much as I love my friends from East 55th and the hood, despite the divide between them. In the thirty years or so since I graduated from Hawken I am astonished at how little contact I've had with my old classmates, black or white. Occasionally, I pass Katie Wasserstrom on the street downtown and we promise to have dinner together. She is as witty as ever. Ben Williams now runs his father's auto body repair shop on Carnegie Avenue. After serving as undersecretary of education in the Clinton administration, Raymond Pierce returned to Cleveland to make an unsuccessful bid for mayor. He now serves as dean of the law school at North Carolina Central University. Others built well on foundations laid at Hawken. There is a judge, a stockbroker, an architect, a doctor, a pastor of a notable church in Washington, D.C.

Anise Jones Jefferson remains my closest friend from Hawken. We are forever bonded by the ride we shared up that magic mountain and our innocent crossing of the divide between the haves and the have-nots. To this day, our every telephone conversation, even those on the fly, includes a reference to Hawken and the unique point of view it has bestowed upon us.

Cleveland is also part of the woman I have become.

After graduating from Smith College, I moved on to Washington, D.C., and other East Coast cities where I worked as a newspaper reporter for fifteen years. In 1999, I returned to Cleveland to co-found *Catalyst Cleveland*, now *Catalyst Ohio*, a magazine that provides independent coverage of the city's schools. I found my beloved city, though touted nationally as a comeback kid, teetering on the brink of blight. Its steel mills shuttered. Its schools in desperate disrepair. Its leaders visionary yet bewildered by an inertia born of deep sociopolitical divides. Despite the good intentions and intense efforts of many, including myself, the schools continue an uphill battle in the face of apathy, politics, and withering poverty.

The woman I have become is in that feeling I get walking downtown streets along which young black men pass ghostlike, bereft of learning, bereft of opportunity. I yearn, pray, chant, and yearn some more to burn my pain into energy that can transform hopelessness and powerlessness into lifeforce, vision and will. Somedays, I believe that only a deep religious awakening—a laying on of hands or a "casting off" of the "transient to reveal the true," something purifying and cleansing as a river catching fire can save my beloved Cleveland.

In 2007, I attended two thirty-year high school reunions. I did not graduate from two schools, yet I feel each reunion was my own. The first was held in June at the Shaker Heights home of a Hawken alumna. Some twenty-five or thirty of the one hundred classmates with whom I had graduated from Hawken School in June of 1977 gathered. The other reunion was held in November at the Mediterranean Party Center on Rockside Road in Bedford Heights. Over one hundred graduates of the 1977 class of East Technical High School gathered.

At both affairs I felt equally welcome and equally awkward. It was that old familiar sense of deep belonging and apartness all at once.

At the Hawken party, we had refreshments, cookies, brownies. I chit-chatted with Steve Kaufman, now an optometrist, and his wife. And Patty Sacks had come back from Denver, Colorado, just to be there.

At the East Tech reunion, we dined on baked chicken, dressing, and a good salad. We stood up and sang two verses of "Lift Ev'ry voice and Sing," the Negro national anthem, with all our hearts. And after the program, we danced like crazy to DJ Gin & Juice. Priscilla Gray, now a scientist at NASA, organized the whole event. Desiree had made sure that I received an invitation, and she was there grinning warmly. I was so happy to learn that many of my classmates had gone on to college and rewarding careers. A classmate whom I had not seen since ninth grade confided with a knowing smile, "Girl, I been through all kinda shit. But, you know what? I just keep on smiling. I just keep on going and praying."

The woman I have become is forever living in two worlds.

A few days after the East Tech reunion, I read two interesting headlines in the *Plain Dealer*: The board of trustees of the Hawken Upper School had voted to open a facility at University Circle, on Cleveland's near east side. The trustees felt strongly that being a part of the city and having access to The Cleveland Clinic and other resources at Case Western Reserve would give students a more well-rounded experience. To do so, Hawken planned to invest nearly one million dollars to renovate an old house.

The other headline reported the homicide of a man in Delaney Village, the new name given to the old King-Kennedy Estates project.

The sharply contrasting promise and sadness of these two reports left a dull ache. Something was changing and nothing had changed. Hawken was, perhaps, seeing Cleveland in a new light. And another black man's life had been senselessly taken in a public housing project.

The woman I have become was angry at the loss of another black life that never had a chance to taste the exquisite education a place like Hawken provides to the privileged—or even a decent public school education.

Once upon a time in Cleveland's public housing projects, most residents had a vision for a better life. Today, upward social mobility has all but ceased there. Those who are born into poverty, like paupers of old, more often than not live out their lives destitute in the city's stark urban core in a contracted universe of eight blocks.

Many benevolent analysts, researchers, reporters, commentators, and critics, myself among them, have tried to examine from every angle—social, economic, historical—why the poor cannot quite seem to get it together enough to pull themselves out of desperate circumstances. Why they can't aspire to middle-class values? Why they can't see—like my mother saw—that education is the ticket out? That Jordan, milk, and honey are just on the other side of E. 79th and Kinsman, with its battered houses, abandoned storefronts, and men without jobs standing on street corners?

Then I see the children in the hallways of tenements and school buildings that ought to have been torn down thirty years ago. I see them in the care of mothers who, too often and for many reasons, just don't understand what an education can do for a child. On a snowy February morning with below-freezing wind chill, I see a girl in a thin jacket and no gloves, braids and beads dancing an orbit around her head. She dashes up the steps into Charles Dickens Elementary School on East 131st Street. Her eyes are shining, eager with inquiry.

I look on her and dare to hope—hope that she will summon brilliant strength and endurance out of deprivation and indignities so that she, too, will dare to disturb the universe. And I dare to hope that she, too, will be given a chance.

Acknowledgments

I AM FORTUNATE TO feel so much appreciation, gratitude, and love in one lifetime.

To my mother, whose grace is amazing. To my father, whose wisdom made him present in his absence. To my beloved sister Beverly "Tinky" Lyles, for all the laughter and all the tears. To my beloved sister Linda, for the fine example. To my brother John, for his keen intelligence. To my brother Scharlton, a gentle giant in his own way. To Mary Elizabeth Moore, who made me fortunate enough to have two mothers in one lifetime.

To Raymond Brown, my partner and best friend. To the power of the Mystic Law. To Nichiren Daishonin, for the wisdom to tap it. To Daisku Ikeda, for the guidance to keep going. To Bibi Potts and Barbara Jenkins for their gentle yet profound insights. To Leslie Morales, for her honest and constant friendship. And to all my wonderful friends in the Soka Gakkai International, especially in Cleveland and Southeastern Virginia, who are always encouraging and supportive of my creative endeavors.

To all the hands that have laid on me. Thank you. May I repay all my debts of gratitude.

About the Author

CHARLISE LYLES was born in Cleveland in 1959. She is an alumna of the A Better Chance program and a 1981 graduate of Smith College. Her other works include poetry published in *Natives; Tourists & Other Mysteries: Emerging Washington Poets; Lips; Maize: Notebooks of Xicano Art and Literature;* and *Whose Woods These Are.* She has read for the Washington, D.C., Ascension poetry series and the Joaquin Miller Cabin Series in Rock Creek Park. A 1990 recipient of an Alicia Patterson Foundation Fellowship, she has worked as a clerk to the *New York Times* chief White House correspondent, as a reporter for the *Virginian-Pilot* and the *Ledger-Star* newspapers in Norfolk, Virginia, and the *Dayton Daily News.* Lyles is the recipient of three awards from the Ohio Society of Professional Journalists. She is the co-founding editor of *Catalyst Cleveland* (now *Catalyst Ohio* magazine), which has provided independent reporting on urban education for nearly ten years. *Catalyst* has also received three awards from the Ohio Society for Professional Journalists and is a winner of a 2007 Clarion Award from the Association of Women in Communication. Lyles was also a Fellow in the Kiplinger Program in Public Affairs Journalism at the John Glenn School at The Ohio State University.